Veritas

Veritas

The Correspondence Theory and Its Critics

Gerald Vision

A Bradford Book
The MIT Press
Cambridge, Massachusetts
London, England

© 2004 Massachusetts Institute of Technology

All rights reserved. No part of this book may be reproduced in any form by any electronic or mechanical means (including photocopying, recording, or information storage and retrieval) without permission in writing from the publisher.

Set in Stone Sans and Stone Serif by The MIT Press.
Printed and bound in the United States of America.

Library of Congress Cataloging-in-Publication Data

Vision, Gerald.
Veritas : the correspondence theory and its critics / Gerald Vision.
    p. cm.
"A Bradford book."
Includes bibliographical references (p.) and index.
ISBN 0-262-22070-9
1. Truth—Correspondence theory. I. Title.
BD171.V56   2004
121—dc22   2004040162

10 9 8 7 6 5 4 3 2 1

This work is dedicated in gratitude to the memory of my navigators Mel, Carl, and Bob, to my anchor Sue, and to Pam and Todd, who keep me nautically true.

Contents

Preface   ix

1 A Guide to the Issues   1

2 The Fundamentals of Correspondence Truth   31

3 Eligible Correspondence Schemes   61

4 Brief Statements of Correspondence   87

5 Deflationism   125

6 The Perils of Deflationism   151

7 Interlude on Progenitors   191

8 Corresponding . . .   219

9 . . . to the World   251

Appendix   279
Works Cited   285
Index   295

Preface

In *The Importance of Being Earnest*, love-smitten Jack Worthing, wooing Gwendolyn Fairfax under the assumed name Ernest, asks her whether she could love him under any other moniker. Gwendolyn replies "Ah! That is clearly a metaphysical speculation, and like most metaphysical speculations has very little reference at all to the actual facts of real life, as we know them." But what might Oscar Wilde's audience, roughly 108 years ago, have had in mind, however dimly, when the pejorative 'metaphysical' was flung at them? Well, by that time metaphysics had been associated with the grand schemes of the seventeenth and eighteenth centuries, forged in conjunction with the emerging sciences (not to say the prevailing theology) and the programs of the late nineteenth century and the early twentieth, which programs aspired to overcome those same sciences. By now these grand palaces of mental architecture have largely fallen into ruin. More recently, as a quick glance in any popular bookstore discovers, 'Metaphysics' has served as a catch-all for just about any sort of New Age nonsense. So things have largely gone sour since the compilers of Aristotle's notes, bewildered by what to call the work that came after his *Physica*, chose the title *Metaphysica*—literally, After Physics.

Popular caricatures aside, metaphysics is still a hardy subdiscipline within philosophy. Indeed, the focus of this essay, the correspondence theory of truth, occupies a tiny corner of this vast subject. If successful, it explains one way in which we humans are connected via our cognitive abilities to, and thus manage to cope in, an environment that wasn't deliberately designed for our comfort or convenience. Like most metaphysical treatments nowadays, it is not the sort of grandiose construction that seeks to subsume all areas of study under a small set of non-negotiable principles. But it does say something about our relationship to the world in which we have been so unceremoniously abandoned to our own devices. Thus, while it may also fall under semantics, epistemology, and a number of other headings, the study of truth appears to have significant metaphysical consequences. If this is yet another immersion in those murky depths, so be it.

No doubt, the truth connection isn't the only sort with which this relatively modest form of metaphysical inquiry is concerned. From the output side alone, reference and predication are other, if related, parts of the same puzzle. And from the input side, the study of perception, *a priori* knowledge, and belief formation, indeed the bulk of epistemology, are central pieces of the same puzzle. They can all be seen as complementary aspects of a single comprehensive enterprise—to sort out our relationship *qua* cognizers to the wider world. Past failures of metaphysics, together with its current critics and antimetaphysical therapists, haven't extinguished the urge to get clear on such matters, nor have they persuasively shown that we should suppress it.

It is hard to keep a lid on yet another issue of concern to philosophers. Not only has the correspondence theory of truth audaciously shown its metaphysical colors; it has been nominated for another role: it is a reluctant entrant in the metaphysical realist sweepstakes. Correspondence has appeared to demand nonmental states of the world to make its sentences, statements, propositions, beliefs, or whatnot true. However, it is not clear that correspondence is well suited to this task. For one thing, the correspondence theory doesn't tell us directly what, if anything, *is* true: that is, it doesn't carry immediate implications for the extension of the property of truth. It doesn't even, as some of its competitors do, give us something to go by, a criterion, for detecting particular truths. Rather, it lays out the conditions for a use of a truth concept (presumably, our current one), but it no more guarantees that anything satisfies those conditions than the conditions governing knowledge and justification protect their extensions against skeptical challenges. In this, it leaves an opening for even so remote a possibility as that the vast majority of 'truths' of which we are capable must be truths only in a revised sense. More important still, despite the assumptions of various of its defenders, the theory by itself doesn't demand that there be any nonconventional, mind-independent, evidence-transcendent truthmakers for any of its bearers (let's say 'propositions'). It merely doesn't close the door on that possibility: that is, it excludes mention of conventionality, mind-dependence, or evidence-dependence from its specification of truthmakers. Thus, certain critics have been quite correct to warn us against employing a quest for the proper truth theory as a way to tackle the issues dividing realists and antirealists. The latter differences (other than realism or antirealism about truth itself) are questions about what things exist and what their character is, not about our theory of truth.

On the other hand, the correspondence theory does bear *indirectly* on those disputes. It appears to be a sensible condition for belief in a mind-independent reality that our theory of truth leave a slot for such a reality. If one's theory of truth permitted no such option, we might be hard pressed to find other reasons for supposing that there must be a mind-independent reality that doesn't link up with our truths. At best, such a reality would acquire the status of a Kantian noumenon. Thus, a popular tactical step for antirealists has been to devise a theory of truth (other than the correspondence theory, of course) whose articles require that the determinants of truth be, in one way or another, mind-dependent, or, at least, metaphysically negligible. Of course, even if the correspondence theory were to rob antirealists of this resource, they might have other resources for advancing their views. Thus, as was noted in the last paragraph, a correspondence theory of truth is no guarantor of metaphyhsical realism, not for any class of items. However, the truth of correspondence would show that this particular avenue was closed to the antirealist. And, given the way things have gone in the past, this must be accounted a setback for prominent brands of antirealism. Accordingly, we should recognize the importance antirealism has placed on the support gained from its reflections on truth. While the correspondence theory doesn't strictly locate the nexus of difference between the two extreme positions, it can't be regarded as a mere spectator to the contest.

On the "third" hand, the realist's interests aren't exhausted by the austere characterization I gave earlier of the commitments of a correspondence theory. While its own truth is compatible with very few truths being of this nature, and with a wholly mind-dependent or socially constructed world, few would be interested in developing or defending such a view if they didn't believe that correspondence with a mind-independent reality constituted at least an important core of truths. Of course, this has to do with the motives behind the theory, not with what is enunciated in its articles. Moreover, the correspondence theory doesn't establish metaphysical realism. (Nor does it refute skepticism, but this, as I explain in the text, is because it is neutral on such epistemological issues.) But if a metaphysical realist believes that the more direct issues can be handled in some other way, the correspondence theory is its natural ally. It introduces the prospect of elucidating in a realist-friendly way just how our truths may latch onto reality.

Several paragraphs ago, I mentioned that an inquiry into the nature of truth was a way of trying to get a handle on an important aspect of the human condition. But although I have shared with many other philosophers a vague notion that some sort of correspondence theory must be on the right track, I might never have undertaken the detailed study reported in these pages if my complacency about these matters hadn't been seriously shaken by a recent development in philosophy. It consists in an influential and growing subculture that sees correspondence and all its substantive competitors as philosophically excessive. The view is, roughly, that older correspondence theories are superfluous, and that truth can be understood more simply, without even raising the sorts of questions tackled by correspondence theorists. From this it follows that the truth of a proposition, or even whether the propositions in a certain area are capable of truth and falsity, can carry no weight in philosophical explanations of our practices. I disagree with these sentiments, and much of the present book is devoted to my grounds for dissent. Readers already initiated into these problems may scoff at so much ado about disputes between deflationary and substantive theories of truth. From the outside it is easy to view them as parochial and tiny in-house differences among a relatively small coterie of theorists. It's a war of the microbes. However, the difference has grown into a major methodological watershed in recent years, and it may hold the key to the question whether philosophy can tell us anything about the world.

Ideas in philosophy, like planets, follow paths of least resistance. We can't study everything in detail, or check up on the reliability of each intellectual gem we acquire from our mentors. Thus, like working scientists, we must take much that our colleagues have given us for granted. Times have dictated, for whatever complex reasons, that the boring old correspondence lore has become one of the things a considerable group of newly minted philosophers regard themselves as entitled to dismiss out of hand. Of course, a failure of philosophers to examine carefully and critically every bit of venerated wisdom isn't a vice. Quite the contrary, vita being brevis, none of us could carry on without doing this for many things. We sort out what deserves our serious attention and set aside certain other matters—with the proviso, if we're alert practitioners, that some of the latter can rudely interrupt our reveries by coming back to life. Thus, communities of philosophers who have other fish to fry may dismiss the correspondence theory as a relic that others have sufficiently refuted for them. Occasionally, of course, brief reasons are given for such cavalier dismissals: "The theory requires facts, and no one has ever been able to show what a fact is other than a shadowy alternative for a truth," "No one has ever provided the detail that gets us past the platitudes" or "nothing so brief can count as a theory," "We can say everything there is to understand about truth in a simple equivalence without raising substantive issues," and so on and so on. Such claims have achieved the dubious status of slogans in certain circles. And, like slogans, they license their holders to proceed without being bothered with the details of what is, to them, a distracting side issue.

Now of course there are large numbers of philosophers, perhaps a majority, who don't buy any of this. But a strain of the philosophical community eschews Correspondence for one or another of these reasons. Moreover, this attitude thrives among some very influential thinkers. A number of first-rate philosophers have taken on this baggage. In consequence, correcting the record on this score has become a high priority for me. It is why I devote a good deal of space replying to deflationary and deflationary-leaning attacks on Correspondence.

Because I have been concerned to put forward what seems (to me, at least) rock solid, I haven't attempted to frame as tightly articulated a complete theory as some readers might expect or hope. I doubt that philosophical illumination is truly advanced by complicated elaborations of theses and subtheses. Once the problems of principle are off the table, the demand for such defensive formulations is less pressing; and if the principled difficulties remain, complex elaborations aren't much help in overcoming them. In this, philosophical explanation may differ from what is usual for leading principles in the various physical sciences (Kuhn's paradigms notwithstanding). Although thinkers do pursue further work based on philosophical suppositions, they do not generate anything like the robust research programs found in the special sciences, nor do they train cadres of laborers to carry out the projects of drawing out the particular consequences of their grand theories. Indeed, once things have become firm enough to do this, they hand over the discovery to a special science rather than continuing to pursue it at a level still recognizable as primarily philosophical. Thus, I have sought enlightenment by going just so far as I had in my possession theses that I couldn't bring myself to deny. I believe I have enough theses to put Correspondence on a firm basis. Of course, a final verdict rests with others.

Since I began by citing the succinct genius of Oscar Wilde, it is only fitting to bring the discussion full circle. When Jack remarks to Algernon "That, my dear Algy, is the whole truth, pure and simple," the latter replies "The truth is rarely pure and never simple." I'll grant Algy *the* truth; however, as applied to *truth* (viz., the concept rather than the range of things that are true), I hope to show that what he says is at best a half-truth.

Veritas

1 A Guide to the Issues

The main business of this essay is to explore the correspondence theory of truth, some of the charges brought against it, and a prominent alternative. If all goes as planned, the upshot will be to reinforce and reconfirm the theory's plausibility. Roughly, the correspondence theory is the view that, when something (say, a proposition) is true, it is true owing to a state of the world. When it is false, that is because the world, or at least the relevant slice of it, is not the way that the proposition expresses it to be. Here is a quasi-official statement of the view:

The truth of a proposition is constituted by a state of the world such that, were the proposition stated, it would state the world to be that way.

Only "quasi" to avoid the impression, first, that this is all there is to say about the subject, and, second, that my explication and defense will be only of this formulation. I shall also try to flesh out some details and defend a broad spectrum of alternative formulations that make use of notions absent (at least explicitly) from my statement of it. The "official" part has to do with the fact that this statement will be enough to go on for much of the discussion to follow, will be repeated when I need to refer back to a plausible summary statement, and is, I believe, a defensible way to state the point.

The view as sketched thus far may seem to be the merest platitude, but discussion of issues raised by the theory has gone on for centuries, and in at least the last century or so it has been so overlaid with claims and counter-claims, quarrels, discussions into minutiae, and the like that we are nowadays confronted with a massive tangle of related inquiries. In the pages to follow, I will address those that seem most urgent or salient, setting aside, with regret, some that drift too far from the focal issues.

It is sometimes remarked that the correspondence theory is the plain man's view. That is scarcely a decisive argument in its favor. Its apparent commonsensicalness is acknowledged by some of the theory's severest critics. But even if we reject correspondence for one of its competitors, it is our most natural way into the study of truth, and truth is worth the probing. Poetic sentiments and clichés aside, the pursuit of truth is crucial to our ends, whatever our ends.

Perhaps the end of deliberation is action. But action without the ability to size up one's situation isn't of much use to the agent. Here truth is much more valuable than any hitherto contemplated alternatives. Critics may cavil at that. The correspondentist, so the tale goes, claims that Maud succeeds in fetching her umbrella from the rack in part because she believes that her umbrella is in the rack *and that belief is true*. To this the critic responds that the explanation begs the question. Maud succeeds because she believes that her umbrella is in the rack *and* her umbrella *is* in the rack. Invoking *truth* to bring off the success is superfluous. However, this objection neglects an important point. We may grasp it by asking why the combination

(i) Maud believes that p and p

should account any more for Maud's success than the combination

(ii) Maud believes that p and not-p.

Some may be perplexed at why we so much as raise such a question—the answer seems so clear. But try stating the reason for its obviousness without using truth or a barely disguised substitute. There is a further explanation for (i) to account for its preference, an explanation absent in the latter case: in the former case *the belief is true*. If we were barred from adding that further bit to finish off, to explain, the effectiveness of (i), there would be a mystery about why it is integral to Maud's success. On the other hand, (i) is not a further explanation of Maud's belief's being true. Truth, here, is an explanatory terminus in a way that (i) needn't be. Of course, conversationally (i) is a customary end point: that is, those who understand what (i) says will normally be satisfied with it as an explanation of Maud's cognitive achievement. But, per the explanation in this paragraph, this is because the belief's truth is taken as implicit in (i)'s second conjunct.

The critic's mistake, once pointed out, may seem too obvious to belabor. Nevertheless, we shall encounter it more than once again in subsequent discussion. It is not the truth predicate, or the mention of truth, but the fact that p is true, whether we mention it or even have a truth predicate in our language, that does the work. It is what guides our understanding of (i), on which the critic relies, and thus it is also what guides our assent to his reformulation of our case.

This may not be the only reason that truth is important, but it is reason enough. We must act, plan, avert, prepare, understand, etc. in a largely indifferent environment—one that hasn't been laid out by benign forces specifically for our sustenance or pleasure. Truth has been of inestimable value in making such action effective. Indeed, despite the fact that we are, and may forever be, largely helpless vis-à-vis the greater world in which we must fend as best we can, truth has made our action effective enough that we are able to engage in purely theoretical enterprises (including this one) aimed at better understanding that world well beyond any immediate practical value it may have for mating, clothing, feeding, or defense. Thus, we become interested in even more truth—truth not tied to what is popularly understood as practical activity.

That relation to action has been for many the chief reason for studying truth, but it is not the end of the story. Given the fact that we find ourselves in a largely alien environment, it is not so much *action* as (mental) *interaction* that may be found the most intriguing. Briefly, we are cognitively connected and disconnected in various complex ways to our surroundings. Some of the connections involve gathering information, and for them perception and ratiocination loom large. Others involve our abilities to think and talk about our cosmic environment, and among the central notions here are reference, attribution, and truth. Belief and related attitudes are crucial to both the input and output sides of our interaction. Thus, truth is a significant part of a larger puzzle about humanity's ability to cope in the global situation in which it finds itself. I believe this nest of issues is the more arresting of the two for those of a philosophical cast of mind.

Some may believe that this way of putting the point already assumes the answer to the most important question we shall be studying, since one major competitor of correspondence is the view that the route through truth doesn't disclose anything about a connection to external reality. But even if things don't pan out for correspondence, this strikes me as a fair way to start. Our inquiry must begin somewhere, and I believe this is as good a description as any of a legitimate first stab. Even those who believe that they have discovered that truth has been a false lead in this regard have done so by first testing such a path and finding it wanting.

The correspondence theory is a natural ally of this view of truth. It is not its only ally by any means: as we will see, other substantive theories can be fitted to this task. But there is a kind of alliance between correspondence and sizing up our situation that blends nicely with this brief capsule of the human condition.

Considerations of this stripe demonstrate the subject's centrality and importance. They are my excuse for giving this much-dissected topic yet another airing.

1.1 A Selection of Theories

Let me get down to business by first mapping the neighborhood in which the correspondence theory resides. That theory is but one, albeit the most common, of a number of what may be called "theories of truth" that have graced the philosophical literature, particularly in the past century. To avoid distracting sub-plots, I begin with a simplified overview. Qualifications can be interjected as needed.

In the main, three traditional theories of truth have contended for supremacy. The most popular is the correspondence theory.[1] We already have a brief statement of it. Its import is that the truth of a proposition consists in its satisfying a relation (correspondence?) to a state of the world, the latter often identified as a "fact." Occasionally discussants add that, with few exceptions, the reality that constitutes truth (= the truthmaker) be mind- or cognition-independent. As shown presently, as a requirement this is too strong. I shall take it as sufficient for the theory that nothing in its conception of truth imposes any cognitive constraints. Also, in mentioning states of the world, I will leave it open whether all those states are empirical. For example, one possibility is that in addition to the empirical facts there are (mind-independent or conventional) mathematical and/or moral facts that serve as truthmakers for their respective propositions. Of course, as I explain in the next chapter, acknowledging distinctive mathematical or moral facts is not required by the theory. Not only might a correspondentist deny that these utterances were either true or false, but if one accepted

---

1. Where there is a threat of confusion between the theory and the relation, I use 'Correspondence' to designate the theory (similarly for 'Coherence' and 'coherence'). Otherwise, where it is less cumbersome and context eliminates threat of confusion, I use 'correspondence' to designate the theory.

that they were, the theory doesn't demand a set of facts of just type X for each kind X of truth evaluable propositions. However, we should be mindful that the possibility of such facts is not ruled out just by the articles of correspondence. (Various other implications of correspondence are explored in the next section.)

Next is the **coherence theory**. Its distinctive truth bearers are seldom purely abstract propositions; it takes beliefs as canonical.[2] These may be actual beliefs, however those are counted, or beliefs that would be held under more or less idealized conditions. A coherence theorist maintains that truth consists in the coherence among a certain body of beliefs. With few exceptions, coherence nowadays amounts to a certain evidential relation,[3] ranging from mutual entailment between all the beliefs in the system to their mere consistency. For purposes of the present discussion, let me say simply that *the corpus of beliefs* (or, as some prefer, *the theory*) requires only that its constituent beliefs be mutually supporting. This demands more than mere consistency but less than entailment. The usual types of support will be, in a wide sense, inductive and/or explanatory. Nevertheless, entailment may figure as a non-exclusive kind of support, and consistency may be regarded as a necessary condition for inclusion. There is much room for confusion here because some coherentists regard inclusion in a body of mutually supporting beliefs merely as a *criterion* of truth. This is a coherence theory of justification rather than truth. But others (of interest to us here because they clash with correspondentists) take it as *constituting* the truth of individual beliefs. Mutual support, then, is a truthmaker for coherentists.

Finally, we come to **pragmatism**. In its simplest form, pragmatism holds that a belief's or a proposition's truth is constituted by its "working" or "usefulness," where such notions are construed in an appropriately epistemic sense. Working is not a matter of general agreeableness but a matter of satisfying expectations of future experiences raised by the belief in question. It points to *success* in anticipating the future, of an appropriately cognitive

2. Versions whose bearers are a broader selection of propositions (or sentences) encounter difficulties over which bearers to include and how to construe a comprehensive set of them. (For some details, see chapter IV of Vision 1988.) Here I limit consideration only to versions current sympathizers have found most defensible.

3. There are some notable exceptions—e.g., F. H. Bradley. But Bradley's identification of truth with reality (1914, 110) may also class him as an identity theorist rather than a coherentist as he is commonly interpreted. (Cf. Baldwin 1991.)

sort, as the truthmaker. As one proceeds through the world, true beliefs do not go unsatisfied. However, a spate of quite different views have been classified as pragmatist. For example, that truth is what we will come to believe at the end of inquiry, or when we achieve an ideal epistemic state, or that it is what we are warranted, or ideally warranted, in asserting, have been ranked as pragmatic theories of truth. So too has the disparaging notion that truth is nothing more than what we are (or take ourselves to be) entitled to believe at whatever happens to be the current stage of our understanding. Indeed, a motley assortment of recent thinkers call themselves pragmatists, and implicate truth in this, only because their doctrines are more practical, naturalistic, or concrete than what they believe to be the current gold standard in philosophy. But it seems that the vast majority of them are not offering us truthmakers; rather, they disdain the search for them in favor of other endeavors. In fact, very few of the thinkers classed as pragmatists have sought to understand truth in the manner of a correspondentist or a coherentist. The closest I have encountered to a straightforward statement of a constitutive version of pragmatism is a remark by F. C. S. Schiller that "social usefulness is the ultimate determinant of 'truth'" (1912, 60), and even this may have been, by the author's own lights, an enthusiastic overstatement. The other occupations in which pragmatic discussions of truth seem engaged include replacing our current notion with a better one (say, warranted assertibility), offering *criteria* for recognizing truths, and searching for only particular species of truth, or some combination of these. The truth concepts pragmatists put forward have been attempts at measured reform rather than efforts to describe faithfully the range of our current notion. Nevertheless, pragmatism has been considered one of the three major substantive theories of truth since the early years of the twentieth century .

Coherentism and pragmatism, to the extent that they make proposals about the constitution of truth, can be considered "epistemologized" or "epistemic" theories of truth, since they identify the truth of a bearer with something like our grounds for accepting it or our ability to apprehend it. I shall explore this connection in greater detail in the next chapter, but the typical choice of belief as the focal truth bearer is an important step in this direction. Also, the verificationist view that the truth of a bearer is the method of its verification (if anyone ever held this view) would be an epistemic theory of truth. Occasionally epistemic theories simply begin by identifying truth with knowledge. Whether this is a deliberate departure from an ordinary concept or an oversight, the result is an epistemologized version of truth.[4]

Past this point there are complications galore. For one thing, not everyone accepts this roster of options. For some, pragmatism is absorbed into coherence. For yet others, in which those two views are distinguished, some of what I have classified as pragmatist has been deemed coherentist. For example, this has been held for versions that first identify truth with warranted assertibility and continue to give a coherentist account of warrant. Then there is the possibility of a mixture of views. For example, one may hold that correspondence works well for certain areas of truth but that, say, coherence works best for others. I shall follow an emerging practice in calling a view that mixes the various theories above, and some views yet to be mentioned, **pluralism**. All instances of that hybrid with which I am familiar hold that correspondence correctly captures truth for some discourses—say, for contingent, empirical propositions—but doesn't suit other subject matters.

In addition, we should consider various accounts which I believe can be regarded as variations on a correspondence theme. Adherents of such views purport to be robustly realist and non-epistemic about truth, but regard themselves as stopping short of correspondence for one reason or another. For example, some don't consider their views correspondentist because they do not believe that brief formulas, such as the one I have displayed, are (or can be) developed sufficiently to count as a theory, or because they believe that their theory can be adequately summarized without subscribing to what they take to be the distinctive and controversial elements of a correspondence theory (e.g., corresponding, facts). Yet others may be wary of the title because they think the world contains too few actual facts for most true propositions to correspond to, so that most of what count as truths link up only with ersatz facts. This makes the correspondence relation, at best, indirect in most cases. The view may be held because one thinks that the only worldly states of affairs that could constitute truth involve the particles and laws of an ideal physics, and few of our true utterances are about those. In addition, depending on one's view

---

4. Bradley (1914) is an exception: after identifying truth with knowledge, he identifies both with reality.

of propositions, it has been held that propositions are not distinct from facts, or from reality in some grander sense. Such views have been called **identity theories**. (See, e.g., Hornsby 1997.) They cut a broad swathe, some assimilating propositions to extra-propositional reality and others assimilating extra-propositional reality to truth bearers. There are also questions about what to do when one supports a view of truth as an explicit reform, not as an account of our current notion but as an improvement on it. As I noted earlier, some thinkers who call their theories pragmatic are in this line of business rather than the traditional one. And there are some newcomers on the scene. For example, although the view is difficult to distinguish from pluralism, at least one recent entry (Lynch 2001b) regards truth as a higher-order, more abstract, *functional* property that may be realized by any, or some combination, of the views I have mentioned. Thus, were we to focus our gaze more sharply, we would discover a very cluttered, partly disorganized landscape.

However, the picture is far from complete. Another group of thinkers accept a cluster of theories that reject all those preceding. These **deflationists** hold that an examination of the concept truth and/or the predicate 'is true' shows that truth has no nature, and, therefore, traditional metaphysical inquiries about truth are pointless or worse. Using $\langle \ldots \rangle$ to abbreviate 'the proposition that' and 'iff' to abbreviate 'if and only if' (that is, biconditionality), deflationary writers may employ the schema

($\mathcal{R}$) $\langle p \rangle$ is true iff p,

or, if one prefers sentences as truth bearers,

($\mathcal{D}$)   'S' is true (in L) iff p

taken by them to show that any instance which can be stated with a truth predicate is equivalent to one that can be stated without it. I shall freely refer to both schemata, and their instances, as *equivalences*. (In ($\mathcal{D}$), the right-hand side of the biconditional is intended as a translation into a metalanguage of the object-language (= L) sentence, whose name—or, more precisely, structural description—appears on the left-hand side. In target cases the object language is usually included in the metalanguage, so that the quoted translation of the metalanguage sentence can serve as a structural description of something in the object language. Thus, for an appropriate L, the following is an instance of ($\mathcal{D}$):

'Coal is black' is true (in L) iff coal is black.

The general idea is that the right-hand side achieves the left-hand result more parsimoniously simply by "disquoting" the sentence described on the left-hand side—hence the moniker 'disquotationalism'—and placing it in the metalanguage.)

The equivalence of the bearer of which 'is true' is predicated with one just like it, but without that predicate, is taken to show that 'is true' is redundant or superfluous, or that truth is not a property. Certain deflationists, *soi-disant* **minimalists**, concede that truth is a property but go on to qualify this by claiming that it has no nature (viz., no truth conditions of its own). All deflationists agree that there is no deep philosophical problem about truth and/or that truth hasn't metaphysical implications. We may also include under the deflationary banner a variety called **prosententialism** in which the phrase 'that is true' is taken as canonical but is rendered as a proform, likened to a pronoun, in which we should not recognize separately meaningful words—better to write it as 'that-is-true'—but rather should see it as an unstructured demonstrative or indexical. Other uses of 'true' can then be modeled on this basic form. The result is that, once the analysis is complete, 'is true' isn't even a predicate expression; this cuts off any prospect that it expresses a property.[5]

However, some who place such equivalences at the center of their theory of truth are not deflationists. They may be correspondence theorists, or lean in that direction. At any rate, these dissenters generally find something more in the formulas, and they invariably regard themselves as realists about the concept and property truth. They construe the right-hand side as presenting more than merely a proposition that happens to be equivalent to the left-hand side. ($\mathcal{R}$) and ($\mathcal{D}$) themselves are mute on these differences: much depends on what one sees implicit in them, a theme to which I shall return in chapters 5 and 6.

For the deflationists, traditional truth theories—what we may now call *inflationary* theories, and what are also called *substantive* theories—are misguided. According to deflationists, each of the rejected theories makes metaphysical, or at least epistemological, sense out of a notion whose total explanation does not warrant raising any such issues.

To round off our survey, we must add a view I shall call, following Scott Soames, **nihilism**. The rough idea here is that no theory of truth is possible.

---

5. Some redundancy theorists, including Ayer (1946, 1963) and Stoutland (1999), also hold that 'true' isn't, or doesn't function as, a predicate.

One reason given is that truth is too fundamental to our thought to be understood in any other terms. These authors hold that it is futile to attempt even an informal account that would allow limited and thus potentially benign forms of circularity. We must recur to truth to explicate a host of other rather basic notions, including perhaps propositionality, belief, meaning, and assertion. But this only exposes truth's fundamental character: it cannot in turn be explained in terms of these or other notions. This outlook is frequently confused with deflationism because both reject inflationary theories *en masse*. But there is a vast gulf between the two views. The deflationist believes that we can achieve an account of truth, although it is more austere than inflationary ones and doesn't involve certain sorts of familiar metaphysical commitment. The nihilist may (but need not) allow that we can say some things about truth. But the nihilist will deny that anything we say can add up to an account of the concept or property. Moreover, nothing in nihilism prohibits truth from being deeply metaphysically implicated. It is simply that the nihilist doesn't claim that this can be captured in an account of truth, since there can be no such account.[6] Occasionally nihilists may phrase this as truth being too basic to be understood in more primitive terms, and this is sometimes taken as tantamount to stating that there can be no reductive analysis of truth. Since some prominent deflationists (e.g., Horwich) also see their opposition to inflationary theories as stemming from the irreducibility of truth, this is another reason why the differences between deflationism and nihilism may be missed. But we must bear in mind that the deflationist believes that there can be an adequate account of truth, while the nihilist does not. Some nihilists, including Davidson (1996), express their opposition to deflationism, along with other truth theories, quite explicitly.

Figure 1.1, the customary "oil refinery" flowchart, highlights the major distinctions.

In addition to this thick stew of views, there have been many, and occasionally very broad, differences between theories falling under any single rubric. A more detailed map would contain further qualifications. However, I shall not attempt to bring greater order out of this chaos. Additional distinctions can be introduced as they bear on particular issues. The map, such as it is, is intended only to provide enough guidance for an exposition.

---

6. Partial accounts aren't ruled out in certain nihilist views on record. Moreover, although partial, they might display the metaphysical links of truth.

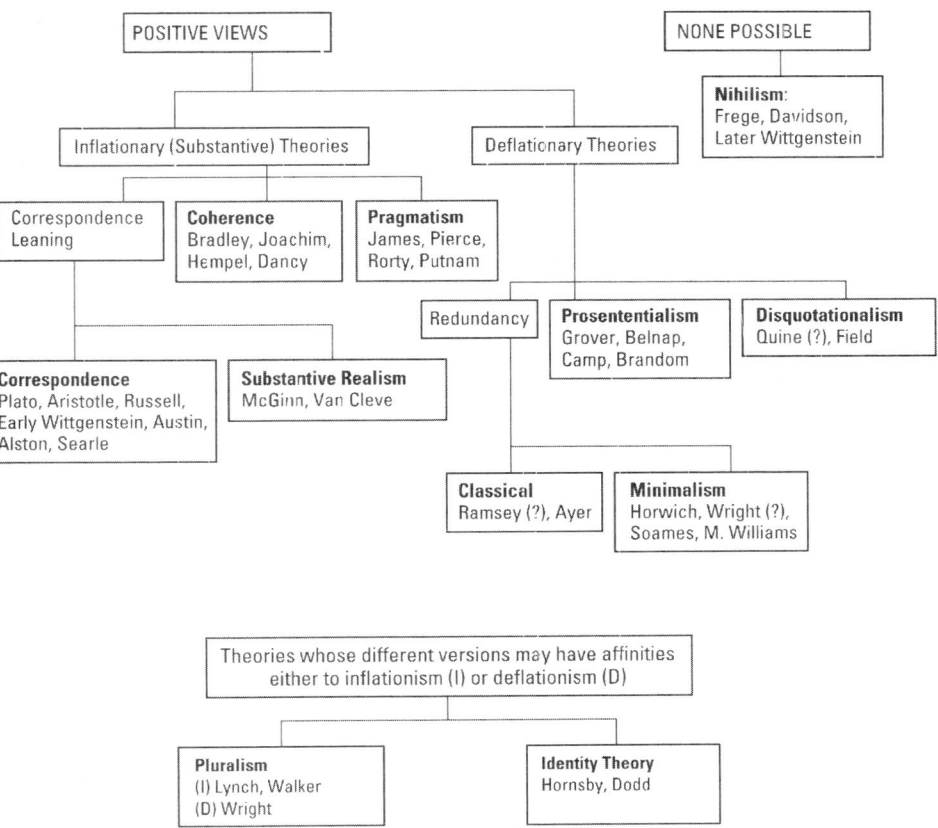

Figure 1.1
Theories of truth.

1.2 Elucidating Correspondence Theories

Once again, the central theme of this essay is the correspondence theory of truth. The basic idea is very old indeed. In Plato's *Sophis*t (263a,b), a Stranger (Plato's alter ego for the nonce) and Theaetetus are discussing statements made with the sentences 'Theaetetus sits' and 'Theaetetus flies.' The Stranger asks Theaetetus what sort of character we can assign to each of these statements. Theaetetus replies "One is false, the other true." The Stranger tacitly agrees, and continues to flesh out Theaetetus's answer: ". . . and the true one states about you the things that are [*or* the facts] as they are . . . whereas the false statement states about you things *different from the things that are.*" Pace Rorty (1979, 306ff.), there is no indication that Plato is inventing a new concept of truth. Indeed, this is an echo of a remark Plato earlier put into Ctesippus's mouth, at *Euthydemus* (283e–284a), that one who speaks falsely "speaks of things that are, but not as they are." The classical scholar Francis Cornford (1957, 310) adds: "Ctesippus is evidently quoting a popular definition: 'The true statement speaks of things that are, or states facts, *as they are*'." (See also *Cratylus* 385b.) The Stranger is eliciting from Theaetetus something that, when made explicit, the latter should acknowledge as beyond dispute. Aristotle, in an oft-quoted remark, agrees: "To say of what is that it is not, or of what is not that it is, is false, while to say of what is that it is, or of what is not that it is not, is true." (*Metaphysics*, book Γ) These are glimmers of Correspondence.

Philosophers have embroidered on this idea, although not as much as one might expect, and there has been much debate about what more, if anything, is wanted for an adequate theory. But here, instead of tackling that issue (it is confronted in chapters 4 and 8), I want to offer some initial clarifications. For a brief statement of the view, one that will not obscure its core idea behind a veil of elaborate refinements, I shall proceed with propositions as canonical truth bearers. This isn't intended to exclude statements, beliefs, sentences, judgments, or other candidates as truth bearers. At this stage, propositions may be taken as the determinate content expressed by all such bearers, and is perfectly neutral with respect to questions of reducibility. Correspondence then can be stated as the view that what *makes* a proposition true, or *constitutes* its truth, is a particular (more or less general) worldly circumstance to which the content of the proposition is related. As I am using 'worldly circumstance' throughout this essay, it is merely a cover term for what others may call facts, states of affairs, situations, events, moments, thick individuals, complexes of particulars and properties, or any similar truthmaker. (As the occasion arises, I may use one of the more specific terms listed instead.) The view needn't assume that such circumstances are nonconventional, or that they are not the products of human endeavor or cognition. The sole requirement is that it not be an inherent feature of the notion of a *worldly circumstance* that it is (like a proposition) semantically evaluable. If it turns out that all states of the world are semantically evaluable items, this will be the outcome of further inquiry, not a consequence of this particular theory of truth. (More on this shortly.) In sum, our formula implies that propositions have truthmakers (or, constitutive conditions for their truth), and these truthmakers need not be semantically evaluable items.

Stating things thus may make the relationship of correspondence to what has been called "metaphysical realism" easy prey for unsympathetic critics. The relations of those two views must be qualified and further elucidated to avoid both misunderstanding and facile rejections. So I proceed to some disclaimers.

First Disclaimer
The mere acceptance of correspondence doesn't imply that there are very many truths, other than negative ones, of the type it describes. (Of course, every held theory has a conversational implicature of the truth of its own articles; but we can ignore that exception here.) A set of conditions for something's being true doesn't guarantee that there are truths any more than a definition of 'horse' or 'planet' guarantees that there are horses, or planets, or any more than a detailed description of the Loch Ness Monster guarantees its existence. Correspondence yields something important about the conditions affirmative truths would have to meet, but isn't by itself a guarantee that the conditions have been met.

Second Disclaimer
If metaphysical realism is the view that there exists a mind-independent reality, including objects and properties, a correspondence theorist needn't be a metaphysical realist. Indeed, due to the winding path the history of philosophy has traveled, there are instances of idealists, even absolute idealists, who have advocated correspondence—e.g., McTaggart (1921). For an idealist, truthmakers will be cognition-dependent states, although even so seemingly safe a generalization has exceptions. (For example, I take it that Berkeley is certainly an idealist, although he holds that God or God's mind, neither of which is a cognitive content per se, is the ultimate truthmaker.) Or one may embrace antirealism (more of which in the next paragraph) by placing cognizability restrictions upon what counts as a state of the world. Still, it is possible to hold that the very same sort of relationship that the correspondentist had in mind when conceiving the world differently accounts for the truth of propositions about those mind-dependent states.

Just as one can refer to Vienna or to the content of Smith's thought of Vienna, correspondence may be to either type of state of affairs.

For reasons such as the foregoing, I maintain that Putnam, who is not alone in this, employs an unduly restrictive notion of correspondence when he remarks of its states of affairs that they are "to be thought of as nonmental nonlinguistic entities which determinately obtain or do not obtain no matter what we think or say. . . ." (1981, 273; cf. Johnston 1993, 98) To reiterate a point made a few paragraphs ago, what is distinctive about correspondence is that it has nothing to say about the case-by-case mind-dependence of truthmakers. Accordingly, if one chooses to impose as a desideratum that truthmakers be mental or linguistic, this must be based on considerations independent of that theory of truth. As long as the extension of one's truthmakers doesn't flow from the nature of one's theory of truth alone, idealism, cognizability, and other varieties of mind-dependence can be strictly consistent with standard versions of correspondence.

Consider a recent revival of an attenuated verificationism commonly known as antirealism. The leading tenet of such Brand X antirealism is that there is no sense to the notion of a proposition the conditions for whose truth transcend (roughly) human abilities to encounter them (or to manifest them in behavior). Those propositions would include all or some of the following: statements about the distant past (say, beyond living memory), unrestricted universal generalizations, counterfactuals, claims about the "private" mental states of others. Brand X antirealism is not identical with idealism because the situations it allows as correlates for sensible propositions need not be mind-dependent or cognition-dependent in any sense beyond being accessible. But it does impose cognitive restrictions on the sorts of facts or circumstances that a proposition can sensibly be about. Some leading proponents of this restriction have also supposed that correspondence implies realism, and thereby regard their case for antirealism as refuting or heavily qualifying correspondence. But, pace certain antirealist claims, this view doesn't rule out even a hearty correspondence theory. Even for standard realists, most propositions we are likely to entertain or utter express situations that are, in fact, cognitively accessible. Nothing in correspondence rules it out as the correct account of the truth of those propositions. Indeed, imagine that all of reality just happens to be cognitively accessible to creatures such as us, although this is not because of a restriction on what is possible. Perhaps there is an *a priori* proof that this couldn't happen. Nonetheless, it is at a minimum (epistemically) conceivable. The correspondence theory itself doesn't imply that our world is constituted otherwise. If that were so, correspondence might be the correct account of what truth consisted in in such a world: verification transcendence would be, at most, a counterfactual hypothesis.

However, there is a serious tension between, on the one hand, idealism or other forms of antirealism and, on the other, correspondence; it accounts for the widespread assumption that the views are in conflict. Correspondence does imply at least that truth is cognition-independent in the sense that it is irrelevant to the eligibility of a truthmaker that we have access to it. This implication will be examined at greater length in the next chapter, but for the present it should be noted that if correspondence truth is taken in isolation, excising whatever other metaphysical views one may have, it makes perfectly good sense to suppose that something is true although no one will ever be able to determine that it is so. For example, we are now able to frame two mutually exclusive hypotheses about what happened exactly one hour after the earth cooled enough to support life, but it is possible (perhaps likely) that no one will ever be able to determine which, if either, is true. Moreover, because of our limited cognitive capacities, there may be true propositions that no subject may ever be able to frame. None of this is ruled out by the correspondence theory alone. Thus, this theory of truth is not the source of whatever cognizability requirements a form of antirealism may impose.

This may lead antirealists to choose a truth theory that conforms more closely to their general outlook. If one part of the antirealist package is that there be some substantive (= nondeflationary) theory of truth or other, this could be a natural inducement to replace correspondence with a coherence theory, or perhaps even with pragmatism. Crudely put, an advantage occasionally cited for idealism, or for antirealist metaphysics generally, has been that it brings the world within the ambit of experience, justification, meaning, and/or knowledge (if not our own, then God's or the Absolute's). By contrast, correspondence seems to leave the world at arm's length, a target we can miss without ever being able to confirm whether we have avoided doing so. A common theme among idealists, pragmatists, and verificationists is that metaphysical realism, the view that there is a world of mind-independent objects, implies skepticism. Since we presumably know that wholesale skepticism is false, it is then tempting to conclude that neither metaphysical realism nor its natural corollary, the correspondence theory, can be right. (The relation of correspondence to skepticism will be examined in greater detail below.)

Although there is nothing strictly inconsistent in, say, being an idealist correspondence theorist, there is at least an incongruity between, on the one hand, a theory of the world and knowledge that makes reality accessible *ex vi termini* and, on the other, a theory of truth that, for all it says, may have inaccessible truthmakers. Coherence, in which a belief is true because it fits evidentially into a larger assemblage of beliefs, seems more attuned to our actual way of estimating our body of truths. Correspondence as a theory of the constitution of truth has nothing to say about the criteria we use for determining truth. On coherence, the counterfactual "If there were no beliefs, there would be no truths" should be true. In fact, given its most popular versions, it should turn out that "If there were no beliefs, there would be no trees" is true as well. For "there are trees" would depend on the truth of the belief that there are trees. No such belief, no such truth. (This is controversial only because it depends in part on the method for evaluating counterfactuals. In fairness it should be noted that some coherentists, for this reason or others, vehemently deny that their theory has such a result, or that their views are incompatible with metaphysical realism as described earlier.) The first of these counterfactuals would be false on a correspondence theory (assuming truth bearers that don't imply any actual beliefs) using the same method of evaluation, and the second would certainly be false. Consequently, while it is possible for antirealists (i.e., those who deny the existence or intelligibility of a mind-independent or response-independent reality) to be correspondence theorists, the relationship of the doctrines is strained. In insisting that correspondence is compatible with various forms of antirealism, I am not contending that those committed to antirealism should, or are likely to, adopt it. In this sense, correspondence-leaning theories are natural allies of realism.

Third Disclaimer

We have been juggling two senses of 'realism' that may be directly implicated with correspondence. In the first, cited above, the correspondence theory is a natural ally of a realist belief in a mind-independent world. In yet a different sense, one's theory of truth *itself* may be considered realist. In this second sense, to have a realist view about X is to have a theory in which X, while remaining a legitimate notion, is not mind-dependent. Deflationism as such does not make truth mind-dependent. And whereas it purports to be a complete account, it leaves no room for the addition of mind-dependence. On the other hand, a theory whose terms imply that truth is mind-dependent is an antirealist account of our subject. Given the current state of the literature, antirealist accounts invariably tie truth to an epistemic (or a potentially epistemic) state. Earlier it was noted that some epistemic theories identified truth with warranted assertibility, or with what would be known by ideal observers (say, in a final science), or with mutual evidential support. These are all varieties of cognition-dependence. Certainly correspondence is a realist theory in this sense, but so is deflationism. Truth is similarly realist on all versions of nihilism to the extent that I have described them. In the past some deflationists have rebutted the charge that their view of truth is antirealist (or nonrealist) by citing the fact that their theories aren't epistemic. But the rebuttal so construed stands a good chance of missing the point of the objection. Certainly deflationists do not identify truth with mind-dependence of the sort just reviewed. However, the more serious charge of antirealism likely to be leveled against deflationism is that it implies that the truth of a proposition does not involve, conceptually, any connection to the (nonmental) world: that is, it is antirealist in our first sense.

No attempt has been made here to cover in its entirety the sprawling topic of realism versus antirealism. There are many different kinds of skirmishes between the camps in which truth may be invoked. Here I confine my attention to those disputes most directly concerned with truth's constitution, as opposed to its extension. While the latter issue may eventually envelop questions of the nature of truth, it is always possible to make one's position on those issues compatible with any of the leading truth theories, and, as Horwich (1996) has shown, abstracting from his deflationism, it is also possible to moot those issues in nontruth terms.

Fourth Disclaimer
Since the ominous specter of skepticism has been raised, its relationship to correspondence warrants further comment.

Briefly, skepticism is an epistemological thesis about either knowledge or justified belief (or both). It states that we have no knowledge (justified belief), or much less of it than is commonly assumed, and for both versions the snag is at justification. As the problem concerns correspondence, it takes off from the question of how we can come to know or to be justified that a proposition is satisfied by its truthmaker. The skeptic draws attention to the fact that on correspondence truth is constituted by something that has nothing to do with any criterion we may have for detecting it. On this account, it is unclear to some how we can ascertain that any particular proposition is true.

A first observation is that any contention that correspondence implies skepticism, whether or not that is regarded as a blemish, is mistaken. The relevant point, stated accurately, is only that nothing in correspondence prohibits skepticism. Correspondence by itself does not rule out a skeptical challenge. Whereas skepticism becomes (or so it is claimed) a nonissue given the implications of popular versions of coherence and pragmatism, clearly it is not ruled out by correspondence. However, many proffered refutations of skepticism are compatible with correspondence, ranging from Moore's appeal to common sense to contextualism and various externalist theories of knowledge (e.g., relevant alternatives, subjunctive conditional accounts, reliabilism).[7] A larger theory that included correspondence could, but need not, also contain one of these refutations of skepticism. This would be an expanded view, but it would in no way impair the articles of correspondence. Given correspondence's compatibility with such refutations of skepticism, the former couldn't imply skepticism. This is not the occasion for critically evaluating those antiskeptical ploys, and it is conceivable that all of them fail. Still, correspondence is in no worse a position for countering skepticism than a number of well-supported theories of knowledge.

Skepticism cannot take root unless perception (and perhaps reason) is (are) equally vulnerable, for perception is the prime source of our justified beliefs about the nonmental world. The objector might respond here that the mind-independence of truthmakers forces us to adopt just such a vulnerable account of perception. To assess that charge, we would need to look much more closely at recent theories of perception than this inquiry permits. In this context, I can only state dogmatically that the response doesn't seem at all plausible. But, in the end, correspondence is not obliged to do more than be compatible with promising independent epistemological

7. See, e.g., the selections and the introductory essay in DeRose and Warfield 1999.

solutions to problems of skepticism. On the other hand, if all the solutions alluded to should fail, it would show that skepticism should be taken seriously, not that correspondence is flawed *qua* theory of truth.

A more basic question is "Why should we demand as a test of the success of a theory of truth that it be able to solve the problem of universal skepticism?" To explore my own misgivings about this supposed requirement, I want to draw a distinction, neither sharp nor exclusive, between certain epistemic, skeptical challenges and a synoptic metaphysical bent, at least as those challenges relate to correspondence. For various reasons (some historical), the separate types of issues each outlook has raised have become entangled. And it is not stretching things too far to call the anticorrespondentist metaphysical posture a type of skepticism, although antirealism and quietism have been more popular tags for many of the views in this cluster. The looming fact about this metaphysical outlook, under whatever title, is that it *is* incompatible with correspondence. So let us look at it a bit more closely.

The metaphysical animus in question despairs of the intelligibility, sense, meaningfulness, etc. (not merely the justifiableness) of connections between concepts or words and mind-independent objects or properties—truth connections among them. It includes examples that extend over a far-ranging vista, and here I must satisfy myself with a C-ish summary (on an indulgent grading system). In its broadest terms, the view—virtually a collection of philosophical methodologies—states that there is no way outside our forms of life, our language games, the coherence of our beliefs, our conceptual schemes, our contingencies, our horizons, or whatnot—no exit to the uncognized world. The outlook has been a staple of coherence theories. Walker (2001, 155) puts it in the form of a rhetorical question: "How can we say anything about a reality that is genuinely independent of us and of our ways of thinking about it?" And Strawson (1992, 86), while not endorsing the view, has written that "the Coherence Theory insists that you can have no cognitive content with, hence no knowledge of, Reality which does not involve forming a belief, making a judgment, deploying concepts." Yet another tradition in this constellation, Absolute Idealism, has sought to establish the view that the knowledge and the unqualified truth value of individual propositions are, *sub quadam aeternitatis specie*, distortions. In their campaign against propositional truth, knowledge, and simply propositionality of any kind, proponents of Absolute Idealism occasionally avail themselves of, among other things, a farrago of objections from the philosophical tradition, including objections drawn from epistemic skepticism. Some of these lines of thought are intended to lead us away from all metaphysical commitment rather than to alternative ones. In the hospitable way I have conceived the outlook, it is also used to scotch any metaphysical explanations involving mind-world or word-world connections. At any rate, that seems to have been its chief employment for post-Wittgensteinian thinkers who make bottom-line use of notions such as "language game" and "form of life." Many of those who cite conceptual schemes or social constructions appear to agree. (Derrida's notorious apothegm, "There is nothing outside the text," looks like a clear affirmation of the outlook, despite efforts of sympathetic commentaries to blunt this appearance.) This leaves us with a myriad of ways, too many to enumerate, to describe how antirealists believe we arrive at this juncture. But all the paths described here employ some metaphysical assumptions or other to agree that the sorts of connections needed for correspondence are unavailable to theorists.

The cardinal point here is that the foregoing metaphysical outlook, unlike its epistemic cousin, does conflict with correspondence. That may seem to be an invitation to a lengthy discussion of metaphysical skepticism. However, aside from incidental comments, the topic will barely enter my further deliberations. When such views are mentioned here, it will be only in connection with issues that may be resolved or clarified without probing too deeply into differences over the larger methodological divide this outlook represents. One reason I ignore the topic is that it appears to embed, and depend on, very different overviews of how to do philosophy and what any philosophical explanation can achieve. I do not deny that these are important issues, but serious consideration of them would shift the present essay's focus from philosophical to metaphilosophical. Rather, I shall try to show how correspondence can be defended on grounds that do not take us too far afield from the particular territory it purports to cover. This will serve, at the very least, as a standing challenge to advocates of this sort of metaphysical skepticism to show why correspondence is not perfectly respectable as it stands. Another reason, connected, is that transcendental arguments designed to demonstrate the impossibility of philosophical explanations, much less dismissive gestures (all too common on the current scene), strike me as futile when confronted with powerful concrete examples of such explanations. If the case can't be rebutted on its own terms and on specifics, a general prohibition against a view of its kind based solely on procedural reasons looks fairly amateurish alongside a worked-out proposal. I am writing for those who agree with me about this.

Nor will much be said about the substantive (inflationary) competitors of correspondence. When correspondence is viewed in these pages as under attack, its source is almost exclusively deflationary. Deflationists claim to abolish all metaphysical consequences from their theory of truth, realist and nonrealist ones alike. Their narratives converge with those of metaphysical critics to the extent that they employ methods designed to show that a statement of the basic articles of our theories of truth does not, contrary to popular belief, (sensibly) state anything about proposition-world connections. And at least some prominent deflationists base their views on a more generic anti-representationalist semantics. I shall have more to say about certain of those arguments in subsequent chapters. But many deflationists do not generally reject the possibility of philosophical theses about content-world relations; their rejection of inflationary truth theories is *not* just a special case of this sort of comprehensive antimetaphysical animus.

Against this assortment of opponents, I shall (in the following chapters), first, propose a basis for claiming that correspondence underlies our common understanding of truth; next, mount a series of forays to show that those who believe we can get along with less, or that correspondence formulas are either inadequate or vacuous, have failed to make out their case; and, finally, expose fatal shortcomings in various deflationary counterproposals. All this is interspersed with elucidations and constructive remarks intended to strengthen the case for correspondence.

Thinkers may differ over the breadth of a correspondence theory. Various of them hold that nothing is a correspondence theory unless it explicitly includes a correspondence relation and takes facts (or something close enough to them, such as Armstrong's states of affairs) as the paradigm worldly truthmakers. For example, Davidson (1996, 269) excludes Aristotle and Tarski from the list of correspondence theorists on the ground that they do not "introduce entities like facts or states of affairs for sentences to correspond to." Lewis (2001a, 175) writes that correspondence says "truth is correspondence to fact," and he takes this quite strictly. Of course, Lewis's narrow view isn't quite so wooden. Indeed, Lewis (2001b, esp. 610,

613–614) sympathetically explores the prospects for different varieties of factual truthmakers. Nevertheless, our current pretheoretical notions of correspondence and fact, undetailed as they may be, are taken as the patterns for any terms we may use to replace them; and this sets the agenda for any further explication (and further explication there must be) to be given. Thus, for example, if one rejected facts for nominalist reasons, acknowledging only individuals and their properties, or had an ontology of events but no facts, a correspondence theory would thereby be precluded on this conception.

At the other extreme, my earlier characterization of correspondence mentions neither fact nor correspondence: it is noncommittal on both counts. The only thing that matters with regard to these two aspects is that something that need not be, as such, a subject of semantic evaluation is a determiner of truth. This type of correspondence can accommodate the following characterizations of the view from Tarski:

... the truth of a sentence consists in its agreement with ... reality. (Tarski 1949, 54)

... a true sentence is one which says that the state of affairs is so and so, and the state of affairs is indeed so and so. (Tarski 1956, 155)

And it acknowledges the passages from Plato and Aristotle as at least forerunners (proto-versions) of correspondence. I have elected to go with a broad interpretation. Is either choice more reasonable, or is this simply a matter of taste?

It might be claimed on behalf of a narrow interpretation that something like it is needed to arrive at a definite thesis, or perhaps even to prevent the claim from dissolving into vacuity. It is the obligation of the broad choice to avoid those pitfalls. But it appears that this is easily discharged by showing how the broad position is incompatible with the others on the map. How could something that conflicts with coherence, pragmatism, deflationism, pluralism, nihilism, and any of the other well-defined, explicitly anticorrespondence views in the literature be vacuous? Still, supporters of a narrow characterization may claim that correspondence must yield an additional kind of explanation, one going farther than that implicit in my remarks about conflicting with other views and choosing a slice of nonmental reality as a truth determiner. The requirement isn't very clear. The best one can do is to examine each clarification of it as it comes down the pike. Provisionally the following will have to suffice: when spelled out properly I

A Guide to the Issues

have found that the demand either has been met even by brief summaries of the theory or that the imposition it places on such theories is highly questionable. I spell this out in greater detail several paragraphs hence.

But why choose the broad characterization? The short answer is that we forfeit a valuable lesson by not recognizing the similarity of efforts to get at roughly the same thing—viz., the relation that makes for truth between our thoughts and utterances on the one hand, and the potentially uncognized world on the other. Much, if not most, of the energy expended in debates about correspondence and its competitors has been over whether nonmental states of the world (or its *thick* individuals) are truthmakers. And it would redirect us away from this focal issue if it was allowed that this were so, but still that a correspondence theory was out of reach because of a rejection of one or another definition of a technical term in a narrower version. Correspondence is not so much a specific theory—say, one associated with Wittgenstein's 1922 effort—but a cluster of them. It is more like a picture or an outlook that directs its adherents to the particular varieties constructed in accord with the blueprint—better yet, outline—it provides. It is this interesting similarity against which the most influential and toxic critics of correspondence have reacted, and thus it raises the issues that seem to have been of greatest interest to the various parties to the dispute. If we define correspondence more narrowly, we will be more inclined to focus on the pros and cons of specific formulations, and be in danger of losing sight of more basic, broader issues.

It seems to me undeniable that the various more detailed correspondence theories have been attempts to refine the insight summed up earlier by Aristotle. Other substantive theories have claimed to be able to accommodate Aristotle's formula, but none I think can claim to be attempts to elaborate or refine it. If one wishes to avoid a term such as 'theory', which comes with some baggage in philosophy, one can call this the correspondence *project*. It would be as much an oversight not to see this in Aristotle's epigram, Tarski's formula, and Wittgenstein's (1922) discussion as it would not to see dogs and wolves as belonging to a common biological family, even from a strictly Linnaean perspective.

This particular mapping of the dialectical landscape sets the agenda for subsequent discussion to a large extent. I note this if only because it may surprise, not to say disappoint, some who are well-acquainted with this knot of issues. For my defense concentrates heavily on deflecting objections from these various quarters. This may be surprising because an impressive list of friends and critics alike have seen correspondence's main task to be to produce a highly detailed version, one that would spell out the distinctive notions involved in it. Thus, one might anticipate the main effort of a defender to be directed toward the discovery of a rigorous statement of correspondence, perhaps containing a series of complex clauses to protect it against the odd counterinstance. And in chapter 8, enough of the missing detail is supplied to indicate at least a direction in which such elaborations might go. However, I do not believe a philosophical understanding of correspondence is chiefly advanced by a series of such defensive clauses. Of course, we should never shirk our responsibility to seek rigorous statements of our views. But the history of such disputes indicates that formulations seem relatively unproblematical once the principled objections are no longer threatening and pretty fruitless while they remain. Thus, I shall be primarily interested in examining more closely attacks that are part and parcel of deflationary (and antirealist) outlooks, and postpone offering at least one set of promising details for the correspondence relation and the nature of truth determiners. This does not mean that questions of detail are without exception deferred to chapter 8. Various remarks must also be entered early (e.g., chapter 3) about the relation and truthmakers. But most of this is a contribution toward explaining why imposing a demand for greater detail is, if not an outright mistake, at a minimum a miscalculation of one's priorities.

Although the heart of my defense is contained in chapters 3–6, here is a brief outline of at least one reason why the demand at the outset for a more detailed formulation seems (to me at least) a distraction.[8] The point now being ventured is that the sorts of general assumptions needed to support such a demand are, at the very least, questionable. For one thing, it is never made reasonably clear just how much detail will satisfy critics. (No doubt, this will differ for different thinkers.) For another, critics point to the fact that at least many correspondence theorists appeal to a general notion of correspondence and their specification of truthmakers is equally latitudinarian. This is regarded as a defect rather than a virtue. Why should the inability to say anything further, in the absence of more specific qualms about what has been said already, be a defect in a view?

8. Of course, detailed formulations aren't wrongheaded. Quite the contrary! However, the complaint now in our sights is that the theory isn't defensible—perhaps doesn't even make a definite claim—until one is produced.

Much of the criticism seems to converge on just this fact: namely, that nothing so brief can be a satisfactory explanation. Why can't explanation just stop here and nevertheless suffice? Is it that a philosophical explanation must never run out of further things to say? Or perhaps the assumption is that there is a natural stopping point in this type of explanation, and we have yet to arrive at it. If so, without demanding much precision, where in general is the natural stopping point located, and what grounds are there for any such claim? Such questions are seldom if ever raised. Of course, some opponents do go on to say why such brief outlines are unsatisfactory. Perhaps there are too many correspondence relations, and picking out the right one without introducing circularity into the account seems an insuperable task. Or perhaps a professional suspicion of claims of simplicity for one's favorite concept places under the same cloud all claims to the effect that nothing more remains to be said. Such objections are legitimate, and I shall attend to them in due course. The relevant point here is that even if one considers my answers unsatisfactory, objections of that form can be addressed. But to rest with the charge that the account is unacceptably brief is too breezy a critique to warrant further concern on the correspondence theorist's part. Until opponents back their demand with a clearer conception of what is being sought, and why it must be sought, it is hard to know even how to address the complaint that the correspondence theorist must provide further detail before being credited with having placed before us a serious candidate.

1.3 Metaphysical Implications

Deflationists maintain that, unlike their view, correspondence has metaphysical implications. I won't probe this issue in any depth here, but I want to call attention to two questions that have been at the heart of claims for the superiority of deflationism. First, is it true that correspondence has metaphysical implications? Second, and more important, if the answer to the first question is affirmative, how exactly does this yield an advantage for deflationism?

We can dispatch the first question quickly. Despite the various qualifications entered earlier with respect to correspondence's involvement with metaphysical realism, we may say that it has at least quasi-implications for there being genuine truthmakers. It is obvious that at least some propositions are true, and even if the world were to consist only of social constructions, correspondence would require them as truthmakers for propositions about them. Coherence and pragmatism also need truthmakers, though perhaps they do not leave open the possibility that these will be mind-independent (non-epistemic). However, we are now concerned with correspondence. So, for our purposes, a blunt answer to the first question is Yes.

It is the second question that looms large. It supplies the contrast with the nonmetaphysical alternative that deflationists regard as a significant point in their favor.

I am assuming here that 'metaphysics' isn't simply a scare word. In the heyday of logical positivism, legitimate philosophical theses were so circumscribed that any view which had metaphysical implications of any sort, including much of epistemology, was forbidden (e.g., as nonsense, or as not cognitively meaningful, or as emotive). But the complaint of current deflationists is different: their view, lacking as it does such metaphysical implications, has the virtue of (relative) methodological *simplicity*. The fewer the commitments of a theory, the better.[9] One reason for this might be that a simpler theory supplies fewer hostages to fate. Another might be that a more parsimonious theory (or so it is thought) has fewer ontic commitments. And if one view can do all the same things starting from a more modest, unified, base, doesn't that indicate that we are on to something? In this light the loser's additional commitments appear gratuitous. (This is one reading of Ockham's Razor.) Thus, a metaphysical theory in this sense isn't faulty per se, but is inferior to a more economical view that carries out just as much of the originally appointed task.

But ultimately these prescriptions aren't very telling. Here are but two of the reasons.

First, what deflationists regard as correspondence's additional commitments, the correspondentist may consider its fertility. Having more substantial implications provides a different virtue—fruitfulness. No doubt, this must be tempered by other virtues, such as relative parsimony. Fertility unconstrained can fuel bizarre theorizing. But philosophers typically take their list of methodological virtues from what can be extracted from the practice of theoretical commitment in the sciences. And while simplicity is

---

9. On ambiguities here, and on potential tradeoffs between ontology and ideology, see Oliver 1996, esp. pp. 5–9.

frequently cited by philosophers, the scientific virtue of fertility is often overlooked. Of course, if the excluded commitments were to dubious theoretical entities, parsimony might have bite: who needs more epicycles? But is the potentially uncognized world a theoretical entity that any serious investigator would want to avoid if possible?

Second, if one grants that correspondence has implications that deflationism lacks, why doesn't this demonstrate that the two theories don't accomplish the same thing? It would appear that having different commitments, when none of those can be independently shown to be bogus, is a sure sign that the same tasks aren't being achieved by the putatively competing theories. What is needed is a description of the tasks for a theory of truth acceptable to deflationists and correspondentists alike. It is unclear that one is in the offing. Deflationists do commonly purport to give just such a description. But their efforts seldom give serious consideration to what correspondence seeks to achieve. The correspondentist is likely to be inclined to complain that the deflationist's assumptions about the point of having theories of truth always leads to a stunted list of its objectives. We shall look more closely at these deflationist characterizations in chapter 6. For the present it is enough to understand the character, and limitations, of the deflationist charge that correspondence engenders metaphysical commitments. Insofar as it is an objection to correspondence, this is only against the background of a competing deflationary view which is, in some sense, more austere. And we have given two reasons, and raised one suspicion, why this summation of the situation is dubious.

1.4 Pathologies of Truth

Old campaigners in these wars may be surprised that the Liar Paradox (or similar semantic antinomies), a salient issue in many such discussions, hasn't been accorded a central place in our deliberations. Here I shall explain why. But first let us consider a version of the paradox. It states that if one attempts to find a truth predicate in the very language one is examining (say, English), one will encounter sentences such as

(L) (L) is false.

(L) says of itself that it is false. If it is true, then (L) can't be false, which is to say that it is false that (L) is false. So, (L) must be *false*. But if it is false, what it states is true—namely, that (L) is false. Therefore it is *true* that (L) is false. (L) is clearly defective, but there appear to be no linguistic regulations already in place that it violates. Call such instances of contradictory truth-values pathological. One might be tempted simply to devise a rule excluding pathological instances. It doesn't even matter whether the rule is patently *ad hoc*. But take the nonpathological sentence uttered by Smith:

(L') Everything Brown says is false.

And suppose that Brown says only

(L") What Smith said last night is true

and that (L') is the only thing Smith said last night. Each sentence (and each statement made) by itself is fine. Neither is a peculiarly paradoxical utterance in isolation. However, if Brown's sentence, (L"), is true, then by (L') it is false. And if what Smith says, (L'), is true, then by (L") it is false. We cannot place the blame on self-referentiality. (See, e.g., Yablo 1993.) In sum, the problem doesn't seem to reside in an isolated group of bad sentences, but is an inescapable consequence of having a truth predicate of bearers in the very language whose bearers are being described.

Reactions to this predicament vary. At one extreme it has been taken to show that a definition (or even a more relaxed consistent account) of the concept of truth is impossible, or that our truth concept is irredeemably muddled. Nevertheless, for various reasons the present work will largely ignore issues stemming from the paradoxes. My reasons can be summed up by saying that even with this threat, the questions over the competing truth theories still present us with issues to be resolved. To wit:

First, many sentences (and their consequences) are nonpathological. Our concept of truth was no doubt forged for those sorts of instances. Indeed, it is obvious why they must certainly precede the constructibility of pathological instances. Thus, even if the concept carved out from nonpathological instances is ultimately confused, there is merit in finding out just what that concept is. Revision is always a possibility, but too many proposals for revision or regimentation in philosophy have simply been founded on inadequate (occasionally perfunctory) overviews of the pretheoretical notions reformers would have us discard. Such hastiness has been a prime ingredient in half-baked theories. So before discarding efforts to understand the overwhelming majority of benign instances, much less contemplating the practical impossibility of discarding the notion of truth, it is a good policy to examine in greater detail just what, if anything, it is that seems to account for the benign instances.

Next, all the theories discussed in section 1.2 have in practice adopted a policy of ignoring the Liar. They have given accounts of truth despite the prohibitions against doing so that certain theorists would draw from the Liar, and even nihilists who refuse such accounts have not avoided them because of Liar-type paradoxes, but because, quite the contrary, truth is too fundamental to explain in more basic terms. Some may be working on the assumption, or hoping, that the paradoxes are eventually resolvable, or at least that it can be shown that they don't have devastating consequences for nonpathological instances. Whatever their assumptions, the point to emphasize is that they all agree that there is something to be studied here regardless of the problems introduced by the paradoxes. All the competitors are in much the same boat in this regard. We are each confronted with working our way through the options this slate of theories presents us, and the Liar doesn't give a leg up to one of the competitors over the others.

Accordingly, there will be little further mention of pathological instances of truth here. This is not because their study is uninteresting, or even any less interesting than the one on which we are about to embark. Rather it is because the two projects don't seem to share so intimate a common fate. If tomorrow someone were to produce, *mirabile dictu*, a universally acknowledged solution to Liar Paradoxes, the differences between the various accounts of truth would persist. So work on sorting through them remains to be done in any eventuality. Accordingly, I shall proceed in subsequent chapters to try to impress on readers the attractions of correspondence, and the drawbacks of accounts of selected opponents. I now turn to the first of those tasks.

2 The Fundamentals of Correspondence Truth

In chapter 1, I cited Plato and Aristotle as early advocates, or at least precursors, of the correspondence theory. Unfortunately, this alone doesn't firmly secure their niche in the correspondence pantheon. Many—including Tarski, whose correspondence-leaning sentiments were also highlighted in chapter 1—have expressed dissatisfaction with such truncated versions. This is not an objection to correspondence as such, but rather to allowing these sorts of brief summaries to count as its enunciation. Occasionally the dissatisfaction stems from correspondence's not meeting preconditions set down for a *theory* of any kind. Perhaps it suffers a lack of significant detail, or of sufficient precision. In other circles, as we will see in chapter 4, it is denied that the foregoing passages even begin to state anything remotely leaning toward correspondence. In this spirit some have claimed that apparent statements of the view, such as those just mentioned, are platitudes, acceptable to the supporters and opponents of correspondence alike; they don't so much as show up on the theorist's radar screen. For reasons such as these we may be unable to stop with such abridgements. Complications ensue. The lesson to be taken from this thick stew of claims and counterclaims is that even if these brief statements should prove in the end more adequate than critics declaim, we may be obliged to provide further explanation to show that this is so. Nevertheless, I believe the statements from Plato, Aristotle, and Tarski are useful starting points: they give at least a glimmer of what correspondence is striving for ("the correspondence project," as I dubbed it earlier).

2.1 Non-Negotiable Intuitions

Before diving into the conflicts and complexities, let's continue a while longer at this very informal level. For it is here, without the distractions of the ensuing debate, that we may ask for an account of the basic insights that have led philosophers to think they can sum up the nature of truth in such general formulas. As was mentioned in chapter 1, correspondence has an undeniably primal attraction, absent in its competition. So, whether it deserves the exalted title of "theory," or is defeated by flaws infecting all its fleshed out versions, its central articles are compelling in ways worth exploring. Furthermore, the compulsion seems to be more than a human quirk, but something residing in the subject matter itself. Let's see if we can unearth the basis for this outlook.

In this section I explore two basic intuitions that account for at least part of correspondence's attraction. In the end they won't distinguish a correspondence theory from each of its competitors, and they may not exhaust its pull, but they are powerful motives for inclining to a view of this general sort.

Truth attaches to linguistic or thought content. I have chosen the title 'proposition', used as neutrally as possible, to capture that content. But because our entry to understanding thought content has always been through familiar linguistic forms, which we then assume our thought contents mirror, it is simplest to choose linguistic or quasi-linguistic entities as prototypical truth bearers. And, for simplicity, I begin with the least complicated propositions, those expressed by uses of singular subject-predicate sentences. Thus, in an appropriate context, one may assertively utter "the apple is poisoned," or "Johnson won by half a second," or "the storm washed out the bridge," and suppose that each is true. Assume that all indices are fixed (part of my reason for starting with propositions); that is, it is settled which apple, which person named 'Johnson', which storm and which bridge are being referred to. Potential ambiguities have been eliminated. On a commonsense level, possessors of the concept TRUTH[1] will agree that if the world had been different in quite specific ways, the truth or falsity of these propositions would have been different. If Lucretia hadn't tampered with the apple, a proposition expressed by "the apple is poisoned" would have been false; if McGurk had passed Johnson in the race, the

1. SMALL CAPITALS are used for concepts. Some uses of *italics* designate properties. Often, italics are used just for emphasis. When nothing turns on it, the context makes clear which of these is meant, and wherever remaining uncommitted is harmless (or useful), I will not flag the word in question with either device and/or use the idiom of 'notions'.

The Fundamentals of Correspondence Truth 33

proposition expressed by "Johnson won by half a second" would have been false; if the bridge had been sturdier, it would have withstood the storm. (I am ignoring overdetermination, both for simplicity and because it ultimately makes no difference to the point at issue.) Change the world counterfactually and you change the (contemplated) truth of certain propositions about it.[2] This seems as well-entrenched a bit of information about that concept as its possessors will have. It is difficult to believe that anyone could be said to know what truth is if without knowing this much.

I sum up this first insight in the following formula.

Variability The truth-value of a proposition would be altered were the world to change in certain definite ways, or, if the truth-value must remain the same, it is because the world cannot change in relevant ways.

One could call this and the succeeding principle platitudes. I generally avoid putting things in this way only to avoid confusion with a narrower understanding of 'platitude' adopted for minimalism (see chapter 4). The qualification in the second disjunct is explained below.

Those familiar with the recent literature may be aware that—shocking as I hope it strikes most readers—this diverges radically from what has become a common theme. (See section 6.4.) It is often stated that the first thing, and perhaps the only thing, one must know about truth is one or another of our earlier equivalences ($\mathcal{R}$) and ($\mathcal{D}$):

($\mathcal{R}$) $\langle p \rangle$ is true iff p.

($\mathcal{D}$) 'S' is true (in L) iff p.

On that view, grasping ($\mathcal{R}$) (or ($\mathcal{D}$)), or its instances, is grasping virtually all one needs to know about our truth predicate. For the present, let us grant that knowledge of the equivalence of one's choice, or systematic knowledge of its instances, is rudimentary for anyone who has mastered the concept, although, as I shall argue, much depends on just how these formulas are taken. However, as Variability makes plain, neither formula is more central to a mastery of TRUTH than the fact that the actual state of the world is crucial to whether certain propositions are true or false. One's grasp of a concept

---

2. Bigelow (1988, 132) seems to aim at the reverse side of this point by claiming that "truth supervenes on being." That is, "you could not have a difference in what things are true unless there were a difference in what things exist." The spirit of the remark is fine, although doubts can be raised about its strict accuracy.

is manifested not merely in picking out instances, but in knowing how to modulate one's behavior in changed circumstances, in knowing what counts as a relevant challenge to a judgment about that thing, and in knowing the appropriate response (or whether there is one) in such contingencies. A quick glance at deflationist expositions indicates that they neglect Variability (purposely or otherwise). Indeed, many employ the schemata precisely as a basis for arguing that there is no need to consider the implications of worldly changes in one's truth concept. In contrast to any such view, I maintain that we must place up front this very basic understanding about changes in worldly circumstances, not changes in propositions, that are as clearly indispensable to anyone credited with a concept of truth.

Perhaps some are tempted to regard Variability as an implication of the equivalences. It might be said on behalf of that view that if 'p' fails so does '$\langle p \rangle$ is true' (or "'S' is true"). Two reasons tell against this move.

First, the equivalences are missing a crucial ingredient—namely, that it is a state (or moment) of the (actual or possible) world, not a sentence or a proposition, that accounts for the difference in truth-value. Thus, if one wishes the right-hand side to prefigure the point of Variability, it is not 'p' qua formula, or as something that is (or could be) equivalent to the left-hand side, that matters; it is a worldly circumstance. Indeed, it is hard to see how someone relying strictly on the formulas can construe this point. The proposition itself doesn't change because something else in the nonpropositional world (other than an act of redefinition) does. So it is difficult to see how we can understand 'p' (or its instances) changing in this context if it is regarded as nothing more than a proposition expressing less cumbrously what is conveyed on the left-hand side. Then what, according to this rejoinder, changes? The truth of p changes, but it is no explanation to say that if the truth of p changes then the truth of p changes. On the other hand, if the p that changes is taken as nothing more than a state of affairs (or fact), then the point is just the one insisted on by Variability. Rather than the equivalences accommodating Variability, the equivalences will have to (broadly) accommodate themselves to Variability.

Second, while the equivalences are confined to a single attribution of truth, Variability requires that we compare an evaluation of a single proposition across changes in a situation. It is hard to see how the mere recognition of instances of, say, ($\mathcal{R}$) contains that information. But even if we stretch our imaginations so as to hold that (R) contains implicitly all that is needed to suppose that a proposition can contain each of two values, Variability also shows the ground of this difference. It is not there to be read off the surface of the equivalences.

This point can be made even with interpreted formal systems. Consider a model consisting of individuals and properties. Properties are given by their extensions. One of our individuals, d, is referred to by (i.e., satisfies) singular term 'd', plus one-place predicate 'Σ', whose extension is given by Σ:{. . . , d, . . .}. That is, d is a member of the set satisfying its extension. Then '$\Sigma(d)$' is true. By removing d from Σ's extension we change the world, or, in this case, the model, thereby converting a truth into a falsehood. Of course, given the purposes for which models are contrived, there is little point to doing this. But the circumstance Variability is meant to capture can nevertheless be brought out by comparing models. The latter preserves just the fundamental datum about TRUTH that I have claimed underlies our grasp of it.

We can also view Variability from the complementary angle of justification. Not that truth and justification come to the same thing, but epistemic justification is linked to truth. One point of gaining such justification for one's belief is to increase the chances that it will be true. Not everyone accepts this. There are schemes of justification, standardly called 'deontic', in which justification is no more than a self-contained epistemic duty. On that view it is an autonomous practice, gaining nothing conceptually from a connection with truth. But that position is difficult to comprehend. Why shouldn't deontic justification be nothing more than a simple prejudice? We have other habits, some equally unshakable, that aren't consecrated as duties; indeed some are naked bigotries or mere idiosyncrasies. Why should justification be otherwise, arrogating to itself an honor analogous to a Kantian moral requirement? I do not mean to deny that justification is an intellectual duty. But I do not see how this can be sustained without something like the link to truth adumbrated above.

In view of that linkage, it is not open to a critic to declare that when I seek (epistemic) justification, I am seeking anything other than to acquire a true belief. Now suppose I want to know whether the proposition expressed by the sentence 'the restaurant is open' is true. I was told it is, but it is important enough for me to gain further assurance. Why would going to the restaurant to see for myself be a relevant, in fact the most relevant, thing to do in the circumstances if the state of the world is irrelevant to truth? What else could be the point of this procedure?

I am not claiming that the place we go to gather information is always the location of the state of affairs in which we are interested. It need not even be the most reliable. If the shelvers in the library are incompetent or lazy, whereas those who enter information in the catalogue are highly efficient, checking the catalogue may be a more reliable way to discover whether a book is in the library than looking for it in its proper location. To say the procedure is most relevant is not to say it is most reliable. But there is nothing indirect about my going to the restaurant or the shelves. (An indirect method might have been to look up the restaurant's hours in an advertisement.) So that is not an issue here. The recognition that going to the restaurant is direct, that it is the most relevant thing one can do, matters.

This is easily explained on Variability. But how does the view that knowing one of the equivalences, or its instances, is sufficient for a concept of truth absorb this point? Suppose someone thinks that going to the restaurant is irrelevant, but not because she is a skeptic, or holds a version of sense-datum theory that would make this dicey at best, or believes people's sensory faculties are flawed. She merely insists that it doesn't matter to the truth of the proposition in question. However, she is disposed to accept all the instances of ($\mathcal{R}$) within her ken. Can we hold that this last fact is nevertheless sufficient for her to have a concept of truth? An affirmative answer is absurd. What could be a more fundamental bit of conceptually encapsulated understanding of truth than its being answerable to the world?

A second basic datum concerns truth's indifference to whether or not anyone knows it to be so, or can determine in principle that it is so, or even that anyone can contemplate the proposition. Let us call this 'the cognition-independence of truth'. On it, the truth of a proposition doesn't depend on the ability of anyone to know or entertain it or any other proposition. For what may appear to be a problematic case, consider Descartes' "I am" (*sum*). Its truth, though not its statability, is independent of his recognizing it. This is not to claim that some truths will never be believed (though undoubtedly that is so), but only that their being believed is not essential to their being true.

"Never?"

"Well, hardly ever!"

Let me explain.

Cognition-independence is put forward here as underlying any theory intended to capture our current truth concept, including but not restricted to correspondence. It does not imply that mental states can never be relevant ingredients in truthmaking. Recall from chapter 1 that occasionally it is claimed that correspondence requires all truthmakers to be independent of anyone's cognition. Under those circumstances a correspondence theorist should be stymied by the question "What makes the proposition that Theaetetus is thinking of Athens true?" The truthmaker in this case—Theaetetus thinking something—is certainly part of the mental world. No doubt this truth is cognition-dependent, but not in a way that need worry a correspondentist. For one thing, its dependence is the result of the particular subject matter (viz., Theaetetus's mental activity), and is not due to articles of the truth theory itself. Second, in examples of this kind, the mental state involved in the truthmaker is not in the proper location for an epistemic theory. That is, it is not a state of the judger of the truth, but occurs in the content being judged. A blanket requirement of cognition-independence is too broad to capture the intent of its framers.

A second potential threat involves what we may call "conventional facts," discussed in the next section. But the threat vanishes once it is recognized that the actual framings of the conventions in question are not as such the subjects of the propositions that are considered as being made true by virtue of those conventions.

I leave open the possibility that other considerations—say, about the nature of propositions—will reintroduce additional restrictions on what propositions can be true. Perhaps they will rule out the intelligibility of truth bearers that fail to link up with our cognitive capacities in a certain way. The only commitment following from the truism of cognition-independence is that these requirements not originate from a restriction on the very concept of TRUTH. If imposed, they must enter via independent considerations (say, concerning the meanings of sentences). I am not suggesting that we impose a requirement that the truthmaker be accessible. In fact, none of the current proposals for an accessibility requirement seem to me to pan out. Rather, I am emphasizing that, for anyone attracted to such a view, the restriction, as long as it is not implied by the theory of truth, is compatible with the cognition-independence of the truths that this theory allows.

The commitment to cognition-independence should be distinguished from a spate of attempts to interpret it narrowly and from restricted principles that may flow from it. These views, of greater or lesser strength, state that it is possible for a certain truth to be beyond a speaker's ken, or that some truths may never be known, or even that some truths are unknowable in principle. (See, e.g., Wright 1999, 227.) They may be attempts to specify more particularly, and in some instances to reduce the polemical impact of, Cognition-Independence. The dispute over which of them correctly portrays the gap between the true and the cognizable is a matter for further investigation. It may stem from this second intuition, but the intuition is more primitive, and is not merely one among a selection of its attempted analyses. Rather, the relevant point here is that there is a difference, however one accounts for it, between the epistemic or psychological status of a person's particular cognitive state with regard to a thing and the fact that the content of the state is true. The paramount consideration in this context is that we countenance this difference as a component of our standard conception. As with Variability, it will be useful to have an official formulation.

Cognition-Independence Nothing in the account of truth itself indicates that truth is, ever will be, or can be entertained by minds of roughly our capacity.

The qualification "by minds of roughly our capacity" is needed because the permission can't extend to omniscient beings. The very idea of omniscience implies that there is no true proposition of which an omniscient being is ignorant. But that bit of *a priori* legerdemain shouldn't affect the legitimacy of our intuition. To see this we need only observe that omniscience doesn't distinguish between an epistemic restriction on truth as such and an unerring ability to track epistemically unrestricted truths. Cognition-Independence rules out the former, not the latter.

Here is an illustration of the pull of this principle. Imagine I venture a radically underdefended hypothesis, *p*, to which my unimpressed companion replies "No one will ever know, or even be able to know, that *p*." I don't contest the justice of the reproof; however, I can respond "But it might be true all the same." This is certainly not a telling rejoinder in typical scenarios, but the point to be noticed is that my interlocutor should be able to understand it. She might not like it, or my intransigence in the light of my feeble debating position. She might respond "So what?" or regard me as irrational or inane. But her grasp of truth prevents her from questioning its intelligibility or conversational admissibility. To do otherwise would betray corruption (she might say "refinement") brought on by an overexposure to philosophical theory. It would be a baffling response, exhibiting her lack of the grasp of the commonest denominator of a shared notion, at the level of the simple grasp from which, *ex hypothesi*, we are starting. Similar cases are legion. We get this much simply by cashing in the cognition-independence built into our truth concept.

2.2 How Other Views Measure Up

Coherence and pragmatism are the two main substantive competitors of correspondence. Each takes truth bearers to be beliefs; more significant, they take truthmakers to be bodies of belief and successful experiences, respectively. Undoubtedly, such deviations from Cognition-Independence are customarily deliberate. For that intuition is the source of the "gap" that lets in the bogy of skepticism, and both positions are standardly motivated in part by their claim to be able to close this opening for skepticism. But whatever the story, they are superficially incompatible with Cognition-Independence. If we give that datum any weight in defining TRUTH, the best such views can hope for is a revision of our current concept.

Coherence theorists and/or pragmatists may reject the claim that they are concerned with actual bodies of belief or actual experiences. This may create an appearance of bringing them closer to accepting Cognition-Independence. For example, consider versions of each view in which the relevant beliefs are those belonging to the set held only on that glorious day when humanity achieves an ideal epistemic state. That may be tough to square with their initial motivation to banish skepticism. But, even if that ideal were attainable, Cognition-Independence still eludes both theories. It is not a condition attaching to us provisionally because we are in less favorable circumstances. It is put forth as a permanent feature of our concept. If it holds now, it must also hold in those circumstances. Thus, on Cognition-Independence when we achieve epistemic (or scientific) utopia, our grasp of every truth (and only truths), will be due to the fact that we have become, like an omniscient, infallible trackers of truth. That we have attained truth in those circumstances may reveal something about us, but not, as this view would have it, about the character of TRUTH.

The discussion of Coherence in the preceding chapter gave my grounds, albeit briefly, for avoiding the admixture of epistemology with the semantics of truth. Aside from what they view as the desirability of having a truth theory leaving no room for skepticism, defenders of epistemic versions of truth may point to a perplexity about thoughts or words linking to a reality which is independent of our ways of conceiving it, a cognition-transcendent reality. (Such views were briefly alluded to in the last section.) I confess a failure to be gripped by the perplexity. It seems quite natural that our nontranscendent practices might have consequences for a realm outside their apprehension. Why regard our more basic practices as *inhibiting* the further development and expansion of thoughts rather than *enabling* it to proceed beyond the materials used, perhaps needed, to get it started? It seems the very fact that we seem to understand perfectly well the contested propositions is some evidence that this is precisely what happens. Of course, critical reflection can show that people don't in fact understand certain things it is widely believed that they do. But when that charge has been made to stick, there have usually been content specific grounds for making it. In this case what we have is a blanket prohibition against anything that exceeds our ability to confirm or recognize it. However, even if we set aside the problem posed by our question, the perplexity doesn't lead ineluctably to Coherence. A range of thought (or assertion) confined to what we can conceive or confirm might still employ cognition-independent worldly circumstances as the truthmakers for its (delimited) collection of intelligible propositions.

This critique is too generic to cover all varieties of these views. To give one example, as noted in the previous chapter a minority of coherentists have ventured nonepistemic versions of that view. But if a coherentist chooses truth bearers other than beliefs (even idealized ones), this immediately opens the view to difficult questions about conflicting coherent bodies of propositions and about the notion of an absolutely maximal body of propositions (a notion that may not make clear sense). At any rate, I have chosen beliefs (or, the tenets of theories) as truth bearers not only because this seems to me the most defensible form such views take, but also because these are nowadays the forms in which coherence and pragmatism are most likely to be defended.

Next there are other (perhaps overlapping) varieties of explicitly epistemologized theories of truth. They too fly in the face of Cognition-

Independence. Heidegger[3] and Rorty (1979, 176), among others, take the bearers of truth to be knowledge rather than propositions. This assures us that nothing will count as truth other than what falls within the ambit of what is at least a potential mental state. At one point in his career Rorty seems to have addressed himself to this sort of issue. While defending the notion that truth was nothing beyond what pragmatists labeled "warranted assertibility," he then confronted the truism "warrantedly assertible but not true." In response he stated that it is an implicit reference to another, perhaps not yet invented, conceptual framework in which the statement in question wouldn't be warrantedly assertible (Rorty 1979, 289). I'm uncertain who would want to make such a remark, but in any event it strikes me as an unnatural—nay, a desperate—reconstrual of a much more straightforward comment. How can 'warrantedly assertible but not true' mean to anyone "can be imagined to be unwarranted on someone else's conceptual framework"? While not quite as willful as Humpty-Dumpty's attempt to foist off on Alice his meaning "a nice knock-down argument" by 'glory', it is closer to that sort of playful nonsense than to a serious effort at a gloss. We must look harder than that for a reading that will defuse Cognition-Independence.

A subtler version of epistemologized truth may be implied by certain versions of verificationist semantics. On such views, a truth condition, and thereby a truth, makes sense only if we can imagine a situation in which it is possible (practically speaking) for someone of roughly human capabilities to confirm it or individuatively manifest that it is true. There are different varieties of this view too. Depending on the generosity of the details, they lead to different ways in which Cognition-Independence is wholly displaced or severely restricted.

What of the compatibility of the foregoing views with Variability? Here coherence's compliance is at best partial. Given the implicit holism of

3. "According to general opinion, what is true is knowledge." (Heidegger 1962, 259) Heidegger's own epistemic notion of truth can't be easily assimilated to either coherence or pragmatism. For him, underlying correspondence is a deeper truth notion amounting to *disclosure* or *revelation*. The argument for this is etymological. He traces the underlying notion to the presocratics. We might have said that Heidegger is in a different line of business were it not for the fact that he believes his view replaces, and thus is relevant to, correspondence. Bradley (1914) too unceremoniously identifies truth and knowledge, but, as I mentioned in a note to chapter 1, he identifies both with reality, and eventually with absolute mind. So in the end this seems to have no implication for our homely notion of knowledge.

coherence theories of truth, it is unclear whether a coherence theorist could allow a localized alteration in the truthmaker (the whole body of beliefs) to alter the truth of a single proposition. That will depend on the version of coherence theory. On the other hand, it certainly seems as if a pragmatist could acknowledge that a change in one's subsequent experience would determine a difference of truth-value. However, neither changes in bodies of belief nor those in experiences may be the right sort of worldly changes required by Variation. Thus, on this score there may be further complications. In whatever way they work out, neither view can be easily squared with Cognition-Independence.

Other substantive views may be less affected by the two intuitions. For example, recall that the identity theory identifies truths with facts. One of its mainstays is the view that, despite appearances, the phrases 'it is true that . . . ' and 'it is a fact that . . . ' convey the same thing. Nevertheless, the identity theory doesn't seem to violate either intuition. It follows that the intuitions cannot be taken exclusively as evidence for correspondence. If we are to rule out the identity theory, we must do so on the basis of other flaws (such as those discussed in the section on facts in the next chapter, or in its handling of false propositions).[4]

Next, let us turn to pluralism. Recall that this view allows that correspondence works for some language fragments (say, contingent truths), but provides a different kind of truthmaker for others—perhaps coherence, perhaps deflationism, perhaps a hitherto uncharted view. I have something to say in chapters 4 and 8 about Wright's version of this view. For now, observe that it may be able to handle Variability and Cognition-Independence by limiting them, or at least the first, to contingent truths. On behalf of that view a pluralist might argue that extended beyond contingencies Variability seems to have the disastrous consequence that necessary truths are possibly false (in a non-actual world) and that necessary falsehoods are possibly true. Also, a pluralist might reject Cognition-Independence for language fragments such as morality, mathematics, or counterfactuality on the grounds that it is difficult to discover any mind-independent facts to support such truths. Perhaps coherence, or even deflationism, is a better fit in those areas. Let us consider these points in turn.

4. For an exploration of the difficulties of a sophisticated version of this view, see Cartwright 1987; David 2001; Engel 2001.

The Fundamentals of Correspondence Truth 43

First, the invariability of necessary truths. The inability to discover a possible situation (= world) that would alter the truth-value of a necessary truth doesn't demonstrate that Variability has no employment there. Quite the contrary, we may satisfy ourselves of a truth's necessity by considering selected possible worlds and failing to find one in which its relevant fact doesn't obtain. (Recall the second disjunct of our formulation of Variability, that "if the truth-value must remain the same, it is because the world cannot change in relevant ways.") To illustrate, consider Kripke's (1980, 49) claim that proper names are rigid designators. A commonplace procedure would be to canvass, as thoroughly as circumstances allow, selected possible situations in which the actual name of something attaches to something else. For the sake of argument, suppose we fail. That is evidence for the truth of the thesis. I am not contending that this is the only way to satisfy ourselves that something is a necessary truth, nor am I endorsing Kripke's thesis. Nevertheless, the procedure just outlined would be irrelevant, not merely optional, if Variability wasn't a consideration here. What would be the point of asking ourselves whether the state of affairs in question obtains in any possible world if the states of such worlds were not determinants of truth? Quite the contrary, our very understanding of necessity legitimates such considerations. Therefore, necessary truth is not an inducement to adopt a nonvariability addendum in our theory of truth, but rather a reason for its indispensability to the original intuition. We needn't suggest that this thought experiment determines necessity. But it is always available, and it shows how closely connected 'necessary' is to 'the facts are never otherwise'.

On to the supposed failure of Cognition-Independence for areas in which facts appear soft or non-existent. Provisionally, let the following two points suffice.

First, nothing in correspondence rules out facts that are altogether conventional or that presuppose conventions. Consider the fact that I paid $5 at the box office to see a movie. Is this the same fact as my having extended my arm into an open window and having placed down a rectangular piece of green printed paper with a picture of Abraham Lincoln on it? This isn't an uncomplicated question. But if it is the same fact, this will only be because some more naturally described items (viz., certain green printed rectangular pieces of paper with pictures of Lincoln) are identical with conventionally described ones (viz., $5 bills). In either case, my candidate fact is described in terms of certain conventions of commerce. It doesn't follow from those conventions alone because it also requires in the present instance, *inter alia*, a contingent bit of purely physical behavior on my part. But if a fact at all, we may say it is a conventional one nonetheless. And, of course, once such cases are acknowledged, we realize that we are up to our figurative hatbands in conventional facts: that liquor stores are now open on Sundays in Pennsylvania, that Tony Blair succeeded John Major as Prime Minister, that February has 29 days in a leap year, that three of a kind beats a pair, that they safely crossed the Cambodian border into Thailand, and so on.

Against that backdrop, filling in with your own favorite example, suppose I commit a morally wrong act. Let us also suppose, plausibly, that my having done so is a conventional fact. Moreover, as in the movie ticket case, it requires my contingent performance (or nonperformance) of a bit of behavior (or nonbehavior). On this scheme we can still say that, on the correspondence view, it is true that I committed that wrong and this is shown by its correspondence to a fact. Of course, this isn't compatible with every noncognitivist view that has graced the literature, but by making the fact conventional it will leave room for much of what noncognitivists have wanted to say about ethical discourse. We will explore this option further in chapter 9. But for our present limited purposes we can see in this a potential resource against pluralism.

Second, let us be more concessive to the pluralist, and declare conventional facts *facta non grata*. There is now a threat that the issue will become merely terminological. What is to prevent someone from claiming on the very same evidence—namely, the lack of correspondence-friendly truthmakers—that the propositions in question aren't truth-apt. No doubt, there is some standard or other for the acceptability of these propositions on either alternative. But what compels us to regard that standard as truth-or-falsity? This may be closer to the way in which antirealists about local matters (say, scientific theories, mathematics, or ethics) have traditionally viewed attempts to extend truth-values to their targeted subject matters. There is a further question about whether to count utterances that are not truth-apt as propositions, but all this can be sorted out consistently. (On this issue, and for other correspondentist possibilities, see section 3.4.)

This isn't a recommendation for any such antirealisms, and, as we shall see in chapters 4 and 9, there are other things to be said that may prevent the difference from collapsing into a matter of terminological preference.

However, this view and the preceding option show that pluralism isn't forced on us just by the terms of engagement. Moreover, the correspondentist alternatives are a way to preserve another intuition (which I shall not defend here), namely, the univocity of truth. Against this the pluralist has the burden of explaining why each of his senses should be taken to address our broader interest in truth as such. Perhaps pluralism can meet this challenge. However, on balance the univocity of truth plus the clear application of Cognition-Independence for some truths poses a challenge for pluralism that correspondence doesn't confront.

The currently popular alternative to correspondence is deflationism. As outlined in chapter 1, its signature tenet is that TRUTH demands no worldly conditions for its possession—truth has no nature (qualifications aside). As we noted in the previous section, this runs directly counter to Variability. If the state of the world is a determinant of truth-value, then surely truth has a nature. On the other hand, nothing in the articles of deflationism itself is incompatible with Cognition-Independence, but for the special reason that truth doesn't depend on *anything*. Generally, deflationists seem to oppose all epistemologized theories of truth, although their adherence to Cognition-Independence derives ultimately from the fact that they believe there is nothing much to be said about truth, epistemically or otherwise. The sole exceptions to this are the rare cases, alluded to in chapter 1, in which deflationist tenets are deployed as a springboard, first, for rejecting correspondence, and, next, replacing it with a very different, almost always epistemic, theory.

How does nihilism fare in light of our basic requirements? Here the situation is cloudier. If the nihilist accepts Variability, how can she continue to maintain that there is nothing significant to say about truth? Of course, she might claim that such platitudes don't amount to a theory of truth, and nothing fills the remaining gap. However, to the extent that we can get even a partial account of truth implied by these fundamental apprehensions, the founding idea that truth is too basic to frame any account for could be gravely compromised. If we ask whether the principles defended in the last section, together with perhaps some truisms established later, add up to an account of truth, the nihilist may find it difficult to answer negatively. As we shall see, much depends on what one recognizes as a philosophical account. Thus, the dispute may ultimately be more terminological than substantive (which may in turn hinge on differences in one's commitments regarding philosophical methodology, and thus one's expectations for an acceptable resolution).

To sum up: Substantive competitors are challenged at least prima facie by Cognition-Independence because of their commitment to mental entities (viz., beliefs, satisfaction) as canonical truthmakers. Pluralists can incorporate the requirements in a limited way, but the typical reasons for not extending them further are weak. The identity theory can acknowledge Variability and Cognition-Independence. Its weaknesses lie elsewhere. Deflationists generally have no difficulty with Cognition-Independence, but the whole point of their theory may be viewed as an attempt to write Variability out of basic truth theories. Nihilism is not supported by the intuitions, and it is unclear to what extent it can accommodate them.

Any imposition of our two intuitions assumes we are discussing truth on its current understanding, however sketchy and imprecise that may be. This leaves an opening for proposals to reform our current notion. The only previously canvassed noncorrespondence views likely to be attracted by this option are coherence and pragmatism. But if reforms are to be serious, they must be grounded in the discovery of significant defects in our current concept. One excuse typically given for undertaking the effort is correspondence's inability to dispose of the problem of skepticism. For reasons given here and in the preceding chapter, I don't regard that as a problem for a theory of truth. What then remains as a basis for replacing our current notion with a revised one? There are two general directions in which critics have sought to show that correspondence fails its inherited tasks:

(a) Its advocates have been unable to give more than the briefest formulations of the view, and these fall short of the illumination demanded of an acceptable theory.

(b) When attempts have been made to overcome (a) by supplying details, there have been difficulties in explaining correspondence's characteristic devices. For example, the relevant relation between truth bearers and truthmakers has never been satisfactorily explained, and the sorts of items presented as truthmakers have either been seriously flawed or, at a minimum, doubts have been raised about their ontological legitimacy.

Both charges deserve answers. I address (a) in chapter 4 and (b) in chapters 3, 8, and 9.

Perhaps we are now in a position to take the next step, and probe further—although still at a very sketchy level—into the mindset of a correspondence theorist.

2.3 Methodological Preliminaries and Clarifications

In chapter 1, I commenced my inquiries about correspondence with a compact, quasi-official formulation:

The truth of a proposition is constituted by a state of the world such that, were the proposition stated, it would state the world to be that way.

Although no more than a brief sketch, that serves our present needs. On its basis, let me introduce some further clarifications, elaborations, and qualifications.

1. Instead of using propositions as truth bearers, I could have chosen sentences, statements, conjectures, beliefs, and so on. Propositions do seem to me to express the most fundamental of the various things said to possess truth, although I won't defend that view in these pages.[5] Still, there are importantly different conceptions of propositions. On one common conception, they are contents or meanings (including references), roughly, of our beliefs and declarative utterances; on another, they are more abstract yet, consisting of the first sort plus the contents of anything anyone could believe or state (perhaps even things that no one could believe or state). On some views, certain declarative utterances aren't propositions just because they aren't truth-apt (see point 4 below). Thus, there is the threat of complaint or confusion in using a term even so colorless as 'proposition' in my formulation. I shall continue using it for simplicity, intending at least the first sense (viz., contents of beliefs and statements) and remaining largely neutral (until confronting some issues in deflationism) on any others. But where I say "the truth of a proposition . . . " one may substitute "the truth of a truth bearer . . . " whenever the safety of one's claim trumps smooth narrative.

2. Nothing in the theory as stated presupposes that there is a truth predicate, a truth operator, or the word 'true' (or a synonym) in the language or thought system in which true propositions occur. The correspondence

---

5. For a defense, see, e.g., Vision 1997a; Alston 1996, 13–22; Horwich 1998a, 86ff.; Soames 1998, 13–19.

relation could have constituted truth even if we, the theorists, didn't have the word 'true' with which to construct its theory. (Quoth the bard, in *Two Gentlemen of Verona*: ". . . truth hath better deeds than words to grace it.") At bottom, it is not, as such, a theory about the meaning or use of the predicate 'is true'. Nevertheless, given some popular assumptions, correspondence can serve as the basis for a theory of the meaning of 'true', and information about the predicate 'is true' (or its uses) is a good entry into our subject. Indeed, once in possession of a truth predicate, it will be an invaluable source of insight about its property if we are carefully selective in its study. This doesn't imply that it is the last word on the subject of meaning, and the formula doesn't presuppose that subjects need the concept for their propositions to be true. Correspondence does affirm that there is a property of *truth*, although not as such an intrinsic one. The job of the theory is to supply the conditions under which a proposition would be true, not directly to explicate our use of its concept or even to secure instantiations for it.

3. Because the theory is most directly about a truth property, rather than a predicate or a concept, accepting it leaves open an intriguing middle ground: it has been maintained that *truth* may be a correspondence *property* without thereby being a part of the common *concept* TRUTH. This proviso has allowed the introduction of a version of deflationism in which it is claimed that the issue of correspondence is to be resolved independent of an investigation into truth's concept, as well as a version of correspondence that concedes deflationism about the concept. It should be clear from the discussion of Variability that I don't subscribe to dividing the issues along these lines. It would be difficult to regard Variability as anything less than conceptual information about truth. But the option is bookmarked here because it has attracted deflationists and correspondence theorists alike. Deflationists may appeal to it to show how modest are their claims for their thin treatment of the concept; correspondentists may adopt it to acknowledge what they regard as deflationary insights. I shall examine this compromise further in chapters 5 and 6. However, like many middling positions in philosophy, it has the disadvantage of not being a natural outcome of arguments that led philosophers to adopt the conflicting views it moderates. There could be tensions between this compromise position and both the arguments for correspondence and those for deflationism. Ultimately, that will depend on whether the original arguments can be viewed as over-

stating what they show. Certainly deflationists have often implied that their view shows *truth* (and not merely its concept) to lack any metaphysical interest.

4. Next, I should say something about what I have thus far casually referred to as the "truth-aptitude" of propositions. To say that a proposition is truth-apt is to say that it is of a type for which it is appropriate to be either true or false. This needn't be taken to imply that a truth-apt proposition invariably succeeds in taking one of the two determinate classical truth-values, but only that it belongs to a class such that some of its members—perhaps excluding peripheral ones—take truth-values. As noted earlier, there is an ongoing controversy whether evaluative, mathematical, and other sorts of propositions (stated with subject-predicate sentences) are truth-apt, or, if not, whether they are still genuine propositions. Given some natural background assumptions, this last issue can become a dispute over nothing more than nomenclature. Here it will be convenient to call just about anything expressed by a declarative sentence a proposition, independent of its truth-aptness. We shall have to allow for a few exceptions—for example, questions stated in the declarative, performative utterances such as "I promise to meet you tomorrow"—but those sorts of cases do not interfere with our chief concerns.

On the other hand, the adoption of one or another view about what counts as a proposition has influenced the acceptance of certain theories in this area. Candidacy as a substituend for 'p' in ($\mathcal{R}$) may amount on some views, in effect, to nothing more profound than having the surface marks of—that is, looking like—a substituend for 'p'. Thus, utterances that something is chic or funny could count as propositions satisfying ($\mathcal{R}$). If one takes this route, it may appear that, since it is hopeless to find truth determiners for a range of propositions broad enough to include these specimens, there can be nothing more to truth than the equivalence itself. Or consider some versions of pluralism. A pluralist doesn't need to include those sorts of examples, but one pluralist strategy may be to posit what O'Leary-Hawthorne and Oppy (1997) call a "supersense" for truth, as stated in an equivalence, of which the various more substantial kinds of truth are species. A pluralist of this type might be a deflationist at a supersense level while accepting a variety of lower-level substantial senses of 'true'. Thus, how propositionality and truth-aptitude are distributed may influence the type of theory one adopts. Some of the complexities are taken up in later chapters. Here I have emphasized rather that it is also possible to separate the issues of propositionality and truth-aptitude. For my statement of correspondence I consider only propositions that can be independently determined to take truth-value, however one decides which those are.

5. Certain vexed questions surround the philosophically charged notions of *definition*, *meaning*, and *analysis*. They can't be ignored: they go to the heart of the standing of various claims put forward in this essay. Thus, in an abbreviated fashion, here are some thoughts on this knot of conceptions.

To begin with, correspondence falls short of what many would consider a *philosophical* definition. Typically, though not invariably, a definition provides the meaning or content of an expression or a concept. "Philosophical" standardly adds to "definition" an expectation that this be an *analysis* (very likely, conditions (a) and (b) below). Indeed, some deflationists (e.g., Horwich (1998a,b)) demand that any alternative to their own view be a *reductive* analysis. While the notion of a reductive analysis is itself understood in various ways, it has been, and perhaps still is, customary to suppose that such an analysis will yield all or most of the following:

(a) a set of necessary and sufficient conditions for the concept in question that are

(b) more illuminating than what is being analyzed
and given in

(c) a vocabulary that, in addition to being wholly independent of that in which the analysandum is rendered, has one or more of the following virtues:
(i) It is relatively simpler than the vocabulary of the analysandum.
(ii) It is a micro-vocabulary in comparison to the macro-vocabulary of the analysandum.
(iii) It is more accessible to direct experience than the analysandum.

Although this sort of analysis had been pursued well before 1900, as an explicit policy it is associated with the work of Moore, Russell, and members of the Vienna Circle. More recent examples in the work of a number of prominent philosophers attest to its continuing attraction.

I side with deflationism in holding that the quest for an analysis of truth meeting the entire set of traditional desiderata appears doomed from the start. The fact that there are at best a paltry number of such generally acknowledged analytic successes in philosophy feeds the suspicion that obtaining one for this subject is highly unlikely. The daunting restrictions introduced by conditions (a) and (c) reinforce its unlikelihood. In particular, pace (a), an account of what constitutes *truth* may not supply an equivalence. Consider the following analogy. An account of the positions that constitute checkmate doesn't tell us that it is the object of a player to checkmate her opponent. In that respect it falls short of what one grasps by CHECKMATE. If truth has an evaluative dimension—say, is the *telos* of belief— this will be left out of correspondence (and coherence) accounts. I am not claiming that truth in fact has such a dimension. And if it does, this may concern accounts of belief rather than those of truth. But if we were convinced that we should include this information in our truth theory, it would be wholly orthogonal to the interests of correspondence or any other familiar substantive theory of truth. It is not something on which a correspondence theorist must take a stand. Thus, any of the speech-act affiliations of truth predications, whether or not they belong in 'true's' concept box, pose no threat to the correspondence project.

Now let us turn to (c). Few of the proponents of substantive theories have assumed that the vocabulary in which the account is delivered is in some ontological or epistemological sense simpler or more primitive than that in which the predicate 'is true' occurs. More important, even if we could make sense of the claim that truth's explanans is simpler, it has seldom been part of the goal of correspondence to make sure that the account was given in more basic terms. Nor is that the only way to purchase an understanding of a concept. Quite plainly, there is no philosophically significant sense in which talk of something corresponding to a fact, for example, is simpler, or otherwise ontologically less problematic, than talk of its being true.

What, then, does correspondence accomplish? I hold that it *explains* a central fact about truth. Some may hold that explaining an analysandum requires an additional clause—clause (iv), say—under condition (c) of analysis. For them, all explanation is a kind of analysis. But I cannot shake the conviction that thereby skirting all of (i)–(iii) is a distortion of the conditions philosophers from Hobbes and Descartes to the present have set for what are nowadays called "analyses." Beyond that, it seems to me unimportant how the term 'analysis' is employed.

Despite the failures of (a) and (c), there is an important sense in which describing the present enterprise as an analysis of a concept strikes a responsive chord. For that I turn to (b), emphasizing the term *conceptual* in the phrase 'conceptual analysis'. A natural way to express what a correspondence theorist is after is to say that she is trying to make explicit what is merely implicit in one's grasp of TRUTH. Moreover, correspondence places up front a feature distinctive of this particular concept, not a general condition for the possession of any concept. That this feature is essential and central may come out in what one would be expected to say when. But it may also emerge in other ways. One particularly fruitful strategy for extracting a concept's commitments, suggested earlier, is to see the sorts of conditions its masters take themselves to be responsible for holding. This is made apparent by a partition between those apparent challenges a possessor must respond to, at the risk of otherwise failing to understand the concept, and those she can (but needn't) dismiss as irrelevant. Although these sorts of considerations do not speak to the entire analysis package outlined by (a)–(c), they are central concerns when philosophical subjects of the so-called analytic type are pursued. So there is still good reason to regard them as leading features of conceptual analysis.

On this notion of conceptual analysis there is a quick refutation of the compromise positions, alluded to in item (3), of both deflationists and correspondence theorists alike. Recall that on such views the acceptance of a deflationary or minimalist account of truth's concept leaves in place at least the possibility of a further correspondence account of its property. To maintain this position one must allow that there exist worldly circumstances, of the right type to be truth-constituters, or at least that it is possible that they exist. But if this is so, and correspondence falls outside our concept of truth, we must allow that the following combination is compossible:

(a) the statement that *a* is F is true

(b) there is (in the abstract) such a thing as the worldly circumstance that *a* is F (or of *a*'s being F)

(c) that worldly circumstance does not obtain.

The compromise view is committed to (b), at least notionally, because it is a *sine qua non* of correspondence holding for the property of truth. If correspondence as the correct account of our truth concept is rejected, then (a)–(c) must be, for this sort of theorist, at least conceivable. It seems to me obvious that the combination it describes is not conceivable, thereby eliminating the possibility of such compromise views.

Some may be inclined to see what I have been calling 'making explicit what is implicit in a concept' as doing no more, say, than exposing its central but nonetheless contingent features. This marks a bedrock metaphilosophical divide which it would be unprofitable to examine sensibly at so general a level. I am not moved by grandiose pronouncements on this issue, and I believe that whatever generalizations about such matters may be in the offing should be derived from decisions about what sense we can plausibly make of concrete instances. But in any event this isn't the place to try to resolve that difference. I am dealing only with those who acknowledge that conditions for analysis are not ruled out *ab inititio*. Within those ranks, I have relaxed the requirements for what counts as a conceptual inquiry and thus what can advance our conceptual understanding. Working on that assumption, it is enough to claim that if there are points to be made about the concept, we are entitled to call this a conceptual investigation whether or not it succeeds at meeting conditions (a) and (c) or even aspires to do so.

6. Although we needn't aspire to a set of necessary and sufficient conditions, we can take steps to clarify what is meant when we say that truth is *constituted by* the relation of a proposition to a state of the world. Certain critics have imposed requirements for clarification that defy satisfaction. Specimens of this type with which I am familiar strike me as unreasonable demands. However, several more things can be stated about the way I understand constitution in this context, and that may help clarify the nature of the view intended here.

First, I draw no distinction between a proposition's truth *being constituted by* X and *consisting in* X. X's *making* a proposition true is just the converse of a proposition's truth being constituted by X. Whatever nuances may differentiate these relations in some contexts, in the present one they amount to much the same thing. A thinker employing one of these notions in stating his thesis about a truth bearer is offering an account of the constitution of the truth of that bearer. Although certain deflationists may claim that nothing constitutes truth, as a rule they don't reject the intelligibility of the notion. That is enough to go on for the present.

Second, although on occasion causation figures in a thing's constitution, I am distinguishing what it is for something to constitute a proposition's truth from what it is for something to cause its truth. To illustrate the role causation may play in constitution, consider: a skin condition is a sunburn only if it is caused in a certain way, an impression is a footprint only if it has been made by a foot, and, in terms of clades, a creature is a panda only if it evolved in a certain way. In the last case, for example, a panda cannot have been concocted in a chemistry laboratory or have been born in a distinct evolutionary line somewhere in a planetary system in nebula M121. However, in the case of truth, the causes of something's being true are not, as such, its constitution. Fred may have caused the truth of the proposition *that the wall is green* by painting it. That has nothing to do with what the truth of that proposition consists in. Causing a truth determiner to obtain is not as such a way of constituting the truth of the proposition which expresses that the determiner obtains.

Third, although correspondence offers a constitutive *relation*, we may throw some light on what this amounts to by comparing these relations to constitutive *rules*, both through their similarities and their differences. Constitutive rules create or define (thereby make possible) a form of behavior.[6] Without the rules of chess my moving what looks like a rook across what looks like a chess board cannot count as checkmating an opponent. We may contrast these with regulative rules, rules that regulate a form of behavior inside a pre-existing activity, but do not define the activity. Violations of the so-called conventions of war, such as those against the use of poison gas or those governing treatment of captured enemy soldiers, do not prevent something from being a war. The violated rules are those for conducting an independently constituted activity. Similarly, the principles of engineering promote the building of a good wall. But one may luckily build a sturdy wall while neglecting such principles wholesale. Merely pointing to the violation of the rules of sound construction doesn't show that the product isn't in fact what it looks like—a sturdy wall. These too are regulative rules. On the other hand, no leg-swinging behavior counts as kicking a field goal without the rules of football. In this respect the constitutive relation implied by correspondence is like a constitutive rule.

However, constitutive rules—in contrast to relations—create or define behaviors that are themselves conventional. Two people may go through all the same moves as in a certain game of chess, but they may not be playing chess if, say, they are spies exchanging coded messages rather than competing to win by capturing an opponent's king. Constitutive rules come into existence at a certain time: behavior preceding that time cannot be

6. Much of this follows Searle (1969, 33ff.).

described in terms of the activity these rules create. Of course there are borderline cases. In particular, the behavior definitive of our more basic social conventions—those that aren't mere games (e.g., the rules of primitive exchange)—very likely evolved virtually imperceptibly out of a prior naturalistic base.[7] Still, for a conventional activity we can imagine photographically indistinguishable forms of behavior occurring before the institution of the rules, but which don't count as the behaviors in question (e.g., playing football, chess, bridge, paying a debt, marrying) just because the rules are not in force. This distinction is not always sharp. Throwing a game doesn't show one hasn't played, though playing to win is best viewed as a constitutive rather than a regulative rule of competitions. So occasionally even some constitutive rules can be violated as long as a certain critical mass of them plus other conditions remain in place. There is no general meta rule to determine when a violation, or collection of them, reaches the point of nullifying the activity.

On the other hand, constitutive *relations* are not confined to activities, conventional or otherwise. In addition, they cut across the conventional-natural divide. The second difference is of prime importance here. Such relations may be constitutive of natural as well as artificial phenomena. Thus, and ignoring *recherché* cases, something is a fingerprint if and only if it is a mark left by the tip of the fleshy part of someone's finger touching a surface. That doesn't make being a fingerprint conventional. Similarly for correspondence truth. The correspondence relation determining truth is, save for specialized subject matters, indifferent to conventions that may be in play. Of course, we can't avoid the contextual relativity of standards for truth. What passes for having made one's bed at home may not pass muster in a hospital or in the army. And on some schemes propositions themselves are conventional entities. Fortunately, we needn't take a stand on that issue because the rules constituting propositions aren't constitutive rules of actual truth. As long as it is granted that we begin with a particular fully formed proposition and the appropriate division of the world, we cannot imagine that the proposition wouldn't be an apt subject for a truth predicate at some time or under some circumstances just because of a lack of a certain further convention. For correspondence, once the conventions for propositionality and conversational standards are in place the truth of a proposition is simply a natural or metaphysical fact.

7. For details, see Lewis 1969.

This may not clarify for some readers all the issues that have been raised concerning the notion of constitution. For example, on what has been called the truthmaker principle—roughly, that the obtaining of a truthmaker necessitates the truth of its proposition—it has been claimed that the relation of a constituter to what it constitutes must be modal. But, as was argued earlier in "second," the relation is not causal. From this it has been inferred that the modality involved can't be physical, and from thence to the conclusion that it must be one of logical necessity. But logical necessity holds between two propositional items, which, it can be immediately seen, is not the sort of relationship we are after. However, I defer taking up this problem until section 9.1. It appears not to be a matter of initial clarification, but a technical issue within modal semantics. As such, it seems best left for an occasion when each side has more cards on the table.

7. A word about statements: A proposition's being stated is mentioned in the quasi-official version of correspondence. This may appear to tie truth to the activity of stating. But a proposition retains its truth-value in all nonstatemental contexts in which it occurs. If the proposition *that Hitler died in the bunker* is true, it will remain so as a component of propositions expressed by each of the following sentences: "If Hitler died in the bunker, dental records should confirm it." "Either Hitler died in the bunker or he escaped to Paraguay." "It is not the case that Hitler died in the bunker." "Fred believes that Hitler died in the bunker." "Maud has entertained the possibility that Hitler died in the bunker." Although the proposition occurs in each context, it is not stated in any of them. In some of them a simple proposition's truth-value contributes to that of its compound context, stated or not, of which it is a constituent, in others it does not. But as long as it is that proposition, no conceivable circumstances will be such that it can lose its truth-value while the rest of the world remains the same.

While this may seem to minimize the role of statements in the official formula, there is a point to employing them.[8] (I am not distinguishing

---

8. While statements aren't crucial to probing truth, the other direction (the dependence of statements on truth) could be a different matter. Certain theories of meaning or content begin with whole sentences, and some of those take truth-apt sentences as central. Their semantics may then be given in terms of truth conditions (as contrasted, say, with assertibility conditions) attaching to various statements of a sentence. If one's interest is in general semantics rather than truth, and one holds

statements from assertions. They may be differentiated in some accounts of speech acts, but the notions are deployed interchangeably here.) What then is the point of using statements in formulating the theory? The brief answer is that framing the theory in these terms allows us to avoid a more burdensome traditional version of correspondence, one whose difficulties have occasionally seemed to doom any correspondence theory. I explain.

Some versions of correspondence commence with mapping relations between simpler constituents of truth bearers and ingredients of configurations in the world: say, between words and things. In chapter 8 these views are brought together under the rubric 'correspondence-as-correlation'. Notoriously, proponents have regularly stumbled when trying to discover the requisite isomorphisms between whole thoughts (or statements-cum-sentences) and truthmakers in the (nonlinguistic, noncognized) world. We have avoided the problems this approach begets by initially taking as primitive the relation between the relevant state of the world and an imagined assertion of a noncompound proposition. That is the chief virtue of using *stating* in our formula, and I shall take it as sufficient excuse for my use of the popular term 'assertoric content' to refer to the sort of content of interest in researches into truth-aptitude. However, if there is any more intimate relationship between assertion and truth, it has escaped my notice. Of course, once we have made this connection, we may subsequently acknowledge that our propositions (or assertions) have constituents, that it is important to map them onto constituents of the worldly correlate, and that the latter may include referents and properties to which referring and predicate tokens in the assertions correlate. But as long as there is no need to construct our truth correlations from such elements, we are not captive to their implied isomorphism. Beginning with whole propositions contemplated as being stated illustrates why the problem of isomorphism for correspondence is gratuitous. Of course, I should also explain why I am entitled to this starting point—a task I defer, once again, until chapter 8.

I need not take a stand on the feasibility of finding any such isomorphisms, or on discovering worthwhile structures of statements explaining how

---

a view of this sort, there may be an intimate tie between stating and truth. We have the luxury here of remaining uncommitted on that issue. But it is important to notice that while this has the potential to reveal something about statements, it doesn't imply the converse—that truth can't be understood in terms of different bearers.

the latter latch on to a particular worldly correlate. The crucial point is that these are different tasks from the one in which we are now engaged. Consequently, their failure is no mark against correspondence projects as such. The question of the proper theory of truth begins from the recognition that there are bearers of truth-value, and asks what, if anything, determines that they have one of these values rather than the other (or, rather than no value). As understood here, nothing in correspondence requires us to say any more about the internal composition needed to qualify as a subject of truth. One reason this may not have been apparent is that some authors have integrated their truth theories with theories of sentential meaning, and have implied it is required of a truth theory that it do so. But keep in mind that this is a theory of truth—in the order of inquiry, it begins only where potential truth bearers have been secured, or at least assumed. This is not to deny that the character of truth bearers has implications for one or another theory. Deflationists and coherentists both rely in their different ways on emphasizing one among the various bearers. Still, the bearers enter their deliberations fully formed. Thus, while there can be no objection to a combined theory of meaning and truth, we must beware of building into truth theory a requirement that it be part of a more comprehensive semantic theory. The independence of truth from a theory of meaning removes a popular reason for supposing that we must first understand the inner structure of bearers in order to apprehend the word-world relation of truth.

8. I have tried to frame correspondence as neutrally as possible between competing specifications without having my characterization degenerate into vacuity. Thus, my formulation doesn't mention "facts," "states of affairs," or "situations." However, there really is no reason why propositions should have one, or primarily one, kind of truth correlate, any more than that a referring expression should only refer to one kind of thing.[9] We can always use one of these as a generic cover term for the variety of truth-makers. Indeed, I previously stated my own intention to use 'worldly circumstances' for just such a purpose, and in chapter 8 I also take 'state of affairs' to be that sort of covering term. But it should be made clear that this is only an umbrella term, not an attempt at explanation or to link the theory to a more specific, well-understood expression.

9. This point is nicely stated by Goldman (1999, 61–62).

Much more will be said about one of these potential candidates for worldly circumstance, *facts*, in the next chapter. However, given the sorts of opponents on which I shall concentrate, it is relatively unimportant whether these serve universally as truthmakers as long as we locate one such. The point can be made vivid by comparing two sorts of opponents of correspondence whose objections go in diametrically opposed directions. The first sort maintains that nothing in the vicinity of worldly circumstances ever constitutes a bearer as true, the second that no single thing constitutes every truth. I concentrate on the first sort of opponent, who seems to me to pose the more basic threat. The second sort, who argues only against the exclusivity of correspondence, is willing at least to incorporate a correspondence clause in her overall theory. But the first sort of opponent isn't objecting to the overreach of the theory, but to the devices in terms of which it is stated. For that opponent, the issue is whether the notion of a correspondence-like relation as truth constituter can be brought off. A single instance of the determination of truth by a worldly circumstance defeats her objection. The second sort, as explained later, is usually someone who would modify, rather than scrap, the claims of correspondence theorists.

Others may be inclined to object to the expression "state of the world," as too global for the truth determiners of most propositions. I trust the following concessive qualification removes this isolated discomfort. Ordinarily propositions wouldn't state anything about the whole world, although my formulation may lead one to believe that it implies that each proposition has something to say about the entirety of reality. If so, we can replace "state of the world" by "state of an aspect of the world" or add "(or state of an aspect of the world)" as needed.

9. If the second sort of critic of two paragraphs ago is correct, truth isn't a univocal notion. But even if there is more than one kind of truthmaker, we want to distinguish all such from uses in which the adjective 'true' may mean genuine, or loyal, or precise, as in phrases such as "true sapphire," "true friend," and "true plumbline." These are no doubt tied etymologically to our targeted sense: they seem to emerge from a common root. But no one would confuse them with the uses of 'true' over which philosophers have been poring. In fact, it will turn out that, pluralists aside, there is a sense in which even correspondence isn't really committed to every true proposition having a distinctive state of the world relevant to its truth. (See chapter 3.)

10. Finally, allow me to insert the following preliminary defensive point. Suppose an opponent charges that this notion of a truth constituter is still too obscure or unclear to play a serious role in philosophizing. And suppose, further, that elaboration of this informal sort is the best that is available to us, so that nothing we could do would bring us closer to correcting this alleged flaw. One consideration seems to me to outweigh all such misgivings: namely, constitution, however poorly understood, is an indispensable notion that will need to be included in anyone's more developed theory of truth. Not that I find anything seriously problematic or wanting in the explanation given here. Yet, even were the problem conceded, constitution would remain a live issue. When attempting a philosophical account, we are in no position to scuttle a notion needed for another one we want to understand just because of our preference for better-behaved subject matters. We must plod ahead. Indeed, as I shall argue much later, even deflationists do (and must) appeal to truth's constitution in word or deed at the end of the day. On their account, what constitutes truth may be slight, but nonetheless it *is* all that constitutes truth. For now that can be set aside. Eventually what matters is that any theorist who claims to be giving an account of truth, and not just some aspect of it, must say something about what constitutes it, or show why it lacks a constitution, a responsibility that cannot be evaded by cutting off one's inquiry before reaching that point. In this regard, I might add that Tarski realized this, although some of those deeply influenced by his work seem to disagree. Thus, while he is praised for his formal achievement, he has sometimes been mildly rebuked for his halting, and allegedly inadequate, efforts to connect that work with the question of what constituted truth. (See the passages quoted in chapter 1.) I believe Tarski's instinct was healthy, and those of the admirers who fault him on those grounds were short-sighted. But the argument for those bold claims will be postponed until chapter 6.

3 Eligible Correspondence Schemes

However strong the initial appeal of correspondence, the argument on its behalf will be incomplete until certain well-known sources of disquiet are addressed. Most of the questions surrounding these objections will have to await chapters 8 and 9. But some grounds for dissent have proved so commonplace that it seems important, for the ensuing discussion to continue smoothly, to give at least an indication that they don't represent insuperable obstacles to the candidacy of correspondence. The most pressing of those is the character of the worldly truthmaker. The notion of fact has come in for the harshest criticism, so I take that as my central theme in this chapter. Another issue, nearly as pressing, is the supposed subject-object gap that inflicts correspondence. There is a certain nagging form of argument designed to make vivid the puzzlement alleged to accompany this gap. I call the argument 'the Berkeleyan Gambit' after the eighteenth century figure who, if not the first to use it, is surely its most stunning advocate. Those subjects will be taken up in order.

3.1 Facts as Truthmakers

My quasi-official formulation of correspondence doesn't explain the more specific character of the worldly, truth-constituting correlate. It seems eminently reasonable to leave this open. Not that we shouldn't believe that there are such things as facts, states of affairs, or situations. Quite the contrary, we appear perfectly capable of providing clear and uncontroversial examples of each. Undeniable cases of *fact* include that Abraham Lincoln was assassinated, that San Francisco is in California, and that my car's antifreeze is leaking. Moreover, that Lincoln was assassinated is a different fact from that my car's antifreeze is leaking.[1] No doubt, some critics don't believe a rigorous definition is so much as possible. Even if the case were otherwise, little hope would be offered that we will ever achieve precise principles of individuation and criteria of identity for such things. Is the fact of Lincoln's having been assassinated different from that of the sixteenth president's having been assassinated, or from Lincoln's having been assassinated in Ford's Theatre? (Cf. Williams 2002, 64.) Once these questions are pressed, the solid ground beneath us seems to give way.

For all that, facts, states of affairs, situations and the like are not *in extremis*. There are perfectly legitimate instances of each of the candidates for constitution. Facts aren't mentioned in my characterization of correspondence, not because I hold them to be especially problematic, but because, as stated earlier, there seems no more compelling reason why propositions should be made true by, or express, one particular category of thing than that singular terms should all refer to one particular category of thing. And using 'fact' as a cover term threatens to produce more confusion than illumination if only because of its tendency to convey the mistaken impression that it is an attempt to explain, rather than merely collect under an umbrella term, the various truthmakers. Indeed, once that is made plain, in chapter 8 'state of affairs' is used as just such a cover term for stating a version of correspondence. There may be some broad conditions we can place on potential truthmakers, such as that they be worldly items, just as there are some broad conditions various thinkers have wanted to place upon the class of potential referents (e.g., that they be well individuated, that they exist). But the attempt to delineate this class more specifically threatens to deflect the inquiry into what is minimally a distraction or at worst a dead-end controversy. The history of disputes over correspondence indicates that the threat is very real. Nevertheless, some of the misgivings that generate the worry over facts can and should be put to rest. I proceed to explain.

Why are facts as truthmakers so widely abhorred? No doubt, details about their individuation raise controversy, but this can scarcely account for so broad a rejection. The lack of such details is seldom an insurmountable obstacle to at least the tentative acceptance of an otherwise eligible notion. We could choose, as some have chosen, to make facts extensional

---

1. Discussion of the notorious Davidsonian demonstration that there can be at most one fact is deferred to chapter 9.

(Pendlebury 1986), or to accord them varying grades of intensionality. Some such decisions may be well motivated. The real difficulty over individuation is that any choice seems to be matched by a different, equally plausible, one. This makes any choice of a fact ontology appear arbitrary. It is a serious problem, but not one that we cannot live with. The satisfaction of ideal standards for philosophical accounts of anything are so rare that *prima facie* it is perfectly reasonable to impute some failures to our own inadequacies or limitations when there are robust examples of the phenomenon before us—that is, we shouldn't immediately jump to disqualify the phenomenon for all serious employment (viz., to illuminate other matters) only because we are unable to provide for it what we are unable to provide for just about any notion that has commanded philosophical scrutiny. One very tentative test for a phenomenon that might outlast obstacles to its precisification would be the availability of good solid examples. And I have claimed that we have this for facts. Of course, that isn't decisive; at best it is only a stay of execution. To overcome this presumption in favor of facts, we would want something that struck at the very heart of the notion, perhaps a transcendental argument for the impossibility of facts. In the absence of so potent an objection, the difficulties in framing acceptable general answers to the questions about identity and individuation won't be decisive arguments against there being facts, or even against their being sufficiently well understood to figure in philosophical accounts of truth.

Most empirical notions we use in good faith suffer a similar fate. For example, we may be unable to answer determinately "two mountains" or "a single mountain with twin peaks separated by a saddle," or (said of the Pope's crown) "a single crown constructed of three crowns" or "three crowns." The former wouldn't show that there weren't mountains, the latter wouldn't show that there are no crowns.[2] Unless we are prepared to jettison the vast majority of our empirical concepts, doing so on comparable grounds for facts is a disproportionate response given our tolerance elsewhere. Indeed, just this sort of problem plagues many respectable workaday concepts that are nevertheless widely used in philosophy. What remains to complete the present case is only to show that the most serious specific objections to the use of facts can be rebutted. It is to that task that I now turn.

2. Indeed, the case of fact may just be another instance of the phenomenon of the *open texture* of empirical concepts, brought to our attention by Friedrich Waismann.

I concentrate on facts precisely because fact-based correspondence has by far the greatest share of unfavorable press among truthmakers. If complaints about them can be deflected, there is even less hope for principled objections to less vulnerable worldly circumstances. But before examining these objections, I remind readers, at the risk of belaboring the point, that not every correspondence theorist appeals to facts. Some prefer states of affairs, situations, events (including static events), moments; others of a more nominalist bent take it that the world contains only individuals and, perhaps, their (instantiations of) properties and relations (that is, thin and thick individuals). Among those who reject facts, some do not regard this as fatal to correspondence (Sellars 1959, 167; Goldman 1999, 61–62; Devitt 1994, 28); others take it as a potentially mortal blow to the theory (Devitt 1994, 37n4; Davidson 1990, 303; David 1994, 20). Some of those who disclaim correspondence because of the difficulty in specifying the right sorts of fact are nevertheless regarded by certain commentators as correspondence theorists because they supply worldly determiners for truth and falsehood. But here we confine our attention to fact-based correspondence.

Perhaps the most common charge brought against facts, or at least against their role in correspondence, is that they are not really separate entities at all, at least not separate from statements whose truth they are supposed to secure. We seem most familiar with facts from constructions such as 'it is a fact that . . .' followed by a propositional clause. But, so the claim goes, we say nothing more with such phrases than we would with 'it is true that. . . .' We can say either "it is a fact that Lincoln was assassinated" or "it is true that Lincoln was assassinated." Facts, it is concluded, are mere shadows cast by truths, no more than a *façon de parler* devised to save us from overusing expressions such as 'true' or 'true statement'. Because a similar result holds across the board for our fact idioms, it is concluded that all fact talk is nothing more than an alternative vocabulary for assertion or truth talk. Here are samples of this widely shared sentiment:

I contend that *"a fact"* and *"a true proposition"* mean identically the same thing. The evidence is that the expression "It is true that . . . " can always be substituted for "It is a fact that . . . " and vice versa; and that nothing can be deduced from what either expression formulates, which can not be deduced from what the other formulates. (Ducasse 1940, 710)

I am inclined to think . . . that it would not deviate too much from customary usage if we were to explicate the term 'fact' as referring to a certain kind of proposition. . . .

What properties must a proposition have to be a fact in this sense? First, it must, of course, be true; second, it must be contingent. . . . (Carnap 1947, 28)

There is no nuance, except of style, between 'That's true' and 'That's a fact'; nor between 'Is it true that . . . ?' and 'Is it a fact that . . . ?' [Facts and statements] were made for each other. If you prise the statements off the world you prise the facts off it too; but the world would be none the poorer. (Strawson 1971, 196–197)

. . . only indirection results from positing facts, in the image of sentences, as intermediaries. . . . In ordinary usage 'fact' often occurs where we could without loss say 'true sentence' or (if it is our way) 'true proposition'. (Quine 1960, 247)

We can, if we like, say that [aRb] is true if there exists a corresponding fact that a has R to b, but this is essentially not an analysis but a periphrasis, for 'The fact that a has R to b exists' is no different from 'a has R to b'. (Ramsey 1960, 143)

We could . . . eliminate the word 'fact' from the language altogether and substitute for it the longer expression 'true proposition'. . . . In ordinary usage they are surely identical, in that whenever we assert that something is a fact we could assert that it is true without change of meaning. (Woozley 1966, 12)

'What we think of as a fact' certainly means no more and no less than 'What we think is true'. . . . (Prior 1971, 5)

['Corresponds with the facts'] gains[s] a use only by being allowed as a substitute for 'is true'. (Blackburn 1984, 225)

. . . not every statement has its fact; only the true ones do. But then, unless we find another way to pick out facts, we cannot hope to explain truth by appeal to them. (Davidson 1984, 43)

The objection purports to show that there are no such worldly items as facts.[3] Were it cogent, it would be fatal to fact-based correspondence. But I don't believe it is. With no very precise notion of fact on offer,[4] it can be argued that the objection fails on two counts. First, even if the rough

---

3. And others have been persuaded by Strawson's criticism to take on board this attitude toward facts without even this much by way of argument. See, e.g., Wiggins 1980; Dodd 1995.

4. This is not to say that the situation is hopeless. I have more to say in chapter 9 about prospects for harnessing principles of individuation and identity. But for starters we might simply treat facts analogously to the way that some theorists (e.g. Kim (1993b)) treat events, say, as property exemplifications. (For whatever reason, while an ontology of events isn't universally accepted (see, e.g. , Horgan 1978), it raises much less of a howl.) Davidson's Slingshot argument aside, which in any case is commonly ignored or resisted, it is hard to see why there is such disparity in the level of opposition for the two cases.

equivalence held, it wouldn't show what critics take it to show. Second, the equivalence doesn't hold. It may seem perverse to pay so much attention to this one objection when there are other urgent problems about facts. But in my experience this general outlook regarding 'fact' talk regularly surfaces informally, as well as in print. And it is worth putting to rest something that seems to play so vital a role, often a surreptitious one, when the question of truth-determiners has been raised.

Suppose, as is widely believed, that the ingredients of facts are described with the same vocabulary and, insofar as syntax can reflect it, they display the same structure as sentences employed to state them. There may be a number of potential explanations for this convergence, but here, in telescoped versions, are two leading candidates:

(a) Facts are nothing more than reifications of a style of speaking.

(b) Since it is a, perhaps *the*, chief job of statements to state facts, it is understandable that the same linguistic resources would be marshaled to formulate both.

Given that both explanations are in play, and given that there is no obvious reason to prefer (a) to (b), it is something of a mystery that so many philosophers embrace (a) and dismiss (b) without further ado. This is quite apart from whatever other reasons—including those mentioned regarding principles of individuation, hard cases, and scope—there may be for rejecting facts. From our current vantage point, the latter set of objections haven't been dismissed, but their charges aren't in question. Our present concern is an argument that begins from the undoubted datum of similarity in the specifications of both facts and truths and concludes that this is to be explained by there being only one kind of item, true statements, not two. However, whenever there are two or more comparably plausible explanations for a phenomenon, it is arbitrary to opt for one of them without explanation.

One may question just how potent an explanation (b) can yield. The following points lend it greater credibility.

First, start from the plausible hypothesis that if a certain state of affairs could be expected to obtain even if a particular thesis is false, then citing it doesn't support that thesis. Even if facts and statements were distinct, and even if originally (say, in the distant past) there had been distinct vocabularies for specifying instances of each, we would expect that ultimately the verbal resources used to specify the one would converge with those with which we specify the other. After all, as noted, a (if not the) chief job of stating on anyone's account is to state facts. So if a form of words was adopted in order to express the content of the one, it is only natural that it would also be used to express the content of the other.

Second, compare this case to that of mirror images. Of course, I can specify something as "the mirror image of . . . " (just as I can use the phrase 'the fact that . . .'). But past that, phrases like 'violets on a mahogany table' fill out descriptions of both the physical world and its mirror images. There aren't two vocabularies, say, for specifying mahogany tables—one for the tables themselves, the other for their mirror images. This is precisely what we should expect. Nevertheless, no one would want to deny that images of tables are distinct from tables. So of what possible polemical value can be the datum that true statements and facts are represented by similar clauses?

However, next, the equivalence doesn't hold. While we can phrase many things indifferently in factative or statemental clauses, some fact talk isn't paraphrasable by truth talk. This is particularly obvious where facts are taken as causes or effects. Thus, consider the following specimens:

That the plane hit an air pocket caused her to panic. (Or, she panicked because the plane hit an air pocket.)

She gathered he was nervous from the fact that he spilled his drink.

There were facts in the Triassic period, but no true statements.[5]

The fact that the plane hit an air pocket may explain her panicking, but the true statement (or truth) that the plane hit an air pocket doesn't explain it. Or, if it does, it explains it in a different way. (If the statement itself caused her to panic, as long as she believed it why should its truth matter?) And her gathering he was nervous from a true statement is, at the very least, more specific than gathering it from the fact (which weakly suggests that she witnessed the spilling). So despite the overlap in "it is true that" and "it is a fact that," which I have argued we should expect in any event, the thesis that they are totally interchangeable idioms isn't even true.

3.2 Forms of Correspondence

The requirement that there be a distinctive fact for each truth may appear to pose another difficulty for correspondence. What sort of fact corresponds

5. See Vision 1988, 57–58; Searle 1995, 206; Steward 1997, 135.

to the truth that there have been wars? Also, is it reasonable to hold that there are negative facts, conditional facts, subjunctive facts, and so on to correspond to the variety of truths we can state? In addition, there are areas of discourse in which, although it is claimed that our utterances are truth-apt, there are no facts to support them—areas of constant philosophical contention, such as mathematics and ethics. There are a number of responses for meeting these challenges. I shall be interested here only in some that illustrate ways to fashion different varieties of correspondence. That will help indicate why the brief statement of the view on which we have been operating, and whose supposed grievous shortcomings are the topic of the next chapter, is a way to summarize a number of varieties rather than merely an offhand concoction.

As mentioned earlier, not every correspondentist appeals to facts. Of those who do so, facts may be only one among a variety of determinants of truth: they could be part of the truth-determination story without being the whole of it. But, although other options also come into play, I concentrate primarily on a response that removes much of the urgency of this charge: to wit, not even fact-based correspondence is committed to there being a distinctive fact for every truth.

First, because facts have ingredients referred to by expressions, reductionist accounts of those expressions or the statements containing them may issue in reductionist accounts of the facts they seem to express. For example, a reductionist may hold that there is no distinctively arithmetical fact corresponding to the truth of $5 + 12 = 17$. Yet the would-be statement may be counted as truth-apt. Perhaps its truth is determined by a collection of facts about sets of sets, or facts about many sorts of concreta such as ducks and pencils. Fact-based correspondence as such is neutral with respect to those disputes. It is required only that at the lowest level there will be some facts, even if not distinctive of that subject matter, that account for the truth or falsity of propositions belonging to a certain class. Thus, the Berkeleyan view that facts about ideas (God's and ours) constitute the truth of statements about tables and rivers is fully compatible with fact-based correspondence. Indeed, for Russell's (1985, 74) correspondence theory, the truth-functional reduction of compounds solves the problem for negative and (some) conditional truths. Russell calls compound propositions 'molecular'. Whereas there are true molecular propositions, there is no need (with some qualification) for molecular facts to correspond to each of them.[6]

Second, at least for the philosophically contentious areas, it is possible to say that the facts supporting such truths may themselves be conventional facts. This option was introduced in chapter 2. It is not as *ad hoc* as it may at first seem, since so many of the facts about which little question is raised involve economic, political, or gaming conventions. Of course, the dyed-in-the-wool physicalist may have misgivings about those sorts of facts as well.[7] But I take it that the laws and looser generalizations in the special sciences that are based on data described in these conventional terms make it at least *prima facie* plausible that conventional facts of these other sorts are admissible. If so, why not admit, say, the fact that Smith acted abominably toward his sister or that 9 is greater than 7? This proposal, plus the one to follow ("third"), takes on greater significance at various junctures in our future discussion—later again in this chapter, and in chapters 4 and 9.

Third, the friend of facts can be even more heterodox. Suppose (what is likely in any event) reductions aren't available, but the notion of truth is extended to a class of propositions, even though no facts correspond to them, because they bear other similarities to the central fact-based notion of correspondence. Indeed, even if we were to insist that fact-based correspondence appear in any adequate analysis of truth, we should expect something like this. There is no *Académie des Idées Générales* to protect perfectly good and precise usages from being co-opted and extended by speakers. This is an immeasurable good: semantic inventiveness has resulted in tropes that have been instrumental to progress and enrichment even in well-tuned disciplines such as physics. But such novel employments do complicate prescriptions for the task and goals of conceptual inquiry. Under these conditions the task of the theorist is not so much to supply necessary and sufficient conditions for a concept. Those may very well be out of reach. Rather, it may be her job to supply necessary and sufficient conditions for the central cases, and persuasive explanations for cases deviating from them. For handy cross-reference, let us call this last

---

6. This is implicit in §4.41 and §4.431 of Wittgenstein 1922.
7. Horgan (2001), apparently starting from facts rather than truths, calls his view "indirect" correspondence only because his austere physicalism doesn't acknowledge the rich range of facts needed to cover most of what we take to be true.

view **Extended Correspondence**. The defender of fact-based correspondence can define her own task in this way.

The crucial point about both the enlarged views just mentioned—the point that keeps them fact based—is that the noncentral cases be viewed as somehow dependent on, and thus secondary to, those in which something clearly recognizable as a fact determines the truth of a proposition. This seems to have been the sort of account that P. F. Strawson (a onetime deflationist) had in mind when he wrote the following:

> Instead of abandoning the [simple model of word-world correspondence], we should rather consider the kinds of case to which it applies without reserve as the primary or basic cases of truth; and then, taking this as a starting point, seek to explain how it is possible and legitimate to extend the notion of truth beyond these limits without feeding on myth or illusion. (1992, 91)

Once the truth-aptness of such utterances is granted, this will distinguish correspondence from one form of pluralist theory (in which quite distinct and unrelated truth constituters work for different language fragments). Furthermore, it seems plausible that such a dependence is in the offing, and that a promising tale about it is available. On the other hand, taking pluralism seriously, TRUTH is radically ambiguous despite some vague similarities: acknowledging it across a variety of widely disparate, otherwise remotely related, truthmakers may seem arbitrary rather than well grounded. (I shall return to this point in chapter 4.)

However, the first and third options come at a price. Not every statement of fact-based correspondence passes muster on them. It will still be possible to say that a proposition is true if it corresponds to a fact, for this merely sufficient condition for truth doesn't presuppose that there is a distinctive fact for each truth. But suppose fact-based correspondence is formulated as follows:

(p)   The proposition that p is true *iff* it is a fact that p. (Alston 1996, 38)

The quantification is substitutional, and each instance is obtained by the consistent replacement of 'p'. Or suppose we maintain that "because a proposition's being true consists in things being as they are said to be, wherever there is a true proposition that p there must also be a fact that p" (Mackie 1973, 56). If 'fact' is being used simply as a place holder for whatever generally non-intentional, worldly situation makes a proposition true (Searle 1995, 213), any conflict with the fact-based options just considered would be merely terminological. But if these accounts rely on a prior, roughly colloquial, understanding of 'fact', which may then figure in an explanation of truth, these views disagree with, say, Russell's on the treatment of truth-functional compounds. On this last assumption, neither of the two quoted accounts has stated a core shared by all fact-based correspondence. However, from the perspective of correspondence theories, there seems to me no drawback both in taking facts seriously and relying on any of the procedures just cited for filling in the details. This is one reason why, as we shall see in the next chapter, the brief statements of correspondence with which we have been working should be considered summaries designed to embrace a number of varieties rather than merely underdeveloped stabs at a correspondence view.

But if we simply use 'fact' (or, for that matter, 'worldly circumstance') as a place holder for whatever the correlate of truth happens to be, that too has drawn fire from correspondence's critics. Davidson (1996, 267) has written of the "awkward blanks marked by the words '[the world being] so and so'." The suggestion is that if this sort of indefiniteness is inescapable, it is a sufficient reason to abandon the correspondence enterprise. And I am confident that plugging in 'fact' as an indefinite cover term wouldn't be regarded by Davidson as an improvement. (See Davidson's fact-bashing quote earlier in this chapter.) However, to counter this we may observe that the awkwardness pales in comparison to that stemming from a refusal to countenance the term 'the world being so and so' even in the most straightforward empirical sort of case from which philosophers typically launch their inquiries. Change the world and you change truth-values. If the proposition is *that this hamster is my pet* and we consider the world changed—that is, consider a different possible world—so that in it my only pet is a goldfish, that very utterance is not true, but false. That is about as close as we are going to come to an irrefutable datum in philosophy. If it isn't a firm basis on which to erect a theory of truth, it is difficult to see how strategies taking off from other starting points could withstand scrutiny. So in the final accounting it is baffling that we can regard "the world being so and so" as no more than an awkward blank, much less how, if it is our predicament, this can be a serious obstacle to a correspondence outlook.

Someone, although certainly not Davidson, may be tempted to respond that by changing the possible world, we thereby change the proposition in question. The referent in the actual world is a hamster; in the alternative world it is a goldfish. In reply notice that the proposition in question (or the phrase 'this hamster') has been, to use a term of art, rigidified (or indexed) to the actual world. It is the original proposition, with its actual reference to a certain hamster, we are considering in altered circumstances. What is true is that the sentence 'This hamster is my (only) pet' could, when uttered in that non-actual world, express a different proposition, or even that (grant for the sake of argument) it might be difficult to see how I could use a sentence to instantiate that proposition from within that possible world. However, the proposition stated by an utterance of the sentence in another world isn't under consideration. Rather, we are discussing our current proposition under changed circumstances.

For yet a different direction in which correspondence might move (indeed, has moved), we might consider rejecting (ℛ) and (𝒟). I begin with some background comments.

A typical recent defense of, say, (ℛ) rests on the view that truth-aptness is no more than a trivial, syntactic matter. This view is known as **syntacticism**. If a proposition satisfies certain syntactical constraints, such as taking negation and being embeddable in truth-functional and intentional contexts, it is truth-apt. Sophisticated versions add that the discourse "must be subject to acknowledged standards of warrant" (Wright 1994b, 327)—we may call this **disciplined syntacticism**—but it is not regarded as a significant upgrading of the body of syntactic requirements. On it, even utterances such as that something is humorous or chic may be deemed true, though it is difficult to imagine that these discourses are fact-stating. On the other hand, some—e.g., Mark Richard (1997)—have suggested we might reject (ℛ) on the grounds that all sorts of believable and assertible propositions don't purport to state facts, and thus don't take a truth-value, although they may be acceptable or unacceptable for other reasons. Of course, this view also requires that we reject truth-aptness as a necessary condition for propositionality, a move syntacticists will be inclined to oppose. But discarding that requirement is not difficult. These dissenters from (ℛ) reject the syntacticist notion, favored typically by deflationists and pluralists, that just because a proposition is acceptable it is truth-apt: "p" may merit a place in the archives without being true. For example, someone might believe that Sherlock Holmes played the violin on the grounds that it is cognitively better (the potential advantages being too great and diverse to enumerate) to hold this than not to or to believe its opposite, but she might not believe that the proposition is true if it doesn't state, or purport to state, a fact or state of affairs. Some instances of ($\mathcal{R}$) and some instances of the schema

p iff it is a fact that p

needn't be true on this combination of views, but that will be no barrier to the correctness of the earlier minimal correspondence formula. In sum, the proponent of this view will admit standards of acceptability other than truth. Reductionist and extended versions aside, nothing in this need be incompatible with holding the version from Alston recently cited—(p) (it is true that p iff it is a fact that p).

This can serve as a model for withholding attributions of truth for recognizable propositions in a number of disputed areas. For example, there are lively disputes over the truth-aptness of declarative utterances in areas such as scientific theorizing, ethics, aesthetics, and mathematics. Similar questions arise about subjunctive conditionals. How will these disputes go? For starters, a syntacticist may defend her view by noting that customary practice sanctions ascribing truth and falsity to all sorts of nonfactual discourses. Taking ethics as an example, she may note that we feel no compunction about saying that *it is true* that someone has a moral right to respond to an unprovoked slander. (Cf. Hill 2002, 54–55.) For a syntacticist, this may be enough to settle the issue. Against this, someone developing the current view could argue it is possible for us to declare that, despite our custom of attaching truth-values to moral judgments, the practice is not to be taken seriously. The syntacticist is likely to respond that adopting anything other than the syntactical view and our everyday practice in using 'true' and 'false' in nonfactual discourse would require of us a deeper metaphysical insight into what makes a candidate truth-apt. And, she continues, it is not plausible to suppose that we have anything akin to such metaphysical insight into the nature of reality.

This last syntacticist response gains much of its force from an unarticulated assumption to the effect that what we are looking for is a uniform method, applicable to any subject whatsoever, to discern whether there are facts (or even a reductive class of such). Granting it, syntacticists might be correct in supposing that there is little prospect of finding a panacea of this sort. But as an assumption about the way the rejecter of ($\mathcal{R}$) must, or usually does, proceed it is certainly questionable. These issues have been locally debated in philosophy for many years. The disputes between cognitivists (say, objectivists) and noncognitivists in ethics have unearthed a wealth of considerations, both pro and con, for regarding moral judgments as taking (or not taking) truth-values. In the philosophy of mathematics, advocates for constructivism and realism, and different shades of each, have likewise presented their cases in some detail. Similarly, while some have elaborately explained why subjunctive conditionals are not truth-apt, others have produced comparably detailed arguments to the effect that such propositions do take truth-values. In none of these cases have we merely consulted our intuitions when confronted with the question "Do utterances of type X take truth-values?" Considerations presented on each side have probed further into the details of particular practices. At a first approach, this leads us to suppose that there are a number of local philosophical questions, quite independent of the articles of truth theories, that have been brought forth to argue whether discourse X is factual (viz., fact stating).

Three qualifications are in order.

First, it is compatible with the realist side in each dispute that some propositions be indeterminate. That doesn't detract from the central differences between the disputants.

Second, some of the disputes are not directly over whether the candidates take truth-values. This may seem at first to favor syntacticists. There is the prospect of interpreting each dispute so that, say, the antirealist side can accord truth-values to the candidate propositions and still maintain that there is a gap between the views representative of their original disagreement. (Compare my earlier remarks on conventional facts and extended correspondence, and see the discussions in chapters 4 and 9.) Nevertheless, disagreements over truth-aptness are natural ways of entering and understanding the struggles. Some have sought, first, to accept the syntacticist prescription, and thereby ($\mathcal{R}$), and, then, to relocate the differences between the parties to the disputes. But, while that doesn't take us any closer by itself to resolving the differences, it may distort their original grounds. (For more details, see chapter 9.)

Finally, even if we regard all these disputes as, *inter alia*, over the truth-aptness of the candidate propositions, this wouldn't show that correspondence is the theory underlying truth-aptness. A coherentist or pragmatist, say, could claim that it is truth on her theory that is at issue. (Of course, on some versions, this may change the character of the debate. But that is a further question.) Nevertheless, historically the disagreements have developed against the background of tolerantly vague correspondentist assumptions. For example, consider the following typical antirealist challenge: What sorts of moral (or mathematical, or counterfactual) facts in the world could support ascribing truth, or objectivity, to such judgments? Perplexities about the presence (or absence) of mathematical or ethical worldly facts appear to grease the wheels of such inquiries. But even were we to allow other truth theories to underlie the differences, the present context is only intended to show how the correspondentist might make use of this material to reject ($\mathcal{R}$) without having to appeal simply to raw intuitions about the extension of factuality.

The syntacticist hasn't exhausted her resources. She may reply that these local disputes have been interminable, as is customary for philosophical disagreements. She may suggest in light of this that we scrap these endless squabbles and settle the matter either by supplying a set of topic independent metaphysical considerations for discriminating fact-stating from non-fact-stating language fragments or revert to using the generous standards of everyday discourse. Since the former is, as noted, unpromising, we are left only with the data of ordinary usage. And, turning to our disputed areas, it is conversationally proper to say that virtually all of Socrates' moral views are true, that it is true that there is no highest prime, and so on.

However, while it is true that the local disputes have not been resolved to general satisfaction—although I hope that no one thinks this follows from the fact that philosophers continue to disagree—it is equally the case that in the past positivistic impatience with philosophical controversies hasn't been more stable than the disputes it sought to replace. Positivisms too have waxed and waned in different eras and among different parties. I believe we should be at least equally suspicious of claims to shortcut long-standing philosophical disputes by replacing them with what advocates take to be their tractable substitutes. Thus, the dismissal of local questions for easier ones is subject to problems similar to those that led positivists to discard traditional disputes.

Moreover, there seems to me a further important complication involved in the appeal to homely, everyday discourse. Suppose that there were a fair philosophical consensus that moral language was nonfactual. (This would entail abandoning not only various naturalistic and non-naturalistic cognitivist views, but error theories as well.) Would the fact that language users in general continued to attribute truth and falsity to moral judgments show that the discourse is both truth-apt and nonfactual? Only on the assumption that language users in general accepted, and were applying their language in light of that philosophical consensus! But there is very little reason to accept this supposition. To show that it was correct we would need more evidence than that language users generally applied truth-values while engaged in moral discourse: we would need evidence showing that they continued to do so after being brought to accept the conclusion of the philosophical consensus, and would be doing so despite that acceptance. And it is perhaps for this reason that (or so it seems to me) we are much more likely to say that Socrates' moral opinions are correct or right than that they are true—a difference that is at least consistent with the earlier point about using standards of acceptability distinct from truth in some areas.

The upshot appears to be that there is a robust practice of trying to determine for various discourses whether their paradigm utterances are factual or not. But it is not the universal solvent that syntacticists pose as the sole considered alternative to their own view. It is a patchwork of local realist-antirealist disputes over restricted language fragments. If one is satisfied, say, that ethics is a factual discipline, even conventionally so, one can then say that its paradigm utterances are truth-apt. If one is satisfied that it isn't, one might say that despite conversational appearances to the contrary, those utterances aren't truth-apt. And it is not at all clear to me that our penchant for using truth and falsity for such judgments doesn't rest on an unguarded assumption that the discourse is factual. Of course, none of this forecloses an option for the correspondence theorist to agree with the syntacticist on the extension of truth-aptness. The present point is only that it is possible to remain a correspondence theorist, be selective about which propositions are truth-apt, but avoid extended correspondence, based on considerations specific to ethics, mathematics, etc. It is not my task here to assess this path, but merely to highlight how it remains a viable correspondentist alternative.

Whereas we have concentrated on the resources available to the correspondence theorist for taking part in these debates, in chapter 9 we shall compare those resources with those available to the deflationist and, by default, the syntacticist. The comparison will disclose further strengths of the correspondence position.

One final remark concerning facts. It is a commonplace that the external world can be cross-classified beyond discernible limits. Metaphysical antirealists make much of this, but realists should, and typically do, acknowledge it as well. Thus far, we are dealing no less with the purely external world just because it has been classified in one way rather than in another. Both a Swiss Army knife and an attached collection of pocket tools may be worldly, mind-independent items, however we choose to organize that part of reality. Nor does the fact that classifications are interest-driven have any tendency to show that it is other than the pure external world being so classified. Similarly, a system of individuating facts in which a chunk of spacetime under one predicate is not identical with that same chunk under another, wouldn't impugn the claim that both chunks are perfectly mind-independent constituents of reality. Lingering doubts about this may emanate from the belief that all classification is imposed by us on the world. That touches on a large topic that we can't explore further here. But the result is, I believe, that that bit of antirealist lore also should be resisted.[8] And, if so, that subverts another line of argument that has sometimes been used to disqualify facts for correspondentist employment.

3.3 The Berkeleyan Gambit

The ploy exposed in section 3.1—that facts are no more than truths—has been a wellspring from which critics have drawn various objections to the effect that one sentence summaries of correspondence, in this case those citing facts as truthmakers, do not amount to a theory. Rather, they are platitudes that any theory can assimilate. We follow up on that sort of reservation in the next chapter. But I mention it here because it is not so much a specific criticism as an underlying discomfort that may very well survive a thorough rebuttal of a carefully formulated objection based upon it. And, I believe it is important to doubters to have that sort of inducement to abandon correspondence if only because the data underlying the latter seem so compelling in their own right. When driven by rather specific, conflicting theoretical commitments, a rejection of correspondence may be tolerable: one simply reviews the relative merits of the competing views and makes a judgment based on the overall weight of the evidence. Correspondence excels in this sort of competition. But occasionally the dissatisfaction with

8. For more on this point, see Vision 1998.

it runs deeper than its merely being an obstruction to a preferred alternative. And it is especially such sources in which I am currently interested. For that reason, I will briefly discuss a procedural worry about correspondence that seems to me related to the concerns of section 3.1. My conclusion is that it is founded on an unsatisfactory way of approaching the issue, a way that shows it already to have a boot firmly planted in an idealist camp.

I choose, for the lucidity of its description, a version of the worry stated by Simon Blackburn and Keith Simmons. The authors believe the problem can be deflected. They introduce it primarily to open a discussion that raises further issues. But it is worth a closer look if only because they don't seem to me to have pinpointed its gravest shortcoming.

Blackburn and Simmons (1999b, 7) begin with a statement of the worry canvassed in the preceding section: "Everyone can agree that a statement is true if it corresponds with the facts. For 'corresponds with the facts' may be just an elaborate synonym for true."[9] From there they continue to describe the correspondence theorist's task as giving an account in which truth is brought about by a relation between entities of two different categories (say, propositions and facts). Their description of what is wanted for such an account effectively captures the concerns of some of the most implacable foes of correspondence:

> Thinking this way, it may appear, involves thinking of two distinct standpoints. There is the standpoint we occupy when we judge that p. Then in addition there is the standpoint we occupy when we step back, and judge that the judgment that p indeed bears the right relation to the fact that p. But then it is reasonable to urge that there are not two distinct standpoints here, but only one. . . . There are indeed mental processes that we can call 'standing back': becoming cautious about p, checking one more time whether p, and so on. But these are all processes of reflecting and checking whether p. (Blackburn and Simmons 1999b, 7)

In other words, if there are really two things—one the judgment that p, the other its relation to a fact—this ought to be reflected in distinguishable standpoints we could occupy. Let us call the first, uncontroversial, standpoint 'epistemic'. Quite clearly, just by judging that p—the epistemic standpoint—we don't gain a notion of correspondence. This sets us off in search of a second standpoint. But upon reflection the other standpoint we sought collapses into the first one. So we don't have two standpoints after all, and

---

9. Compare the passage from Blackburn 1984 quoted in section 3.1 above, in which he is less tentative about the connection.

that undermines the basis for regarding correspondence as an intelligible alternative to the position of simply judging that *p*.

Where does the notion of distinct standpoints acquire this urgency? A difficulty is created here only with the aid of a questionable major premise: namely, if these are distinct kinds of judging, we ought to be able to distinguish them by distinguishing between the cognitive relations in which we stand to their contents. To begin to see the complications in such a requirement, compare it with a notorious move Bishop Berkeley uses to establish idealism. It has come to be called his *master argument*. Berkeley writes that he is "content to put the whole [of his position] upon this issue," and he prefaces it with this remark:

If you can conceive it possible for any mixture or combination of qualities, or any sensible object whatever, to exist without the mind, then I will grant it actually to be so. (1734, 35)[10]

To a similar earlier argument he adds: "I say, the bare possibility of your opinion being true shall pass for an argument that it is so." The challenge is taken up by posing the rhetorical question "What more easy than to conceive a tree or house existing by itself, independent of, and unperceived by, any mind whatsoever?" Berkeley's fictional alter ego, Philonous, is quick to retort that in the very act being supposed one is thereby conceiving, or perceiving, the object. The fallacy in Berkeley's reasoning may be easy to spot.[11] He is transporting the mental episode of conceiving the scene into the content conceived (as a part of the "what" in "what is conceived"), thereby thickening the content with the conceiving. It is as if someone was given the task of thinking of a tree, she tried to do so, but she was then scolded by a Berkeleyan for thinking instead of thinking of a tree.

Berkeley argues that because there is no way to distinguish a conception of a tree from a conception of conceiving of a tree, all conceiving is essentially of the latter kind. Blackburn and Simmons's critic argues, conversely, that because there is no difference (in standpoint) between judging a state of affairs and judging that we are judging a state of affairs, the second is absorbed into the first. Both involve the interplay of attitude and content. And it seems both end up with incoherencies. I am not now alluding to

---

10. See Berkeley 1710, I, §22, where an earlier version of basically the same challenge appears.

11. See, e.g., Williams 1973.

Berkeley's unwarranted inference of reading the attitude of conceiving into its content. That too leads to questionable commitments, such as to an infinite regress, but I cannot find a way to show that the conclusion reached is thereby incoherent. However, Berkeley, like Blackburn and Simmons's would-be objector, must require that the verbal element—conceiving or judging—play two roles simultaneously. Given the sorts of roles in question, this just doesn't make sense.

On the surface it seems easy enough to visualize or imagine each of the following two situations: "my judging that p" and "my judging that I am comparing my judgment with p."[12] Let me label, in their order of occurrence, these three instances of a concept of judgment in the two descriptions. Ignoring any process-product ambiguities (which could be eliminated by wordy reformulation as needed), I flag them as 'judging$_1$', 'judging$_2$', and 'judgment$_3$', respectively. Thus, we may rewrite the situations as "my judging$_1$ that p" and "my judging$_2$ that I am comparing my judgment$_3$ with p." Were we to interject Berkeley into our current dispute, he would demand that we *infer* from judging$_1$ that it is an implicit part of the content. But how are we to understand this result? It requires two things. First, it requires that one and the same judging episode play two roles in a single judgment, that of judging$_2$ (being the attitude) and of judgment$_3$ (being part of the content). And, second, on top of that, in doing this we must somehow preserve the judging$_1$ episode at least by leaving its content, *that p*, in its original focal position for the subject. For that original content can't be lost as a subject of evaluation in the move from the first to the second standpoint.

Of course, reflexivity is possible in propositional attitudes. Where Φ is such an attitude, I can Φ that I am doing so-and-so. This is to read the *subject* of the attitude into the content; it does not read in the attitude itself. But it is difficult to see how I can Φ Φ-ing where the very same token of the attitude is both a psychic episode and its content. The problem here is a first cousin to the felt tension involved in Aristotle's description of the Unmoved Mover, who thinks about nothing other than its (current) thinking. Of course, thinking about one's own past thinking, or thinking about one's dispositional thinking isn't similarly problematic. Nor is taking a

---

12. Problems have been posed for conceiving, from the outside as it were, things happening to oneself (e.g., visualizing one's own funeral). I ignore those here, assuming that such frequent descriptions of this happening in dreams and daydreams creates a presumption that there is an intelligible account of the matter.

second-order attitude to a first-order one. I may want to want to be a better person. There the first-order attitude has a different content (viz., to be a better person) than the second (viz., to want to be a better person). But there is difficulty when both thinkings (or judgings) are (a) episodic and (b) they are the very same episode.

If that is not the difficulty foreseen in the second standpoint, it is hard to know what else it could be. For otherwise there seems no great difficulty in judging that the judgment that p bears the right relation to p. To do so we need only think of ourselves as approaching p with a judgment in mind, and confirming that judgment. Of course, a judgment is not the sort of thing that can be pictured in the way the rest of the scene can be, but I assume the impediment here isn't that mental judgments as such aren't pictorial.

The critic maintains, just as I have, that the second standpoint is impossible. But she does so on the grounds that it is vacuous. For the critic, once the empirical situation has been reviewed, there is nothing left to describe to satisfy the second standpoint. Thus, it looks to her like an empty empirical description. But my point is very different. The description of such a standpoint, if it were to satisfy the critic, would require that the judging had to perform mutually exclusive tasks simultaneously. Thus, it is not the vacuity of the second standpoint that prevents it, but the inconsistent profile of it implied by the critic's requirement. Seen in this light, it couldn't be put forward as a requirement for making sense out of judging that our judgment conforms to the world.

Perhaps it will be contended that in order to get a second standpoint we have to change the content crucially, so that these aren't distinct standpoints *with respect to the same thing*. This brings me to my next point: the impression that we need a second standpoint meeting this requirement seems indefensible.

I begin by asking what the difference of standpoint is supposed to amount to. The best sense I can make of the difference would be a pictographic one, that of seeing the scene from one place and then seeing a more comprehensive scene, which includes the first one, by stepping back and taking in our position in the first scene. But, save for very unusual circumstances (e.g., mirrors), while I can see o I can't see myself seeing o. That prompts no inclination to deny that my seeing o is a different circumstance (content) than the content of my initial seeing, namely o. (The state of affairs denied must be possible if only because *o* might have obtained without my, or anyone else, seeing it.) Moreover, I can see someone else seeing *o*, and it is worth pondering why that shouldn't satisfy the objector. After all, the point of the exercise is that we want to make sense of someone comparing an attitudinal state having a certain content to the corner of the world to which that content answers, and the latter scenario seems to do this. But let us stick with the first person and switch to cases of visualization, both of which are more favorable to the critic. I can visualize both *o* and myself visualizing *o*. Still I can't do the latter without radically changing the content of the former. The cost of change of standpoint is that the content too is substantially altered. Visualizing is of course among the most pictographic of psychological episodes. If the inability to embrace both in a single episode is a palpably weak grounds for denying that there are such contents as someone visualizing *o*, why should anyone believe that the lack of a second standpoint, under similar restrictions, has deleterious consequences for judging something about the relation of our judgment to what it is a judgment about? No doubt, if we could produce distinct standpoints, this might be a useful way to distinguish the two contents. The misstep is only to make the ability to distinguish the two standpoints *a requirement* for there being (or our possessing the notion of) distinct situations.

Is anyone nowadays guilty of this sort of a conflation? Well, consider the reasoning that Rorty (1986, 337) puts in the mouth of the idealist. Although he doesn't subscribe to it explicitly, he does so (as is his wont) by default. That is, it is allowed to stand as an important step in a chain of reasoning by which he reaches a final, clearly endorsed, lesson. In the relevant passage he invokes a coherentist reinterpretation of the superficially correspondentist tenet that "'there are rocks' is linked by a relation of correspondence to the way the world is," and defends that reinterpretation as follows:

> Idealists support this move by saying that the correspondence relation . . . cannot be a relation whose existence could be established by confronting an assertion with an object to see if a relation called 'corresponding' holds. Nobody knows what such a confrontation would look like.

Why is it that nobody knows what such a confrontation would look like? I have just shown that it is easy enough to envisage. A number of reasons might be given for Rorty's claim, and he offers his readers no help there in sorting out which of these he has in mind. A well-grounded suspicion is that a porridge of considerations is at work here, including the view that our would-be facts are really just beliefs (or thoughts) because they are infected by our concepts. One might have supposed that that concerns our theory of perception, not truth. But Rorty has shown a penchant in the past for making knowledge, or its possibility, his basic truth bearer—x is true → x is knowable—thereby enforcing on practical grounds a type of verifiability. And this might get us to the view that there is no second standpoint. Attempts to adopt it collapse into the situation in which we simply confront the world, *sans* assertion. This is all we can verify. Thus, "nobody knows what [a relation of correspondence] would look like."

What, other than the doubtful assumptions just reviewed, prevents my freely imagining confronting an object with my assertion about it? I imagine myself asserting, say, that a bird is on that branch. And at the same time I imagine myself checking the branch to see if a bird is there. Either there must be something about perception that blocks my having unmediated apprehension of the object through that means, or there is something wrong with imagining myself in such a scenario. The latter is easy enough to evade, since Rorty's claim is not confined to first-person cases. I can simply imagine someone else doing the confronting. The first obstacle would require a more detailed examination of the objects of perception than we can mount here. But any view that held that perception doesn't normally give us unmediated access to the world has a mountain of serious objections to overcome. In light of the current state of perceptual studies, the view looks untenable. (For further discussion, see Vision 1996 and Vision 1998.)

In addition, there is the consideration that if we *do* the same thing in both cases—namely, check the facts—no difference will show up to distinguish the second case. Thus, in a case of confirmation, it is futile to add to plain old p's content, "confronting our assertion with. . . . " But this doesn't result from a genuine inability to distinguish these contents, but from confining the purview of "doings" so narrowly as not to allow room for such a difference. On a narrower enough view nothing might be available to distinguish one's solving a problem for fun from solving it to complete a homework assignment. Even the same emotional accompaniments might attach to each activity. Of course, we can distinguish these by going outside the time and descriptive frame of the narrower doing, but then similarly we might distinguish confirming p and comparing our assertion that p with reality on the same basis.

We should not confuse this maneuver with that old pragmatist chestnut "a distinction without a difference" (viz., a comparison of situations in which no difference is determinable). The situations in which the glass is half-full and that in which it is half-empty aren't distinguishable, and aren't different. That has nothing to do with our inability to come up with different measurements. We cannot even imagine a further element, X (say, a tester), such that if X were introduced onto the scene, the outcome could be different. In short, we do not need to defend the view that X is prohibited, perhaps for reasons of prior methodological commitment. Even if we allow X to enter the scene, half-full and half-empty would have the same result. The two situations just can't be distinguished, period! However, in Rorty's case we can think of such an element X—namely, our confronting the first situation. It is simply that Rorty won't allow us to introduce this X for whichever of the foregoing reasons or other commitments apply. If he can defend the view that there can be no such X, he will have excluded the second standpoint. That is the outcome he claims in the quoted passage. Thus, his task is to establish his description of the case over against one in which X makes a difference. He cannot appeal to the half-full/half-empty sort of case to defend that view, for it is precisely what the illegitimacy of X (= the confronter) is supposed to show.

Although I have suggested a way to defend a distinction between the standpoints, it seems to me more forthright to reject it as a desideratum. The demand for a distinctive correspondence standpoint is not a neutral ground rule acceptable to all parties to the dispute: it interjects a substantive antirealist assumption. Presumably it has not been easy to see this. I surmise that because the inability clearly to sort out a distinction between, on the one hand, the subject of an attitude and the attitude itself, and, on the other, its content, crops up persistently across many philosophical eras and a variety of topics. Not only is it a linchpin of Berkeley's outlook, but it also informs a familiar argument for psychological egoism, in the form of a contention that our ends must be self-interested because they are *our* ends. It may also be noted in some arguments for verificationism, and as well for some skeptical defenses of what has been known as the egocentric predicament. Classical logical positivists had the merit of bringing it out in the open, and offered something of a further defense of it by arguing that anything meaningful had to have one or another variety of cognitive access. But most often it has merely been assumed, as by Rorty and by Blackburn and Simmons's imagined anti-correspondentist. In its current embodiment it is a form of the claim that when one reflects upon a subject, the reflecter (or, in this case, her standpoint) either is already considered as a part of the subject matter reflected upon, or can't sensibly enter any other content of a related reflection. And despite the enduring popularity of this maneuver, it lacks the stamp of credibility. Not only is it far from evident why this should be so, but frequently when the motives behind it are brought to light, they can be seen to beg the question. We should withdraw this battered coin from circulation.

4 Brief Statements of Correspondence

4.1 The Soul of Wit

In 1907 William James wrote that truth "means [the] 'agreement' [of our ideas], as falsity means their disagreement, with 'reality'." Although James accepts this unreservedly, he continues as follows: "Pragmatists and intellectualists [his rough approximation to correspondence theorists] both accept this definition as a matter of course. They begin to quarrel only after the question is raised as to what may precisely be meant by the term 'agreement', and what by the term 'reality'." (1907, 87) We needn't trace the subsequent pragmatic development of these notions, in part because it seems as clear as can be that *leading to satisfactory experience,* even if qualified along the lines of 'epistemologically', is not a promising translation of *agreement with reality*: it doesn't pass muster as a piece of lexicography. I don't doubt for a moment that James knew this. He is pursuing a reasoned replacement rather than a faithful restatement. Thus, if pragmatism 'works' or 'pays' (two other ways James characterizes truth), it must be defended on grounds other than its superiority as a candidate for an understanding of our current term 'true'. Nevertheless, James's remark is of interest even to the doggedly unreformed if only because it is an early version of a widely disseminated bit of lore that such brief statements of what some take to be the core insight of correspondence are, on reflection, so inconsequential that they don't tilt the scales ever so slightly in favor of one out of the various competing theories of truth, neither substantive nor deflationary ones. They rule out no candidates. James's own summary of correspondence and intellectualism is outdated and now appears quaint, but I don't suppose he would believe that my own contribution—that the truth of a proposition is constituted by a state of the world being such that were the proposition stated, it would state the world to be that way—improves matters in this respect.

In various quarters it is still held that such summary formulas are too thin or noncommittal to support correspondence: they are platitudes consistent with virtually any theory in the field. It will be useful to begin this inquiry with samples of brief statements of correspondence. Both James's objection and the one I discuss below should apply equally to all of them if the point has any force at all. Thus, to my earlier statement we might add the following ten (sort of) randomly selected samples, each of which its author regards as a statement of correspondence:

. . . a proposition is true just in case it corresponds to facts or the world. (Schmitt 1995, 145)

. . . a sentence is true if and only if it corresponds to the facts (or to reality). (Devitt 1991, 27)

A statement is true if and only if it corresponds to the facts. (Searle 1995, 201)

The correspondence theory of truth says that a statement is true if it corresponds to the facts. (Nozick 2001, 44)

. . . a proposition is true iff it corresponds to a fact and false iff it does not correspond to any fact. (David 2001, 683)

To say that p is true is to say that this proposition corresponds to reality. (Armstrong 1993, 435)

. . . a statement corresponds to a unique state of affairs involving [discourse independent objects and properties], and is true if that state of affairs obtains. . . . (Horgan 2001, 67)

. . . a statement is true if and only if the world is as it is represented as being . (McGinn 2001, 91n)

An item X (a proposition, a sentence, a belief, etc.) is true if and only if X is descriptively successful, that is, X purports to describe reality and its content fits reality. (Goldman 1999, 59)

A statement (proposition, belief, . . .) is true if and only if what the statement says to be the case actually is the case. (Alston 1996, 5)

To this collection we might add the popular medieval saw that truth is the equivalence of thing and understanding.[1] None of these statements of correspondence swerve out of the path of the Jamesian juggernaut. If he

---

1. *Veritas est adequatio rei et intellectus.* 'Adequation' is, roughly, "approaching identity or sameness". Perhaps "isomorphism" is the least unsatisfactory rendering into current philosophical shop talk.

is right, none of us has succeeded in stating the view that we set out to characterize.

Let me specify James's target more exactly. James's view is that such statements are so vulnerable to divergent understandings that they don't even begin to state a theory of truth, correspondence or any other. A different sort of critic, sometimes confused with the Jamesian, insists that there isn't enough contained in such brief summaries to amount to a theory, but doesn't question the fact that these claims are correspondence-leaning. Perhaps, the second critic continues, what is expressed is a generic form of realism about truth. Thus, the foregoing statements aren't noncommittal on the basic issues dividing correspondence from its opposition, although they fall short of supplying a satisfactory theory, definition, or analysis of the type intended. Insofar as this is a matter of larger prior expectations for what a completed correspondence view should look like, I have little to add to the brief remarks of chapter 2 concerning analyses. If correspondence locates the constitutive conditions for the truth of propositions, it covers the principal concerns of those who have debated this issue. At present, our interest is rather in the Jamesian who denies that the samples state even so much as distinctive elements of correspondence. On that note, there are a few initial reasons for rejecting the contention that these summary statements aren't even pivotal tenets of correspondence.

First, a clear import of such statements, *inter alia*, is that (a) something determines the truth of a bearer and (b) nothing in the notion of truth on offer interjects the idea that the determiner is either an experience itself or a semantically evaluable content. (a) implies a rejection of deflationism, (b) implies the unacceptability of any substantive conception—such as coherence or pragmatism—requiring that the determiner be on the order of a proposition or an experience. Moreover, insofar as we see these characterizations lacking nothing more than details, (b) also fails an adequacy condition for some recent popular varieties of antirealism by not requiring cognitive access among the conditions for the truth of propositions.

As mentioned previously, (b) shouldn't be construed to imply that the fragments of correspondence with which we have been presented are incompatible with views placing cognitive constraint on truth bearers (or even with full-blown idealism). Nevertheless, with this much already implied by our summaries, how could formulas that rule out so many actual rivals be empty? Indeed, given that deflationism and substantive competitors are ruled out, even if one doesn't grant that the statements themselves amount to a correspondence theory of truth, could the further development of any theory incorporating them be other than a version of correspondence?

Next, the objection seems to interdict perfectly legitimate efforts to summarize what distinct, detailed versions of correspondence have in common. Consider the many varieties of that view. For example, one could be a nominalist about facts, denying there are any such things, but still be a correspondence theorist. Perhaps the correspondentist will hold that the only existents are individuals and their properties. Also, different analyses of the correspondence relation might be undertaken, or, on a strict interpretation, that relation itself might be rejected in favor of a different kind that propositions bear to the world. Anyone who wanted to summarize what such a variety had in common would construct a characterization at a rather general level. How would this differ significantly from the sort of general statements in our samples? Of course not all of the specimens above are quite so general: some of them mention 'correspondence' and 'facts', and are thus suited only to summarize views with items that can fall under those heads. Still, those summaries are relatively general. Perhaps the last three samples—from McGinn, Goldman, and Alston, respectively—are most inclusive. But even if we take so simple and forthright a formula as Searle's— "... a statement is true if and only if it corresponds to the facts"—this ought to serve as a way to summarize various correspondence views that conjure with those components, although they may differ on further details about correspondence, statements, or facts. It would be indeed singular if for this one subject matter there were no possible generic statement of a variety of related views in the area. And if we admit the possibility of such generic summaries, it is difficult to see how they would differ significantly from those set aside as trivial, or otherwise insufficient to express what is distinctive about correspondence theories.

Nor will admonitions against unrestricted generalizations about truth bolster a claim against such epigrammatic statements of correspondence. Suppose, say, that the Liar Paradox defeated universal theories of truth stated in their proprietary languages. Then imagine we limit the generalizations to truth bearers that don't themselves contain 'true' or 'false'. If the Jamesian objection showed that our formulations of correspondence were empty for the unqualified version, they would be equally so under these limited conditions. Thus, because this last concession wouldn't make any difference to the bearing of the objection, its champions have nothing to gain from concerns about paradox.

While these considerations create a presumption in favor of the correspondence impact of our formulas, they do not deny the objector all room to maneuver. Below we examine a distinction drawn by Crispin Wright between (benign) commonsensical correspondence and what he calls a correspondence 'platitude'. Wright avers that the platitude is toothless, and thus not a statement of the correspondence theory. In legalese, it is simply "boilerplate" or something we chant thoughtlessly. But the various statements he gives of the platitude—e.g., "'P' is true if and only if 'P' corresponds to the facts"—are expressed in sentences that look essentially indistinguishable from our general versions of correspondence. If it is not Wright's intention to deny that such general statements affirm correspondence, how does he distinguish them from his class of platitudes?

Before proceeding in earnest to examine Wright's argument we should be clear about the following. While there is a time-honored tradition of deflating claims, of showing that they convey less, or for that matter *more*, than their claimants suppose, things cannot be quite so facile. To suppose that the would-be correspondence statements say less only because there *can be* alternative interpretations on which they do so, employs a method on which it can be shown that no statement ever states anything. This ill-fated consequence ensues because every claim, even those constituting alternative interpretations, can be reinterpreted. But the fact that any statement *may* fail to state what it seems to in the face of reinterpretation doesn't imply that every statement *does* so fail. Well-motivated reinterpretations aren't prohibited. James is entitled to one only if he gives us some reason for thinking that his view is preferable to what he calls the intellectualist (or sometimes the "copy") theory. That reason will no doubt consist in what he believes to be the virtues of his replacement account. Thus, the reinterpretation cannot be a step in the argument for his alternative, on pain of circularity. For the alternative is itself the motivation for the reinterpretation. In lieu of such a motivation we are entitled to construe the general statements of correspondence as stating just what untendentious readers take them to state. This doesn't render the obvious, *prima facie* construal of our summaries especially tentative or fragile. It is merely a condition that governs anything that is stated. And it is sufficient to insure the standing of those statements against not only their Jamesian decommissioning, but against any unsupported claims of vacuity for our correspondence formulas.

4.2 Correspondence as Platitude

Let us now take a closer look at the alleged inadequacies of brief statements of correspondence.

Earlier I distinguished two sorts of dissenters:

(a) those who believe the brief statements contribute something toward correspondence, but not enough to attain the status of a theory of truth

(b) those who believe that the brief statements are either vacuous, or say something so anodyne as to be compatible with the further development of any competitive truth theory.

Notice that both are compatible with, but don't require, the nihilistic view that no acceptable theory of truth is in the offing. Obstacles to a richer account may lie in the subject matter (e.g., too fundamental to be explained in other terms) or in the investigators (e.g., inherent limitations on human understanding). Insofar as nihilism is the ground of either objection, (a) is its more natural home. However, as before, I shall concentrate on (b). Crispin Wright is taken as the main representative of that view, although later I also consider a related implication of Horwich's minimalism. Wright's version is particularly interesting because he thinks both that correspondence isn't just a platitude and that it is just a platitude. To begin resolving this bold paradox, let us look first at why he believes correspondence isn't just a platitude. At one point, he says:

> I think it's fair to say that this conception of correspondence, shorn of any further analytical or explanatory obligations, comes across as highly commonsensical. In general, we'd want to think both that there is a real distinction marked by the classification of some propositions as true and others as false, and that it is a distinction which cannot generally be understood without reference to things which are not themselves propositions, so cannot be understood in intrinsicist or coherentist terms. (Wright 1999, 207)

For handy reference, let us call this **plain correspondence**. Two features seem to mark it out: first, there are conditions that make a difference between a proposition's truth and falsity, and, second, this difference cannot be wholly understood by comparing that proposition to other propositions (or to itself). The first condition states, in effect, that truth is a genuine property, thereby departing from traditional deflationism, the second rules out the only serious substantive alternatives to correspondence. By elimination, the suggestion is that the only thing left for the truth of a proposition to have "reference to" is something about the ("external") world. This would bring Wright closer to a statement of correspondence rather than merely a dismissal of its alternatives. But he quickly adds this:

> This piece of common sense is not to be confused with the idea that, understood one way, correspondence is nothing more than a platitude. The platitude is that predications of 'true' may always harmlessly be glossed in terms of correspondence to fact, telling it like it is, etc. These paraphrases incorporate no substantial commitment about the structure of truth. . . . (Wright 1999, 208; cf. Lewis 2001a)

And Wright later displays an example of such a platitude:

> . . . for a proposition to be true is for it to correspond to reality, accurately reflect how matters stand, 'tell it like it is', etc. (1999, 227)

Following Wright, let's call this platitude (on this and its other formulations) **trivial correspondence**. It is not easy to discern what accounts for the distinction between the substantive view and the platitude, or even to decide to which class standard brief statements belong. Indeed, the notion he considers commonsensical is *so* commonsensical that it is difficult to see why it too is not, in common parlance, a platitude. Perhaps a clue to the difference is found in the fact that most, though not all, formulations of the platitude highlight correspondence *to* something. One suggestion might be that Wright distinguishes plain from trivial correspondence on the grounds that the appeal to a correspondence relation in the platitudes isn't illuminating, or at least not enough so. (This thought might have placed him in camp (a), save for his insistence on its neutrality between competing views rather than its mere insufficiency.) But if the plain notion doesn't end up by affirming that something about the confrontation of the proposition with—thus its relation to—the nonpropositional world determines the former's truth, it is difficult to know what connection this is supposed to have to the correspondence tradition, or, for that matter, to commonsense. Indeed, Wright later describes as his "second main contention" the view "that there is no alternative but to think of the truth of a proposition as conferred upon it, in the general case, by its relations to nonpropositional reality" (1999, 223). The mystery yet deepens when we examine Wright's grounds for rejecting the view that *truth* is an intrinsic—viz., non-relational—property of true propositions:

. . . the truth-value of any contingent proposition must co-vary with hypothetical changes, in the characteristics of the things it concerns—so that a hypothetical change, for instance, in the location of my coffee cup may entail an alteration in the truth-value of the proposition that there is no coffee on my desk, even though that proposition and the particular coffee cup in question are quite distinct existences. (1999, 208)

It is not easy to distinguish this from the primitive Variability datum cited in chapter 2 and used there to motivate correspondence. But even if the words 'correspondence' and 'external reality' (much less 'fact') aren't incanted in these formulas, hasn't Wright appealed to just the sort of phenomenon that generates this notion as a way to generalize and draw attention to this sort of implication of *truth*? In any event, it is difficult to know how one is to prevent the features Wright regards as commonsensical from entering the very concept of truth and thus being distinguished from what he considers a platitude.

The foregoing strongly suggests that plain and trivial correspondence form an unstable compound. When emphasizing the plain variety, it is puzzling how TRUTH can retain the neutrality Wright wants to impose on certain of its uses; when emphasizing trivial correspondence, it is puzzling how the plain notion can preserve its standing. While this is only one among other themes to follow, it bleakly confronts us when trying to get a grip on the conditions for trivial correspondence being a platitude. But before turning to that critical task let us see how the remainder of Wright's position plays out.

4.3 The Road to Pluralism

Assume that a version of plain correspondence has been established. Its connection with truth in general is explained by Wright as follows.

First note that Wright's official position on truth aptitude is **disciplined syntacticism**, a view described in the last chapter. It states that any discourse satisfying a limited set of syntactical tests (say, taking negation, being capable of being embedded in conditional and intentional contexts) and with a standard in place for distinguishing correct from incorrect applications of its predicates is truth-apt, and thus generates legitimate instances of schema (𝒟)—or (ℛ), hereafter understood. This also satisfies what he calls "having assertoric content." It isn't a taxing requirement. As noted earlier, it is satisfied by attributions of the comic and the fashionable, and—this is the important part—it may be the whole of what truth amounts to for those or other discourses. That there is nothing more than this to truth is the view Wright calls "minimalism," which I have dubbed "deflationism." Accordingly, merely being truth-apt isn't of much interest for resolving burning issues dividing realists from antirealists in, say, mathematics, ethics, and scientific theories.

To moot such issues, Wright suggests a battery of further tests, of which the one he calls **Cognitive Command** (1992, 144) is pre-eminent. Roughly, Cognitive Command governs a discourse just in case, setting aside vagueness and differences in standards of acceptability, it is *a priori* that a difference of opinion always stems from at least one party to the dispute displaying a cognitive shortcoming (e.g., miscalculation, ignorance, carelessness). There is no blameless disagreement where Cognitive Command reigns. In this way, a discourse's truth-predicate may have, in addition to its disciplined syntax, a further set of requirements. Wright also reviews further tests, such as supplying the best explanation of belief (1992, 176ff.), having wide cosmological role (1992, 191ff.), and not conforming to the pattern Euthyphro, in Plato's dialogue of that name, set by his analysis of piety (1992, 108ff.). None is rejected, although problems with each are explored; but Cognitive Command appears the most appropriate tool with which to probe these further issues. Presumably, their application creates a space for plain correspondence.

In addition to plain correspondence, Wright gestures toward other sorts of substantial truth predicates. For example, he speculates that perhaps "the true propositions of number theory [are] those which sustain . . . an appropriate kind of semantic consequence" (1999, 225). Such intrapropositional relations may suggest coherence or an idealized sort of warrant (viz., superassertibility) as the ruling truth notion for the discourse. Again, perhaps in certain other areas of the *a priori* truth is determined by the intrinsic character of its propositions. So although correspondence apparently suits contingent, empirical propositions, it may be out of place for other discourses which are nonetheless subject to substantive truth predication. This seems to be the force of the qualification "in the general case" occurring earlier in the citation of Wright's second main contention of plain correspondence. The diversity of minimal and substantive truth-predicates in play constitutes his pluralism. There are various ways to put this: a currently fashionable one would be to say that although truth is (in some sense) a single concept, it is *multiply realized* in the truth-apt discourses. That would bring it closer to a view earlier identified as functionalism. (See Lynch 2001b.)

Although Cognitive Command and the attendant tests raise issues that go well beyond anything we can, or need, discuss here, several preliminary observations are in order.

First, there is a tension, of which more below, between minimalism and the view that correspondence and the like serve to fill out the content of a truth concept or predicate. If the minimalist truth-predicate is a sufficient condition for a truth concept, and it is the whole of the account for some varieties of truth—apparently Wright's view of comedic discourse—then it seems plausible that anything additional we say on the topic could be nothing more than a further, perhaps deeper, analysis of the minimalist condition already given. For what role can an addition to sufficiency or completeness possible have in the initial account? Quite clearly the substantive truth predicates are not intended to spell out minimalism further. Moreover, Wright gives no evidence to support the view that the equivalences admit any further analysis, and he gives every indication of believing otherwise. Even the use of the notion of multiple realization in this place stretches credibility since the 'in' of being realized *in* different discourses is so different from that of being realized *in* different materials, and there is no comparable structural similarity (other than the minimalist base which all the substantive truth predicates take off from) preserved in its various applications. Multiple realizability seems to lose the rationale given for applying it in, say, functionalist accounts of intentional states.

None of this is intended to deny that features propositions accumulate by passing Cognitive Command etc. may contribute toward adjudicating various local tiffs between realists and antirealists. Nothing said in these pages about the tension between the two correspondences counts against that. But it is hard to see how whatever Cognitive Command and the other tests add to the realism wars can be an inherent feature of the truth concept or predicate. Nonetheless, Wright runs together, without missing a beat, (a) utility in resolving realist-antirealist differences and (b) filling out the remainder of a truth concept (or predicate). Putting the main point conversely, if we insist that whatever is added by passing these tests be an inherent feature of the truth it characterizes, isn't that a powerful indication that minimalism doesn't yield a whole account of that sort of truth (and, thereby, of *any* truth)?

Second, what Wright labels minimalism is roughly equivalent to what I have been calling 'deflationism'. (This differs in minor ways from the view Wright calls 'deflationism'. His rejection of that view is based on a criticism of what he takes to be its positive, ascriptivist, account of the function of truth-predicates rather than, as in my case, on doubts about the adequacy of its minimalist equivalences.) In the next few chapters I shall raise a number of objections to deflationism. Because Wright's minimalism is vulnerable to those objections this is bad news for any pluralism founded on it. This version of pluralism thus falls victim to whatever disorders infect traditional deflationism.

Third, passing Cognitive Command, or any of the other tests Wright suggests, doesn't even purport to introduce plain correspondence. Each of the tests, as evinced in my summary of Cognitive Command, focuses on the obligations or shortcomings of *holders* of the propositions in question rather than on truth conditions. None pinpoint why those requirements lead us, say, to a correspondence rather than a coherence theory of truth for a discourse stamped by them, or tell us what is responsible for imposing those obligations. Thus, plain correspondence does not fall out naturally from this development of pluralism. At most, it might be held that satisfying Cognitive Command shows how a place is left into which some further substantive account or other may fit. But a separate argument would be needed to show that any particular account actually occupied that place. The consequence is that plain correspondence, or any other so-called substantive truth predicate, does not fit the profile of something built out of minimalism by way of applying these further tests. It is also a further reason for rejecting the idea that these further requirements can yield information relevant to filling out a *truth* concept (or predicate)—as opposed, say, to determining an issue for or against realism.

Fourth, although both pluralists and deflationists reject Correspondence, the pluralist's objections are useless for deflationism. Classical deflationary opponents of correspondence rely on criticisms of the distinctive features of the view to launch their objections, usually the relation of correspondence itself or the notion of a fact (= worldly truthmaker). The intended objections, if sound, would show that there can't be a single instance in which truth is constituted in this way. If there were such an instance, this would supply, *eo ipso*, at least a limited endorsement of those very distinctive features. For that reason, a rejection of even a single instance of correspondence truth has been a pillar of traditional deflationism. Similarly, deflationists have argued that there can be nothing to add to explain correspondence's tenets once we are in possession of the equivalences. Anything additional must be superfluous. Thus, the deflationist cannot acknowledge, as Wright does, that correspondence works for some cases. And, conversely, Wright isn't entitled to either form of traditional deflationist support. He can't reject completely the devices by means of which correspondence works because he acknowledges instances of it, while his pluralism prevents him from regarding anything more than the equivalences as superfluous. Although we haven't examined his grounds for minimalism, this is worth noting if only because it is easy to read into Wright's defense of minimalism the customary arguments that others have used to defend deflationism. However, those can do nothing to strengthen Wright's case. Pluralism must rest on wholly different grounds. These have more in common with the sorts of criticisms launched by substantive competitors, as when a coherentist asks provocatively just what a true axiom of geometry might correspond to.

The last point underlines the importance I shall be placing on the particulars of Wright's argument for trivial correspondence. He maintains that he can derive the correspondence platitude from a version of ($\mathcal{D}$). In *Truth and Objectivity* (e.g., 25–26, 74), this is given as a basis for its having that status, although admittedly that is more a hint than an outright declaration. We will examine these matters shortly. But if certain instances of correspondence do not respond to this treatment, as his pluralism dictates, we cannot fall back on traditional deflationary arguments to rescue the view.

4.4 Potholes

What is at stake here? It is an implication of Wright's pluralism that, whereas correspondence works well enough for contingent propositions, other language fragments are better suited for (thick or thin) competing conceptions. The view is highly problematic. In this section I discuss two principal difficulties.

Wright himself brings up the first difficulty: "What makes all these kinds of *truth*?" Of course, one answer is "minimalism." But that is the deflationist's answer, not the pluralist's. It would mark a defeat if his view had to collapse into deflationism to solve the problem. While Wright addresses the problem, not only does he fail to solve it, but it is difficult to see how it can solved on his terms.

A good way to appreciate the problem is to compare it briefly with the sort of answer on offer from varieties of correspondence theories discussed in chapter 3. On some versions there are no distinctive facts supporting certain true propositions. But we can explain how they are nonetheless truth-apt by reductive techniques, in which they correspond to facts appropriate to the subject matter of their reductive bases, or by counting them as secondary, dependent instances. On the latter view, the secondary truths are claimed to bear some of the central features of the correspondence-friendly instances, and it was hypothesized that this may be sufficient to give them truth-value. We needn't endorse either view to make the current point. They are mentioned here only because they make it fairly easy to see how one might argue that many if not all of the instances a syntacticist countenances count as truth-apt. The notion of truth is hierarchical on them; those truths that can't be directly explicated via a distinctive corresponding fact, or any at all, nevertheless acquire their birthright to truth via their dependency on cases in which there are straightforward correspondence relations.

Wright is in no position to employ a similar explanation. Pluralism declines even so tenuous a hierarchical connection between the varieties of truth. Thus, it must negotiate the following rough terrain. The various realizations of truth within pluralism are unranked. That is, the language fragments to which they apply are all equally, and independently, truth-apt. Once again, correspondence occupies no pride of place in this collection. It is suitable for contingent, empirical propositions, but other types of truth may be invoked for different discourses.

Certain correspondentists who reject "extended correspondence" (section 3.2) have held that while many contingent, empirical propositions and others admitting correspondence relations are truth-apt, paradigmatic declarative utterances in some or all noncorrespondence areas don't take truth-values. Let's call this view T-positivism. I am not concerned to defend T-positivism here, but I want to emphasize that its motives and grounding are quite palpable. While it differs from syntacticism on the extension of the truth predicate, it doesn't appear to depart radically from our hospitable and vague pretheoretical notions about truth. It may reject some ordinary truth talk as loose (say, when applied to ethical judgments). But it does so by defending a widely acknowledged common core of truth talk and refusing to deviate from it. Moreover, it can be made compatible with the equivalences simply by placing restrictions on referentiality and/or propositionality.

Now consider a fantastically inverted version of T-positivism. On this view truth-aptitude is denied to correspondence-friendly discourse, but allotted to all other language fragments covered by pluralism, including the branches of mathematics, ethics, humor, and style. Assuming that different accounts of truth cover different remaining fragments, this is still pluralism. We should ask ourselves why, if there is nothing special about correspondence, we aren't naturally tempted by such a view, and why we believe that it does not, as T-positivism does, preserve something like a pretheoretical intuition about truth. Indeed, the concept it installs diverges radically from our current one. It is simply difficult to see how we could preserve enough of the notion from which our investigations begin if we allow truth-aptitude only for the areas (or some proper subset of them) for which T-positivists deny it and for which correspondence was an inappropriate account on Wright's bookkeeping.

In this limited respect the extension of the truth-predicate is relevant to our ordinary notion of it. Thus, even if we allow enough pluralism for our truth notion to cover some subjects that haven't strictly correspondence-type truthmakers (an issue on which we may remain neutral in the present context), this should lead at least to a well-grounded suspicion that the correspondence portion of our notion is fundamental in a way that the pluralist's other discourses are not. It appears to be by virtue of the reflected light given off by correspondence truth that the notion is conceived to have application elsewhere. We are in much better stead considering the latter as dependent on a correspondence account, rather than simply floating free of it.

A pluralist might protest that my original question—"What makes all of these truth?"—presupposes naive Platonism. Wittgenstein has warned us about this snare; he offered "family resemblance" as a prophylaxis. Since then the literature has featured notions such as open texture, multiple criteria, prototypes, and similar solutions as looser ways in which instances may be grouped under a single head. Those forms of correspondence that admit secondary cases aren't threatened by the objection. But even for those cases, we should be careful about extending stereotypes too far. Eventually swans would turn into geese. However, let us assume that truth is a term falling into one of the family resemblance, etc. classes. The pluralist must still say more before he's out of the woods. We cannot suppose that any agglomeration whatever warrants a similar title just because we have so assembled it. Of course, one can choose to give any ragbag collection a single name. But then one cannot expect that the collection so named will throw light on the problem at hand. Naming can be a matter of stipulation, philosophical illumination is not. Thus, even for family resemblance accounts of a term, stereotypes, central cases, are important. It is cold consolation to be told that 'game' and 'number' are family resemblance terms. That simply isn't a sufficient excuse for the unity of every collection. Where correspondence serves as the stereotype, the other varieties, if they are admitted at all, may be admitted on the basis of the ways in which they are able to be seen as offshoots of the central case. But pluralism as such must take in all its cases on an equal footing.

A second difficulty concerns the fact that pluralism creates problematically mixed inferences.[2] Consider the following argument.

Waddling penguins are amusing.
This penguin waddles.
Therefore, this penguin is amusing.

The argument is clearly valid, thus truth-preserving. However, the pluralist will hold that the conditions for the application of truth differ for our two premises. If the truth-predicate applicable to each premise is different, what sort of truth is preserved? The argument appears to conceal a fatal equivocation, though not one occurring in terms appearing in either premise. However, if the chief value of deduction is that a good (= valid) one

2. I follow Tappolet's version of the objection. Williamson (1994, 141) raises basically the same difficulty, but for propositional constituents of compounds (say, disjunctions) rather than for arguments. Wright's reply (1994b, 337), considered below, addresses Williamson's version. Once again, although Wright frames his response in terms of satisfying the platitudes, for simplicity I continue to use the satisfaction of ($\mathcal{D}$).

preserves the truth of a conclusion drawn from a set of true premises, we can scarcely quibble over this merely because the equivocation occurs only at a meta level.

Wright has a response. But so far as I can tell his solution relies on waffling between the two interpretations earlier proposed for his minimalist supersense: roughly, he avers that the premises only need satisfy (*D*). However, either (*D*) yields the concept of truth we are after, or it does not. If it does, Wright's minimalism doesn't, as he intends, "supersede . . . the deflationary conception of truth" (1998, 185), but instead falls in with it. On the other hand, if (*D*) isn't a self-standing adequate conception of truth, how is it relevant to resolving our difficulty?

It isn't easy to see on which horn of this dilemma Wright is impaled. The vocabulary in which he chooses to defend his view against the charge doesn't match up—perhaps is designed not to match up—with the unhappy options I have afforded him. In an earlier discussion of a concessive form of deflationism, we distinguished truth's conceptual content (or, meaning—that difference being irrelevant to the point at hand) from its property. The latter's conditions for satisfaction might be wholly external to the content of TRUTH or the meaning of 'true'. Several of Wright's comments suggest that he is relying on some such distinction. He states that "a truth *predicate* is any that satisfies the minimal set of platitudes: those platitudes enshrine all that can be said by way of explanation of the meaning of the word. . . ." (1994b, 337; my emphasis) He repeats this almost verbatim (1998, 186). Moreover, he adds shortly thereafter in both places that pluralism enters at the level of what *constitutes* truth in various discourses. Such remarks certainly suggest that the platitudes, or (*D*) on our present construal, deliver a complete account of the truth predicate (or concept). Moreover, his way of bringing in truth's constitution seems to conform to what I have been labeling the conditions of satisfaction for a truth *property*.[3] And he had written earlier that "[t]he form of pluralism for which space is allowed by this overarching uniformity is one of, roughly *variable realization*. . . . [W]hat constitutes truth in ethics may be quite different to what constitutes truth in theoretical physics" (1996, 924). If these passages are reliable indicators of his considered opinion, it would place him in the class

---

3. ". . . truth is formally uniform—in the sense determined by satisfaction of the platitudes—but its constitution may vary depending on the type of statement and subject matter concerned" (Wright 1998, 186).

of concessive deflationists, those who hold that the meaning of truth is adequately summarized by ($\mathcal{D}$)—or the platitudes associated with it—while leaving room for an additional issue engaging correspondence and its competitors. But, once again, concessive deflationism isn't pluralism.

At least two things thwart this interpretation. First, Wright also mentions "a variety of truth *predicates* [that] may be characteristic of different discourses" (1994b, 336; emphasis added). Here it appears to be the predicates themselves that may differ, and not merely the satisfaction conditions for a single, thinner predicate. Different predicates, different concepts. Second, Wright seems committed to the view (ibid., 338–339) that the relation between a truth predicate and truth's constitution is too intimate for the division of labor I attribute to the concessive deflationist. No doubt Wright wants the intimacy as a way to restate (and defend) his 'default antirealism'.[4] Whatever the motivation, the device can't work. If we allow that the substantive truth conditions for correspondence are even so much as an aspect of the truth-predicate relevant to the second premise of the above reasoning, the truth governing that premise is different from that governing the first one. Mixed inference is a grave difficulty for pluralism. A similar problem arises for truth-functional compounds whose clauses are evaluated by different truth concepts.

4.5 Laodicean Platitudes

Let's turn our attention to further matters concerning pluralism—in particular, to Wright's list of platitudes. His exposition highlights the members of this list, rather than ($\mathcal{D}$), as the aegis under which the kinds of truth are unified. They form a cluster of notions that round out a conception of truth. Any notion satisfying them counts as a truth conception. Wright lists them (1999, 227; 2001, 760). As Wright mentions, this needn't be a source of tension in his larger view. The platitudes are all supposedly derivable from ($\mathcal{D}$); we aren't wandering beyond the earlier method in any way that could result in conflict. (The claim of derivability for at least one platitude is explained in a bit more detail later in this section and is critically explored in the next one.) Here is a quick review of the roster of platitudes.

4. "We will . . . be default anti-realists . . . in the sense that nothing in our practice of the discourse, nor in the conceptions of truth and objectivity for it which we can so far justifiably profess, will change if that proves to be so." (Wright 1994b, 339).

Trivial correspondence—or, as Wright puts it, *correspondence*—is one of seven itemized platitudes. Though he concedes that his list isn't exhaustive, he suggests that as a whole it yields a rounded picture of truth. For handy reference, the other six (1999, 226) are as follows:

transparency "To assert is to represent as true, and more generally, . . . any attitude to a proposition is an attitude to its truth. . . ."

opacity "A thinker may be so situated that a particular truth is beyond her ken, [or] some truths may never be known, [or] some truths may be unknowable in principle, etc."

embedding "Truth-apt propositions have negations, conjunctions, etc. which are likewise truth-apt."

contrast "A proposition may be true without being justified and vice versa."

timelessness "if a proposition is ever true, then it always is, so that whatever may, at any particular time, be truly asserted may—perhaps by appropriate transformation of mood, or tense—be truly asserted at any time."

absoluteness "there is . . . no such thing as a proposition being more or less true; propositions are completely true if true at all."

On the face of it, the list poses additional difficulties for pluralism. For example, coherence almost always takes an evidential connection as its truthmaker, and evidence—even in the rare ether of theoretical mathematics—is a matter of degree. How then is a coherentist to honor *absoluteness*? Elsewhere Wright identifies what he calls **superassertibility** as a truth predicate, an identification that admits serious doubt. *Super*assertibility differs from more commonplace justificatory notions such as warrant or assertibility by adding, roughly, the following proviso: once obtained, assertibility is never lost by closer scrutiny or the simple addition of further (good) evidence. Here we need observe only that if the notion is to have an assertibility credential of any kind, it is still a matter of degree, and so not absolute. Assertibility, even superassertibility, doesn't imply total justification.[5] If Wright instead identifies truth in mathematics with provability, how are we to incorporate *contrast*? Moreover, *opacity* is characterized too vaguely, as a disjunction, to warrant its being a platitude of any kind. How

---

5. For detailed critiques of superassertibility, see Kvanvig 1999; Brueckner 1998; Pettit 1996; Edwards 1996.

could this sort of disjunction, the requirements of whose disjuncts are so varied, amount to a platitude? At least the third, perhaps the second, of these disjuncts is not satisfied by coherence, or even superassertibility. So is the test applicable to them? Or how is a pragmatist to handle *timelessness*?[6] Moreover, as we shall presently see, (*D*) has problems accounting for *correspondence*. This brief summary is merely a preview of the sorts of difficulties that abound in applying a full panoply of these items to just about any conception of truth other than correspondence. Indeed, assuming that any conception satisfies *transparency*, correspondence seems be to the only one that satisfies the entire list without special pleading.

One response might be to require only that a truth conception satisfy a certain (weighted) proportion of the platitudes: truth is, in essence, a multiple criteria term. This is not Wright's official view. For him each of these platitudes must be satisfied by any conception of truth that doesn't violate our pretheoretic intuitions. Nonetheless, observe that the maneuver doesn't avail us. It is well and good for cases in which we have prior assurance that the term applies to all the members of the family. But where the inclusion of a noncorrespondence fragment is under investigation, this scheme is not justificatory or even explanatory. It throws us back to our starting point. And if that was a problem, as Wright acknowledges, it is unclear why it shouldn't remain a problem on the present proposal.

To elaborate: We have a number of methods of evaluation that seem to resemble each other in their epistemic importance, and we use truth talk about them, at least loosely. This leaves us with two broad options. The first, of course, is that they are all forms of truth. The second is that this is just an unguarded extension of serious conversation, and once the similarities are set before us there is nothing further to be said about the variety other than that they resemble one another in these respects. Taking the first option, we are asking for something more than the similarities that led us prereflectively to consider them all truth-apt. This loose collection of similarities was acknowledged as part of the situation that gave rise to our conundrum. At least correspondence, even the relaxed version recently discussed, attempts to direct us to an answer to this question by creating a hierarchy. It is difficult to see what answer is on offer from the "weighted proportion" proposal for satisfying the platitudes. It gives us no reason to

---

6. See James's diatribe against timeless truth (1907/2000, 96ff.).

prefer preserving truth talk across the board rather than preferring some similarity (as there is between many different, but related, things) and choosing different kinds of terms for evaluating different language fragments.

Pluralist claims to truth, then, should satisfy the whole menu of platitudes, as Wright has at least one time proclaimed. How can this be made out? In a longish footnote (1999, 230), Wright claims that the platitudes can be derived from ($\mathcal{R}$) together with minor and indisputable assumptions. The argument for this was developed at greater length earlier, in *Truth and Objectivity* (1992). Later (2001, 760) Wright hints that ($\mathcal{R}$) "underlies" only *transparency, correspondence,* and *contrast*. That modification subverts the foregoing as a reason for the unity of concepts satisfying the list, but let us look more closely at least at the derivation crucial to instituting a correspondence platitude. In the less sketchy derivation (Wright 1992, 14), *correspondence* is derived from a slightly revised version of our equivalence:

($\mathcal{D}_w$)   " 'P' is true if and only if P."

The official version of the correspondence platitude (ibid., 25) is given as

(C)   " 'P' is true if and only if 'P' corresponds to the facts."

Despite variations in phrasing, it is clear that this is intended as the same platitude described as *correspondence*: "The platitude is that predications of 'true' may always harmlessly be glossed in terms of correspondence to fact, telling like it is, etc." (Wright 1999, 208). While it may look as if (C) is designed specifically for *sentences* as bearers of truth-value—and the derivation is from ($\mathcal{D}_w$) rather than from ($\mathcal{R}$)—different restatements of the platitude make clear that the choice of bearer is largely indifferent. They include "a content is true just in case it corresponds to the facts" (Wright 1992, 72), "to be true is to correspond to the facts" (ibid., 34), "[f]or a statement to be true is for it to correspond to the facts" (ibid., 82), and the derivation is from a variant of ($\mathcal{R}$) rather than from ($\mathcal{D}_w$) (Wright 1999, 230). It seems evident that the main thrust is only that deflationism has "no difficulty in accommodating intuitions about the relationship between truth and correspondence as long as doing so is held to require no more than demonstrating a right to the phrases by which those intuitions are characteristically expressed" (Wright 1992, 27). The choice of truth bearer, within reason, is unimportant.

Wright then assures us that "as long . . . as we stick to platitudes and do not go in for more fine-grained interpretation" nothing is lost by paraphrasing (C) as

(CP) "'P' is true if and only if things are as 'P' says they are." (1992, 25)

If we may momentarily digress from the flow of the argument, notice how (CP) also shows that direct mention of *correspondence* and *fact* are not crucial to *correspondence* being a platitude. That was already strongly suggested by Wright's alternative characterization of the platitude in terms of "telling it like it is" (rather than corresponding to facts). However, (CP) makes explicit that it is not the use of some especially problematic expressions that warrant this diminished status, but rather the attempt to sum up, in a capsule way, a certain sort of outlook. Indeed, in this respect Wright seems to me to see farther than some correspondence-leaning advocates. Various realists have labeled their views *minimal* realism to make it clear that although they are in some sense realists, they aren't correspondentists. The suggestion appears to be that by sticking close to (R), and not explicitly mentioning the relation of correspondence, or even facts, the view does not raise certain contentious issues about the character of word-world relations. But consider, e.g., the last three examples of brief statements of correspondence (from McGinn, Goldman, and Alston, respectively). They mention truth bearers *representing*, *describing*, and *saying* something about the world, reality, or what is the case, respectively. And when the world is the way the bearer represents, describes, or says it is, we have all that is needed for a metaphysical relation of just the type that deflationists seek to eradicate from their accounts. It is unimportant whether it is called "correspondence." If the foregoing replacements for "correspondence" are justification enough to relieve a proponent of the need to provide further details, it is difficult to see why those epigrammatic versions employing that embattled term should be bothered by their absence. The matter here seems to boil down to a case of potential miscommunication. Deflationists and minimal realists may assume that the use of the term 'correspondence' signifies the speaker issuing a promissory note for forthcoming details. But nothing more need be conveyed by such summaries than that the speaker wants to state the view at a comprehensive level and thereby embrace distinct varieties, which are perhaps no more detailed and may not even use the term.

Returning to the derivation, with the addition of the uncontroversial notion

(U)   "'P' says that P,"

we can derive (CP), and thereby (C), from ($\mathcal{D}_w$) in the following steps. (U) allows us to replace the right-hand side of the biconditional in ($\mathcal{D}_w$) with "things are the way 'P' says they are" simply because (U) states that *the way that 'P' tells us things are* is P. This yields (CP). We then obtain (C) through the paraphrasal equivalence of "things are as 'P' says they are" with "'P' corresponds to the facts."

I divide consideration of this derivation into two parts. In the remainder of this section, I examine how, if at all, Wright manages to distinguish the platitude he has derived from plain correspondence. After all, his original claim was that, contrary to critics, classical deflationism does not fail to do justice to correspondence truisms, as is shown by its derivation from ($\mathcal{D}_w$) (Wright 1992, 25). Since this is trivial correspondence, if, as Wright maintains, plain correspondence is to be differentiated from the former, it must be able to escape a similar fate. If it cannot, his position gives rise to a dilemma. In the next section I turn my attention to the *bona fides* of the derivation itself.

For argument's sake, provisionally grant the basis for the derivation. A major concern is that, as previously noted, it threatens to swallow up plain correspondence. More unsettling yet, if it is sufficient to carry along the commonsensical version with it, this would make it impossible not only for correspondence to be a correct view for limited discourses, but it would make it impossible even to *state* correspondence as a substantive view. In particular, if the derivation, and the method it employs, has the consequence Wright claims for it, the various philosophers quoted near the beginning of this chapter failed to stake out any substantive claim about truth. That itself would be a quite amazing result. It certainly calls for closer scrutiny.

What might take us *from* a platitude *to* a substantial claim? Wright isn't as forthcoming as we might hope, but here are a few overlapping possibilities based on (admittedly) inadequate hints in his exposition:

(i)   being able to cash in the crucial notions (say, correspondence and fact)

(ii)   providing a more detailed statement ("a more fine-grained interpretation of the idea of correspondence" (Wright 1992, 25)).

Beginning with (i), perhaps the thought is that merely invoking a notion such as correspondence is empty, though it gives off the misleading appearance of being explanatory. To get beyond a platitude we must be able to flesh out trivial correspondence's more distinctive nature. Suppose this were so. Still, it can't obliterate the fact that (C) says at least as much as the plain notion endorsed by Wright. It is merely that, taken as a serious claim to stake a position on the nature of truth, (C) is unsuccessful at specifying "reference to things which are not themselves propositions" (Wright 1999, 207). But then Wright says little more than (C) does to flesh out his substantial notion, and there is no indication he believes we are in a position to provide a further explanation. Quite the contrary, as quoted earlier, the commonsensicalness of the plain notion depends on its being "shorn of any further analytical or explanatory obligations" (ibid., 207). Thus, if (C), despite conveying as much as—and purporting to convey even more than—plain correspondence, is a platitude, how could the plain notion, conveying even less, fail to be a mere platitude as well?

By classifying (C) as a platitude, Wright intends, *inter alia*, that it be neutral with respect to metaphysical implications of just the sort correspondence places up front. If so, we can be confident that with some not very subtle reworking the same minimal tenets could be made to imply each of the samples of generalized correspondence in section 4.1. (The first five quoted passages are phrased especially closely to straightforward generalizations of Wright's (C), and the others can be brought into conformity with (CP).) If this line succeeds it would prevent any generalized correspondence from expressing its intended position. Indeed, as noted earlier, it is difficult to see how the particular wording of the platitude could matter. For if a simple reformulation without finer-grained interpretation could avert this result, why would Wright expend so much effort to show that no metaphysical position is marked out by this particular formula? But, although it seems as if the alleged trivialities couldn't come from anywhere other than the unspecific character of notions such as correspondence and fact, my own version and those from McGinn, Goldman, and Alston don't mention either, nor does Wright's (CP) paraphrase of (C). Thus, it appears that word-world relations in general and any cognitively independent type of worldly determiner are the real issue, not the specific notions displayed in (C). To sum up the critique, our general formulas fail to convey the thesis that their authors set out to state—namely, a metaphysically charged correspondence theory of truth in which worldly conditions for a bearer's truth are fixed.

Let us then turn to (ii), the platitude's lack of fine-grained detail. Perhaps it will no longer come as a surprise, given the method just described, that the would-be failure of Wright's formula to make a metaphysical claim has nothing to do with its generality, simplicity, or lack of detail, but only with its derivability from ($\mathcal{D}_w$). This is worth emphasis because Wright's method questions our very ability to state or make sense of the view with these formulas. If the platitude is satisfied simply by satisfying ($\mathcal{D}_w$)—and "any competitive philosophy of truth, whatever more it says, must incorporate" ($\mathcal{D}_w$) (Wright 1992, 72)—it is satisfied by deflationism, coherence, or any other competitive noncorrespondence truth theory. If there is nothing but a platitude to consider, it is difficult to see how correspondence can be a statable option. It is incumbent upon us to ask how a more detailed account averts this disaster.

Any further detail would need to say something about relations between words or concepts and the world. If we are allowed Wright's method for rendering the earlier formula innocuous, is there any reason to suppose that those details cannot be similarly disenfranchised? Indeed, given the proliferation of deflationary theories of meaning and reference, along with Wright's own hint of a minimalist account of propositional content, it is quite likely that comparably plausible means will be available for hiving off the metaphysical commitment of any words or concepts.

It may strike some as incredible that all versions of correspondence could be dispatched in such an off-hand manner. Well, it would be tedious to go through a detailed theory point by point to show how it could be rephrased into something Wright would rank as a harmless platitude, but perhaps it will suffice to give the flavor of the tactic. J. L. Austin is unquestionably a correspondence theorist. His version is a central theme of chapter 8. But for now we need only note the following compact but relatively detailed statement of his ultimate view:

A statement is said to be true when the historic state of affairs to which it is correlated by the demonstrative conventions . . . is of a type with which the sentence used in making it is correlated by the descriptive conventions. (Austin 1961, 90)

For starters, we might gloss this in the style of Wright as

A token of "P" says that the world is as the type "P" says it is generally.

If Wright believes that (C) can be paraphrased as (CP), on what grounds can he object to this paraphrase of Austin's formula? We could then explain the differences between two types of referential conventions (demonstrative and descriptive) in equally deflationary ways, for nothing in their particulars (as opposed to their titles) provides any more illumination or fine-grained detail than the correspondence relations Wright readily dismisses in the platitudes. We may then proceed to derive this from a version of ($\mathcal{D}$). The version of ($\mathcal{D}$) would need refurbishing to make room for statements made with sentences as well as the sentences with which they are made, but that introduces no threat to the standard method of generating platitudes. And even if my restatement of Austin's view could use fine-tuning, enough has been provided to show how the method may be extended to detailed versions of correspondence. Indeed, what formulation, however, detailed, could escape this treatment if, as Wright maintains, even the claim "'Snow is white' is true *because* snow is white" (1992, 26) is susceptible to it?

We are now in a better position to evaluate Wright's suggestions (i) and (ii) for overcoming the malaise of uninformativeness. He briefly suggests (1992, 84) that the correspondence theorist must show how her understanding of her claims goes beyond its platitude. But this misses the main point. It is not the lack of detail or further words that account for his result, but merely the ability to be derived from ($\mathcal{D}_w$). Presumably he believes this is a matter of how detailed one's account of correspondence's central notions are. But however detailed they may be, in the end they will be no more than words, and it is on this, and it seems nothing more, that Wright's procedure for reduction to platitude rests. Indeed, he tips his hand in a passage cited earlier, when he identifies 'the moral' of his argument as being that "deflationism [has] no difficulty in accommodating intuitions about the relationship between truth and correspondence so long as doing so is held to require no more than demonstrating a right to the *phrases* by which those intuitions are characteristically expressed" (ibid., 27). "Of course," he immediately adds, "there may be an intended further substantive content which minimalism cannot so easily make its own." But what could a content be that wasn't made manifest in what were just phrases? And, as he avers, "the permissibility of correspondence phraseology as paraphrase of 'true' is the merest by-product of the minimalist platitudes" (ibid., 143).

Close attention to my earlier summary of Wright's supplementary tests for plural concepts may give rise to the suspicion that we've overlooked the crucial point. Weren't Cognitive Command, wide cosmological role, etc. devised to bring out just the distinction we've been laboring to discover? Perhaps, but I don't think that an appeal to these tests (Cognitive Command for short) can avert the problem now before us. Aside from the internal difficulties of these tests, alluded to briefly earlier, there are the following points to be made.

First, nothing in these further tests shows that the *reductio* implicit in Wright's line of reasoning is not still in force: there is still no way to state the position of correspondence nontrivially. Thus, even if Cognitive Command had directly supported correspondence for certain discourses, we would still lack the wherewithal to state the result. And it is unclear what point there is to defending a view that can't be stated.

Related to this, suppose (contrary to my earlier claim) that a discourse governed by Cognitive Command is thereby shown to be correspondentist. What is to prevent the following situation from holding? (a) The discourse is governed by Cognitive Command. (b) The statement of that resulting view is derivable from ($\mathcal{D}_w$). (Remember that it doesn't matter how complicated the derivation from ($\mathcal{D}_w$) is, as long as it doesn't introduce anything more than the sorts of premises passing Wright's test for triviality.) If what I have argued in the foregoing is correct, at least in outline, it is plausible to suppose that any discourse satisfying (a) will also satisfy (b). But following from the equivalences was regarded as a sufficient test for platitudinousness. Thus, it seems as if the resulting correspondence not only can't be stated as other than a platitude, under these, quite plausible, conditions it would *be* a platitude, Cognitive Command notwithstanding.

These remarks reinforce certain of those I made earlier. Wright supposes that passing tests such as Cognitive Command tells us both something about the character of the truth concept being used *and* about the prospects for a realist defense against antirealism. I have nothing to say here about its latter office. (But see the discussion of the extension of truth in chapter 9.) However, even if we acknowledge that role, it is precipitate to read into this a test for the truth concept being employed. The points just mentioned are additional good reasons for that caveat.

Thus, there is likely no means to state, for adherents and opponents alike, a metaphysical theory of truth conditions. Wright's own plain correspondence suffers a similar fate. Whether or not all attempts to state the view are relegated to platitude purgatory, they can be seen, by a method of this type, to be implications of similar truth schemata. On Wright's strategy, pursued consistently, this should be enough to strip them of any metaphysical implications. For our limited purposes, the crucial point is that this has nothing to do with the *generality* of the statements of correspondence. The argument doesn't show that a general statement of the position has any less of a chance of stating correspondence than a detailed one. The only feature that matters is whether the statement of the position, or a whole cluster of such statements, can be derived from ($\mathcal{D}_w$). Whereas this may be simpler to see for sketchy and epigrammatic formulations, no difference of principle is introduced by providing further details.

4.6 The Derivation

The claim under review is that capsule summaries of correspondence are vacuous or at least state too little to conflict with any competitive theory of truth. Wright's trivial correspondence would appear to be a prime candidate for such disparagement, but we have shown that combining it with his plain correspondence is unstable. To the extent that Wright's commonsensical commitment is unassailable, this calls into serious question his claims about the platitude. However that doesn't take us beyond a circumstantial *ad hominem*. If the argument for (C) being a platitude is basically sound, then the charge against summary statements of correspondence (and, indeed, by extension against their detailed elaborations) cannot be dismissed, even if it destroys in its wake his plain correspondence. So we should re-examine the derivation of (C) from ($\mathcal{D}_w$) itself.

An initial problem: Even if (U)—'P' says that P—is true, as Van Cleve (1996) remarks it is only a contingent truth. If sentences are merely syntactic strings, then any sentence might have said something different from what it in fact says. Given this qualification (C) has not been shown to be more than contingent. If the derivation needs such a contingent premise, (C) can't be deemed insubstantial just by being the conclusion. Perhaps those who accept the intended import of the derivation will regard this as the wrong sort of substantiality: (C) may still be a platitude in another way. (The response to follow is different from Wright's own (1996, 916n6).) Although it now yields substantial information about *which* thing makes 'P' true, it does not tell us what it is for 'P' to correspond to it and it does not discover the structural character of P or truthmakers in general (e.g., fact-likeness). Of course, Wright's plain correspondence is no more revealing here than its trivial counterpart. It too gets demoted to a platitude. Still, the point may be that the contingency of (U) doesn't undermine the claim that there is another sort of substantial information still lacking in the premises and conclusion. So provisionally I turn to a different set of problems for the derivation.

Consider 'Does ($\mathcal{D}$) harbor inflationist commitments?' In chapter 6 I argue that it does. But I take it as obvious that, without any accompanying rationale, one can't achieve this simply through the following semi-inversion of Wright's reasoning. For starters, suppose the correspondentist were to recommend as a certitude, on a par with (U), the following:

(U+)   P if and only if P is a fact.

Wright might be agreeable to (U+) because, like the army of thinkers discussed in the previous chapter, he gives every indication of thinking that all talk of facts is no less platitudinous than it is in (C). And, more important, I suspect that deflationists in general would accept this, if only because part of their credo is that they can incorporate with ease all the sorts of loose fact talk that a substantial theory peddles. And (U+) certainly seems to fit that profile. We may then use (U+) to derive, by substitution, the conclusion that ($\mathcal{D}_w$) *can never say less than*

($\mathcal{D}_w$+)   'P' is true if and only if P is a fact,

which can then be taken to show that deflationism can't be stated without a metaphysical commitment. Parodying Wright's line, the correspondence theorist can, and does, make use of the deflationist's phrases, but there is no way the deflationist, whatever her intentions, can state her view without committing herself to those metaphysical consequences. This lampoon is no more or less persuasive than Wright's original. We should be equally skeptical of both.

We may reinforce our skepticism about Wright's reasoning by locating where it has gone astray. A problem can be detected in the key role given to (U), and Van Cleve's earlier observation supplies a crucial clue. Items such as sentences, statements, propositions, beliefs, and judgments are subject to semantic evaluation. Kitchens, birds on logs, rivers, states of affairs are not. Although facts have been a more controversial case, *prima facie* they aren't semantically evaluable. Arguments, such as those highlighted in chapter 3, conclude otherwise. But just because facts don't seem to be semantic entities on their face, if one is to conclude that they nevertheless are, reasons for contravening the appearances are needed. Those examined earlier all fail. In the end, that outcome doesn't matter because we have seen that Wright is willing to restate the so-called platitude in various ways that make no mention of facts. However the important point is that the notion of *things being the way 'P' says they are*, which occurs in (CP), is simply an instance of the general notion of *things being some way*. For *things being some way* it is clear that what is being designated is not semantically evaluable as such. *Things being some way* cuts across the distinction between the semantic and the nonsemantic. This applies equally to the instance to which Wright appeals in (CP). It is only as read thus broadly that we should be inclined to regard "things are as 'P' says they are" as a plausible rephrasal of "'P' corresponds to the facts." And that rephrasal is needed to take us from (CP) to (C).

Now consider the other, front, end of the derivation, from ($\mathcal{D}_w$) to (U). Recall that it was argued that (U)—"P" says that P—is contingent: "P" might have meant something other than what it does in fact mean. But whatever its modal status, (U) is intended strictly as a semantic claim. That is, the second occurrence of 'P' in the formula is taken as a (potential) *meaning*, and meanings are paradigms of semantic evaluations. We are thereby lulled into assuming that we are dealing only with semantic contents. Consequently, when we plug the remainder of (U) into the right-hand slot in ($\mathcal{D}_w$), thus obtaining—with minor alterations for grammar—(CP), the suggestion is that "things [being] as 'P' says they are" is also nothing more than a semantic content. But, as just noted, this pinched reading of (CP) should destroy our easy, intuitive acceptance of the move from (CP) to (C). If we have simply been relying on the right-hand side of (CP) as being a special case of *things being some way*, which is the most natural way to read the phrase, the limitation suggested by (U) is without warrant. It is only as such a special case, without further limitations to semantic involvement, that we should accept *things being the way "P" says they are* as a gloss on *"P" [corresponding] to the facts*. This is the broad reading of the former phrase that (U) is intended to exclude. The argument seems to succeed only by playing on different understandings of "'P' says that P" (from (U)) and "things are the way 'P' says they are" (from (CP)).

The obverse side of this problem is that if we want (C) to be uncontroversially derivable from ($\mathcal{D}_w$), we should adopt an inflated reading of the latter, one that leaves open the possibility that its right-hand side denotes or expresses a state of the world. This is not how deflationism regards such formulas: the animus behind that view, whatever the polemical overlay, is that the right-hand side performs the same task as the left-hand one, but without the mention of truth or the conversion of the content of the right-hand side into a singular term that makes such a mention possible. Put otherwise, instances of ($\mathcal{D}_w$) commit us to nothing more than two semantically evaluable items on either side of the biconditional. It is difficult to see that there is nothing more to instances of (CP), and consequently those of (C), if we remain mindful of all that can be conveyed by notions such as *things being as 'P' says they are*.

The plot thickens. The correspondence advocate will insist on a more robust relationship than ($\mathcal{D}$) between the two sides, one expressed by

($\mathcal{B}$) "P" is true because P.

Or, to revert to the standard example,

($\mathcal{B}$*) "Snow is white" is true because snow is white.

This too seems to be a part of our ordinary conception of truth, but it is hard to see how deflationism can accommodate it. Wright doesn't dispute that ($\mathcal{B}$) is a part of our ordinary conception. Rather he maintains that it can be derived from ($\mathcal{D}_w$) in a way parallel to the derivation of (C). But, as demonstrated presently, this extended derivation also fails, and does so dramatically. Moreover, there is a perfectly general reason why all similar attempts will fail in lieu of an inflationary reading of ($\mathcal{D}$). However, before laying out these claims I want to explain briefly why even deflationists typically don't simply dismiss ($\mathcal{B}$)'s relevance. This will bring into clearer focus just why the inability to derive ($\mathcal{B}$) is so crucial in the present context.

($\mathcal{R}$) (and ($\mathcal{D}$), henceforth understood) expresses a type of covariation. Covariation by itself is not explanatory. To fix that we would need to add something roughly like *dependency*. But it is well known that covariation assures neither mutual nor one-way dependence. (For details see, e.g., Kim 1993c, esp. pp. 142–149.) A and B might covary only because both depend on a third thing, C. If those are the sole relevant connections, A doesn't explain (the presence of) B or B that of A. Of course, once given the background knowledge that C is responsible for both, we may infer from one to the other. But the explanation of their copresence (rather than its bare knowledge) requires the mention or assumption of something beside them, such as the operation of C. In contrast, deflationists tend to claim that the biconditional relationship in ($\mathcal{R}$) brings out all that need be said about the matter. And if that doesn't imply a kind of dependence it is likely assumed that that is because there is none. Without some such claim, it is open to the correspondence theorist to rejoin that ($\mathcal{R}$) is true only because both sides are mutually dependent on a third thing—namely, the fact that P.[7]

Relations such as *because* and *in virtue of* crystallize this sort of dependence. That may account for the fact that deflationists and correspondence theorists alike regard formulas such as ($\mathcal{B}$) as an important test case, despite their ultimate disagreement about its impact.[8] For the correspondence theorist it is a sign either that something important has been overlooked by the deflationist, or that ($\mathcal{R}$), as relevant to the present debate, is to be interpreted more substantially than deflationists are willing to allow. For the deflationist, it may be considered the correspondence theory's last line of defense, and if it can be handled while not committing us to anything beyond ($\mathcal{R}$), the latter will have depleted its final resource against deflationism. But for each of them, as stated earlier, it is something that possessors of the concept TRUTH will want to grant. Thus, ($\mathcal{B}$) becomes a significant test case. Wright and, as detailed presently, Horwich quite properly address it.

How does Wright get from ($\mathcal{D}_w$) to ($\mathcal{B}$)? His only direct argument is contained in the following brief passage:

... there is no difficulty, once CP is secured, in saving [($\mathcal{B}$*)] for minimalism (or deflationism) as well. For, given that 'P' says that P, the question why things are as 'P' says they are is quite properly—if rather trivially—answered by citing its being the case that P. Whence, given (CP), the truth of 'P' can quite properly be explained by citing the fact that P. (1992, 27)

7. Horwich, whose attempted deflationary resolution is discussed shortly, writes that it is likely that a "carefully qualified, true version" of correspondence "could be concocted." Why then not replace deflationism with it? Because, according to Horwich, it doesn't provide "a good account of why it is that instances of the equivalence schema are true" (1998a, 11–12). What is wrong with the account to which this note is attached—namely, that the equivalences hold because both depend on a third thing? Or, for that matter, what deflationary account of the equivalences has Horwich on offer other than that they are obvious? Why can't the correspondentist avail herself of that?

8. Not everyone agrees. For example, Alex Oliver (1996) states of the phrase "in virtue of", that it ought to be banned (69n), that it amounts to "weasal words" (49), and that it belongs to the realm of "murky metaphysics" (49). But past heaping such scorn on the phrase, I cannot discover his objections to it.

Before coming to closer quarters with this reasoning, let me briefly explain why it is highly improbable that any argument of this sort could work. The reason I have in mind extends to any attempt, not only to Wright's, to show that ($\mathcal{B}$) can be brought within the ambit of ($\mathcal{D}$) or ($\mathcal{R}$).

The biconditional in "*p* if and only if *q*" expresses a symmetrical relation, whereas the because of "*p* because *q*" is nonsymmetrical. While it is possible to have "*p* because *q* and *q* because *p*" in special cases (viz., *because* isn't antisymmetrical), there isn't the slightest presumption that if we have one of the conjuncts we are likely to have the other. Indeed, any presumption here is in quite the opposite direction: only in the rare case does the because relation hold symmetrically. Now, if "*p* if and only if *q*" were to imply "*p* because *q*" (with the help of nothing more than trivial and uncontroversial principles), that fundamental difference would disappear. For "*p* if and only if *q*" entails "*q* if and only if *p*," which in turn, by the current derivation strategy, implies "*q* because *p*." This would obliterate the nonsymmetry of *because*. If one quails at calling "if and only if" a relation, preferring to take it as a connective, we can replicate the above reasoning, *mutatis mutandis*, by starting from the fact that biconditionality is commutative and *because* is not.

The problem underlying this failure is the attempt to go *a priori* from a covariation idiom to a dependency one. We do not have to pin down the more precise kind of dependency involved with "because," but it is clear that if anything reflects dependency it does. It is hard to imagine another term more directly designed for its expression. "Is dependent on" and "explains" are no less vulnerable to this sweeping deflationary tactic, and no less nonsymmetrical. We can keep the variety of dependence as open as we want. The first type likely to come to mind is causal, but we can have logical or mathematical dependence as well. Let us also be latitudinarian in allowing a *partial* (mereological) identity between a dependent item and the item on which it depends, as when something is so because it is a part or an aspect of a larger thing that is so. Thus, although it may sound a bit strained, or even ironic, perhaps it is not patent nonsense to say that this table is material because everything in the universe is material. However, the one thing that serious straightforward uses of "because" do prohibit is strict reflexivity. (Notice that biconditionality is reflexive.) X cannot be the case because of X, unless of course we construe the two occurrences of X as designating distinct items despite the similarity of their denoting devices. ($\mathcal{B}$) too is subject to this restriction. It prohibits our reading the "P" on the two sides as expressing the same thing. If the situation were otherwise "'Snow is white' is true because 'snow is white' is true" would be perfectly in order. It is not, though its correlative biconditional—"'Snow is white' is true iff 'snow is white' is true"—is, if a bit turgid, an acceptable English counterpart of a tautology in propositional logic. The restriction above is a straightforward consequence of the dependency vocabulary being deployed. Whether this is also the reason underlying the nonsymmetry of (*B*), it certainly is *a* reason for prohibiting a direct inference that does no more than replace a covariation relation with dependency one.

Let us return to Wright's laconic justification for this derivation. Consider the two-part solution he proposes:

1   its being the case that P (which *answers* "Why things are as 'P' says they are?")

2   the fact that P (which *explains* the truth of "P").

Although mere schemata, the relevant instances of each strike me as paradigms of expressions for denoting extra-propositional reality. It is unclear what mileage Wright believes he can get from appealing to them, unless he has merely assumed that their references to facts and what is the case can be written off as platitudinous. Even were we to grant that (C) is a platitude, that would be to no avail here. What is needed for the derivation is the claim that every relevantly similar occurrence of phrases of the form 'the fact that P' results in platitudes. This would certainly be a doubtful thesis for factative clauses which were cited as *explanations* of something. I can see nothing more to the imputation of the fact of P explaining the truth of 'P' being a mere triviality than the supposition that the explanans must itself be trivial *tout court*. In sum, we have been given no reason to accept—and good reason to reject—an argument from (the assumption that) the phrase 'the fact that P' expresses nothing more than a platitude in (C), to the conclusion that 'explains' brings nothing more to an utterance when it replaces 'if and only if', much less to accept it only because the alleged explanans is *the fact that P*.

Furthermore, it seems clear that the relation in

(i)   *q* explains *p*

is taken to be the converse of that in

(ii)   *p* because *q*.

That is Wright's bridge from 2 above to ($\mathcal{B}$). I provisionally grant this supposition about the relation between explanation and "because." (Shortly I'll present grounds for calling it into question.) Wright's derivation then begins from

(C) "'P' is true if and only if 'P' corresponds to the facts." (1992, 25)

Wright claims in his justification, "given (CP), the truth of 'P' can quite properly be explained by citing the fact that P" (1992, 27). But the relation (or connective) in (C), as in (CP), is only a biconditional. To maintain that this is an *explanation* of the truth of "P" is just the sort of thing that the broader argument seeks to establish. It cannot be assumed. It is precisely because, on a deflated reading, the biconditionality doesn't convey an explanatory notion that the correspondence proponent challenges the deflationist with ($\mathcal{B}$). This would amount simply to arrogating to oneself the disputed thesis which correspondence has defied deflationism or minimalism to generate from its own limited resources.

What of the step from "'P' is true is explained by the fact that P" to ($\mathcal{B}$)—that is, from the language of "explanation" to that of "because"? The trouble here is that *explains* is not the converse of *because*, and this is an additional hitch in the derivation. The differences between them may be subtle, but they are genuine. Both 'explains' and 'because' are non-extensional idioms; each bars the unrestricted replacement of co-referentials. Nevertheless, they have different ranges of allowable substitutions. Explanation relations appear to have all sorts of contextual constraints relating to palpability, the relative simplicity of the explanans, and the like, which are lacking for "because." Philosophers broadly disagree about what counts as an explanation, but all seem to accept some such restrictions. "*p* because *q*" may be true although not explanatory. Of course, the greater restrictiveness of *explains* contexts need not prohibit this step in Wright's argument. I mention it only as preparatory. More significantly, I may also explain to an onlooker what I am doing by giving a more detailed description of my action, but I am not thereby conveying to her that I am doing it *because* of the more detailed description. (E.g., "What are you doing?" "I"m protecting the plants from a frost.") Thus, even if, pace my earlier objection, Wright had succeeded in giving an *explanation* of the truth of "P" with (C), this wouldn't assure him of having accounted for ($\mathcal{B}$) as a platitude.

As was noted earlier, Horwich (1998a, 1990) also attempts to redeem ($\mathcal{B}$) for deflationism. This implies that epigrammatic summaries such as ours cannot state a substantial position because, together with his deflationist interpretation of ($\mathcal{R}$), the very constructions they exhibit, including ($\mathcal{B}$), commit one to no more than deflationism allows. Horwich frames the issue in terms of our concrete instance, ($\mathcal{B}^*$)—"Snow is white" is true because snow is white. He claims of such instances that they do no more than raise questions about the order of explanation (1998a, 105), considerations which can be absorbed by deflationism. The order of explanation begins with "such things as basic laws and the initial conditions of the universe." From there we explain by familiar methods particular things, e.g. snow being white. That explanatory potency transfers to the right-hand side of the formula, which together with the principles governing ($\mathcal{D}$) or ($\mathcal{R}$), explains the left-hand side. We thereby obtain all instances of ($\mathcal{B}$). In addition, Horwich claims that ($\mathcal{B}^*$) is a trivial restatement of

(E) ⟨Snow is white⟩'s being true is explained by snow's being white.

I dealt partially with this last point earlier, when criticizing Wright's conflation of 'explanation' and 'because' idioms. I will make a brief additional comment on it after dealing with the main point, the "order of explanation" contention.[9]

A first observation is that, as in Wright's case, if this is intended as a derivation (as it certainly seems), it would violate the asymmetry of the because relation. Something must have gone awry. We may transfer the lessons of that earlier argument to the present case. However ornately Horwich decorates the narrative, in the present instance it comes down to no more than the situation noted earlier of two terms in a biconditional being explained by a third thing. This circumstance arises when "A if and only if B" holds only because C is the common explanans or cause of both A and B. Basic laws together with initial conditions explain (the fact that) snow is white. Granting the foregoing, those laws and initial conditions also explain *the truth* of the sentence "snow is white" on the left-hand side of ($\mathcal{B}^*$). Horwich claims that only after we have explained that snow is white "do we deduce, and hereby explain why . . . ⟨Snow is white⟩ is true" (1998a, 105). But there is no basis for interjecting the right-hand side of ($\mathcal{R}$)

---

9. For objections to Horwich's earlier (1990, 110ff.) and somewhat altered deflationary apologia for ($\mathcal{B}^*$), see Vision 1997b.

or ($\mathcal{B}^*$) as an intermediate step in this second explanation. One would be hard put to show that the right-hand side of either construction was explanatorily more fundamental for physics or chemistry, whatever the situation for semantics or metaphysics. The proposition *that snow is white* is wholly without a role in bringing off the second explanation. The deflationist solution rests on conflating a scientific explanation with the preconditions for Horwich's would-be understanding of what is conveyed by one of its explananda. Once those issues are disentangled his claim to have accounted for ($\mathcal{B}^*$) is seen to be utterly groundless.

Returning to (E), the changes Horwich must make to the right-hand side undermine the claim that nothing more than deflationism is on offer. The phrase 'snow's being white' is a noun-clause, not a sentence. This difference, although significant, is often neglected. We aren't replacing a quoted part of the left-hand side with its translation into our meta-language on the right. There is no vestige of an appearance that these are equivalent utterances having the same truth-values. On the other hand, 'snow's being white' is quite naturally seen as designating a state of affairs which, were it to obtain, would make the left-hand side true. What is needed for Horwich's purposes would be something along the lines of

⟨Snow is white⟩ being true is explained by snow is white.

The phrasing is inelegant, but suppose it is nevertheless construable. However, if we do understand it, what recourse have we other than to say that we do so by reading it as a clumsy misstatement of (E)? (Interestingly, Horwich agrees that *explanation* is an irreflexive relation (1998a, 106). Thus, a restatement of the last formula is needed if only to remove the appearance that it violates the agreed-upon irreflexivity condition on explanation. What better than (E), which then returns us our original predicament?)

Returning briefly to Wright's attempt to salvage ($\mathcal{B}$) for minimalism, a similar point is germane. Recall, once again, his crucial claim that "the truth of 'P' can quite properly be explained by citing the fact that P" (1992, 27). Setting this out in a form amendable for use in derivations, we might get something like

"P" is true (or, "P" being true) is explained by the fact that P.

The use of schematic letters here may disguise a serious snag in the formula. Working uniformly from ($\mathcal{B}^*$), we get

"'Snow is white' is true (or 'snow is white' being true) is explained by the fact that snow is white."

The right-hand side of either construction—i.e., "the fact that P," "the fact that snow is white"—is no more a sentence than "snow's being white." They are denoting phrases that, in their present forms, may be regarded as denoting facts. In either case, the right-hand side is certainly ill-suited for a redundancy claim or for a claim to the effect that it is a metalinguistic translation of a sentence.

Conclusion

In this chapter we have examined challenges to epigrammatic summaries of correspondence, such as those given in section 4.1, as being no more than trivialities compatible with all the leading views about truth. While we can never be assured that we have exhausted all serious challenges of this ilk, I have tried to take account of those treatments which have been worked out in greatest detail. This bears on another major challenge to correspondence, deflationism. The two treatments of ($\mathcal{B}$) just reviewed are attempts to bring 'because' formulas in line, up to that point, with deflationist claims. As we saw, those efforts fail. The outcome is that our epigrammatic summary is restored to its presumptive legitimacy as a statement of a correspondence theory. It occupies a definite location on the map of competitors, and cannot be discounted as nothing more than a harmless *façon de parler* that non-correspondentists can incorporate.

Nevertheless, we have merely scratched the surface of the issues raised by deflationism. While the skirmish over the foregoing handling (or mishandling) of instances of ($\mathcal{B}$) represents a defeat for that view, if the view is grounded in compelling insights about truth and can be defended on other fronts, the deflationist might be in a strong enough position to maintain either that instances of ($\mathcal{B}$) are to be rejected or that another untested deflationary treatment must be able to work. And this will then have been achieved without excessive hand-waving. At any rate, in the current philosophical climate, a case for correspondence is unlikely to be regarded as complete without a more direct and thorough investigation of its deflationary adversary. The next three chapters are devoted to that task. In chapter 5 the view is explained. In that same chapter one recent version of it (viz., minimalism) is critically examined in light of its distinctive contribution to the general view. Chapter 6 sets out a number of objections to deflationism, most of which I maintain hit their target. In chapter 7, I explore the extent to which two of the early deflationist inspirations, Wittgenstein and Quine, can be said to share the main aims of subsequent theories to which their dicta have contributed so much.

5 Deflationism

5.1 The Essentials

As the twentieth century unfolded, the sternest challenge to correspondence came not from coherence, pragmatism, pluralism, or even from an inability to flesh out further details, but from an assortment of deflationary theories. Provisionally setting aside some minor and some important qualifications, such views affirm that truth has no nature, that it is not a property. And this, it is contended, eliminates the sorts of metaphysical implications associated with traditional theories of truth. Consider once more the schemata for our *equivalences*:

($\mathcal{R}$) ⟨p⟩ is true iff p (again, abbreviating 'the proposition that . . . ' with '⟨ . . . ⟩')

($\mathcal{D}$) "S" is true (in language L) iff p.

Deflationists maintain that one or the other of them, or its instances, is virtually all there is to truth, both to its concept and to its property. Let's begin with the concept. Deflationism holds that ($\mathcal{R}$) (or ($\mathcal{D}$), hereafter understood) captures the essence of truth: nothing remains to constitute its property. Certain recent versions have qualified the view to admit a truth property. Following the lead of its proponents, let us call this brand of neo-deflationism 'minimalism'. (Warning: this terminology isn't universally adopted. For example, some refer to all deflationists as minimalists, others reserve the title for views that make a variety of minor alterations to what they regard as strict deflationism.) Minimalists contend that while, strictly speaking, truth may be a property, it doesn't involve the characteristic metaphysical commitments of inflationary theories. There are no worldly truth conditions for a proposition's truth, it might even be said to be a property without a nature. We will examine minimalism in greater detail below (sections 5.3 and 5.4). For now it suffices to note that despite admitting a truth property, that addition is so heavily qualified that deflationism's major thrust is preserved by minimalism.

This chapter is devoted, first, to outlining the standard deflationist outlook and, second, to a critical exploration of its minimalist variety. A broader examination of deflationism's bona fides is deferred until the next chapter.

We can grasp deflationism's attack without divulging any more about correspondence than is already before us. All versions of correspondence affirm that the truth of a proposition, or at least that of the central ones, is its satisfaction of worldly conditions. Deflationism's batteries don't target the details; rather they are directed at this basic tenet, what we might, once again, label 'the correspondence project'. As seems only natural, deflationism is also incompatible with every other substantive theory of truth. This isn't always clearly discerned. Coherentists and pragmatists have been known to appeal to one of the equivalences to support their own opposition to correspondence. *A fortiori*, they construe an equivalence as showing only that it exhausts the legitimate residue of the correspondence theory's excessive claims. This then opens a slot for their competing view to add something substantive but different, something they do not believe endangered by a proper interpretation of the equivalence. I shall assume without further ado that this narrow construal doesn't take deflationism seriously enough. The claim now under review is more ambitious: to wit, there is nothing to TRUTH beyond what the formulas yield, therefore nothing for coherentists, pragmatists, etc. to add. It is hard to see how the equivalences can be understood as deflating correspondence without at the same time granting its proponents' larger claim to provide a complete and adequate account of the concept.

By focusing on the contrast between correspondence and deflationism I am not insinuating that current versions, say, of coherence are in total eclipse or beyond the pale of serious consideration. But a fair consensus seems to be that in the competition for the best substantive theory, correspondence has the inside track. It is a consensus not only because a large percentage of those who have weighed in on the issue favor correspondence or what might be considered one of its realist variants, but also because deflationary critics almost always play off their view against a pretty nondescript form of correspondence. For reasons such as these, plus the pre-eminence of deflationism in recent discussions, substantive competitors such as coherence and pragmatism will play only a minor role in the polemics surrounding correspondence. (For a fuller examination of substantive noncorrespondence views, see chapter 4 of Vision 1988.) Instead, we concentrate on the struggle between the correspondence project and deflationism.

Capsule summaries of deflationism were given earlier, and further details have emerged in subsequent discussion. But it is now time to furnish a more systematic account of the view and its basic structure. I start with a closer look at its disquotationalist version, the one featuring equivalence ($\mathcal{D}$).

Earlier it was explained why ($\mathcal{D}$) delivers metalinguistically something held to be true only of a proposition in its object language. Tarski took it to be a condition of material adequacy for any truth theory that it produce the right extension. Such instances are known as T-sentences. Insofar as Tarski's views can be located on a map of our current alternatives, he is, as I have said, closest to a correspondence theorist.[1] We may move further from his frugal correspondence-like intentions and toward deflationism by taking ($\mathcal{D}$) as a proper definition of truth. Tarski himself shied away from defining truth for various reasons. He certainly thought semantic antinomies, such The Liar Paradox, made it impossible to give a definition in a language in which its own truth predicate was being defined. Moreover, his characterizations were restricted to individual languages, there being no official way of stating what various truth predicates had in common. Nevertheless, to the extent that we regard ($\mathcal{D}$) as yielding information about the concept of truth, rather than simply grinding out instances, we approach closer to deflationism's quarry.

The account doesn't commence with T-sentences. Rather, the latter are derived from (open or closed) sentences meeting satisfaction conditions. Satisfiers are sequences of ordered classes whose members serve as potential values of whatever variables the sentences may contain: a sentence being true when it is satisfied by the whole sequence, false otherwise. Tarski's focus on sentences of mathematics allowed him to ignore open sentences that were candidates for merely contingent truth. Thus, for him a true sentence

---

1. Other than quoting a few striking passages, I haven't argued seriously for my interpretation. It would take us too far off topic to do so here. But see, e.g., Garcia-Carpintero's (1999) construal of Tarski's views.

could be defined as one satisfying every such sequence. This definition also applies to *closed* (= genuine) contingent sentences—there are no sequences that they don't satisfy. (False closed sentences satisfy no sequences.)

For our limited purposes we can ignore the details of the work of satisfaction. On the other hand, it is more difficult to ignore problems that have been raised for candidate definitions of satisfaction. A natural definition might state that a sentence satisfies a sequence when its values make the sentence true. That would make it impossible to use satisfaction in any noncircular definition of truth. To avoid this difficulty Tarski suggested that we simply list "which objects satisfy the simplest sentences" (1949, 63). But this gives rise to a different sort of problem, raised early, repeatedly, and strikingly by Plato's Socrates: how can a list amount to a definition? I shall not have anything further to say about this matter. For the sake of argument, let us assume that a nontruth-involving, suitably general, delineation of satisfaction is in the offing.[2] We may then ignore any further complications about the way in which the T-Schema, ($\mathcal{D}$), or its instances, the T-sentences, are arrived at.

Let's begin with the popular homophonic specimen that dominates the literature:

($\mathcal{D}$1)   "Snow is white" is true (in L) iff snow is white.

If the quotation marks and 'is true' on the left are removed, what remains on the right-hand side is the sentence's metalinguistic translation. Of course, not all T-sentences are homophonic (e.g., "'La niege est blanche' is true iff snow is white"), and indexicality introduces yet further complications. But the homophonic cases are most illustrative of the lessons deflationists draw from the equivalences.

Now let us turn to ($\mathcal{R}$). While nothing is strictly disquoted, when the left-hand side is *disencumbered* of the context "The proposition that ___ is true," what remains is the right-hand side. Both equivalences give the impression that, as far as these sorts of cases are concerned, whatever content we

---

2. Suppose we listed all the predicates in the language. Then we might follow Quine's example for "the sentence consisting of 'walks', accompanied by the alphabetically *i*th variable": it "is satisfied by a sequence if and only if the *i*th thing in the sequence walks" (1970, 40). The finitude of our vocabulary makes this possible. But there are sticking points. For example, relational terms combined with conjunctions can generate an infinite number of different (atomic) relations ("a loves b and c together", "a loves b and c and d together," and so on).

wanted to convey by using the predicate 'is true' can be conveyed just as directly without it. Simply replace the left-hand side by the right-hand one.

Qualifications aside, the heart of deflationism on either version is the contention that the equivalence yields all we need to say to round off an explanation of the concept and property truth. Should there remain other interesting things to say about relations truth has to various notions, they will not enter an account of its concept. The point to keep in mind for this provisional sketch is that we have in front of us a complete account of truth, and it hasn't left an opening for raising issues about worldly conditions needed for something to be true. On the current view truth turns out to be much less of a pivotal or explanatory notion than traditional theories imply.

To complete this picture we must address commonplace occurrences of 'is true' other than those covered by the equivalences. Sometimes we predicate 'is true' without having before us (in the relevant way) the proposition(s) of which it is predicated. For example, consider circumstances in which the proposition said to be true is described, but not present (e.g., 'what Pam just stated'), or in which we want to generalize for classes of propositions (e.g., 'everything Il Magnifico says', 'a proposition or its negation'). For handy cross-reference all such occurrences of 'is true' will be known here as *indirect*. Here are two explanations consistent with the deflationist outlook for indirect occurrences.

First, they allow us to form a whole sentence when combined with a subsentential phrase. No proposition is expressed by phrases such as 'what Pam just stated' or 'everything Il Magnifico says'. The use of 'is true'—or a thinly disguised surrogate such as 'is the case'—enables us to form a complete sentence for assertion, or, with 'is false', for denial.

Second, indirect uses of 'is true' enable us to state generalizations such as the principle of excluded middle or the claim that everything Il Magnifico says is true. For most generalizations we can use natural language equivalents of quantification. For example, suppose I note that Donald swims and that Daffy swims and observe the same behavior for very many other ducks. Generalizing I replace the names (or other designations) of individuals and say "All (most) ducks swim." But if I want to generalize over "Either ducks swim or they do not," "It is raining or it is not," "I am in Utah or I am not," I would need to quantify not over things, but over propositions or sentences. For reasons which needn't be detailed here this consequence is often thought to be worth avoiding. We avoid it in common forms of speech by saying "Either a sentence or its negation is true." Thus, the truth predicate is useful for generalizing over semantically evaluable items. As it is popular to phrase things since Quine put it this way, the truth predicate is a device for "semantic ascent," taking us from talk about the world (viz., whatever the true utterance may be said to have talked about) to talk about the language used to talk about the world. This is made most evident by ($\mathcal{D}$), in which 'is true' is a predicate of sentences. And it is this change that enables us to state the generalizations in question.

Whereas indirect occurrences need not in themselves advance the view that 'is true' is redundant, deflationists typically take them to reinforce their claim that truth's utility is exhausted by its logical (or grammatical) role: there is no need for a separate metaphysical account of truth's conditions of application. If such indirect uses exhaust the rationale for having a truth predicate, and that is the end of the tale concerning its property, metaphysical codicils are superfluous.

($\mathcal{R}$) and ($\mathcal{D}$) result in distinct varieties of deflationism, depending on whether one takes propositions or sentences as one's canonical truth bearers. And this initial difference, which may seem rather minor at first, expands like ripples in a pond into broad and technical disparities, involving thinkers in issues such as the proper theory of quantification with which to express the view. In a somewhat different direction, various taxonomies divide deflationism yet more finely than I have done. However, our limited focus enables us largely to ignore further differences among versions. Our current interest is confined to the following two aspects of deflationism: (a) its, explicit or implicit, arguments against the correspondence project and (b) whether so sparse an account (in either version) can sustain claims made on its behalf. Further discriminations between separate varieties are irrelevant to much of the subsequent discussion: the points I shall raise usually apply indifferently to either initial form. Exceptions can be noted as they arise.

As mentioned, the equivalences have also been central to the views of some correspondence theorists, or at least realists about truth, such as Alston, McGinn, and Searle. How then does the very same equivalence lend itself so readily to deflationism? Something additional to the equivalences themselves must be responsible for the differences between it and such metaphysically charged views. Two questions then arise: first, what differentiates the deflationary reading of the equivalences, and, second, why prefer it to the one accepted by inflationists? I have already answered the first question: deflationists take the right-hand side of the equivalence to demonstrate that whatever is conveyed or stated with the use of the truth predicate can be fully captured without it. They do not see any significance in the right-hand side beyond that. But what of the second question? What reasons underlie, and support, these deflationary interpretations of ($\mathcal{R}$) and ($\mathcal{D}$)?

For starters, with some idealization we may view deflationism as a construction resting on three pillars.

(1) Logical thesis: The left-hand sides of the biconditionals (i.e., "$\langle p \rangle$ is true," "'S' is true") are logically equivalent to their right-hand side (i.e., "p").

(2) Semantic thesis: The left-hand and right-hand sides of the biconditionals mean the same thing (viz., have the same cognitive content).

(3) Metaphysical thesis: 'Is true' does not express a property, *or* truth has no (substantial) nature, *or* 'is true' is not a predicate, *or* ($\mathcal{R}$) or ($\mathcal{D}$)—plus whatever can be culled from the indirect cases—express all there is to TRUTH.

Occasionally, deflationism is described simply as the view that ($\mathcal{R}$) shows that "$\langle p \rangle$ is true" (or, "'S' is true") and "p" are *equivalent*. That way of stating it combines two infelicities. First, it fails to distinguish (1) from (2): is what is intended logical or semantical equivalence, or some combination of them? Next, it doesn't mention (3). Even correspondence theorists, who one would expect to be more solicitous, have been known to take this for a statement of deflationism. That makes it rather easy game to then conclude that one's own correspondence theory is compatible with deflationism. However, if we view (3), or something along those lines, as indispensable to deflationism, the two views can no longer be reconciled.

Failure to distinguish (1) from (2) may be understandable for those who believe logical equivalence is all there is to synonymy, or for those who disdain theories of meaning.[3] Philosophers diverge widely on their commitments to theories of meaning or content. Thus, (2) is meant to cut a broad swathe through distinct outlooks. It is formulated to embrace the views of those willing to state only that (2) yields an irreducible account of the concept of truth, on many different understandings of 'concept'.

3. For a distinction between (1) and (2), see White 1970, 92–93.

More important than counting the number of deflationists going through something recognizably like (2) is the fact that stopping with either equivalence falls short of drawing any of the lessons in (3). Deflationism as it is understood here must incorporate one or another of the theses making up (3), or something to like effect. Otherwise, nothing distinguishes it from the many varieties of correspondence which are consistent with, or may even incorporate, (1) and (2). Indeed, (1) and (2) do not by themselves even state that this is all that is implied by the equivalences. Moreover, as a matter of historical fact, if not logic, deflationists have supported (3) with (1) and/or (2). While it is *conceivable* that (3) be maintained solely on an independent basis, I ignore versions of that sort in the absence of any clear instances in the literature. (In the next section I will show that a few potential counterexamples to this generalization evaporate on closer inspection.)

To repeat: (3) is vital to this account of deflationism. It supplies a basis for the advertised absence of metaphysical commitment. (We might call it the "Strictly Accurate Redundancy Specification," or "SARS.") However, (3) rests on some combination of the equivalences. And while the equivalences mention (the predicate) 'is true', (3) is about the property of *being true*. Thus, those running an argument along these lines must be supposing that certain features of the predicate disclose all we need to know about its property. Nothing is inherently wrong with the assumption that linguistic discoveries about a predicate lead to conclusions about its correlative (would-be) property. But it is an assumption; it is not self-evident. Thus, its further examination is warranted. (This point is revisited in section 6.3.)

Like almost everything in this area, the articles of deflationism are subject to qualification and minor revision in light of deviant versions. Some of those presenting themselves as deflationists maintain only that their theory extends to the concept TRUTH. They leave open the possibility of a different tale about truth's *property*. This is a relatively recent, ultra-concessive wrinkle in the ranks of deflationists. The standard view has it rather that (1) and (2) yield grounds from which we may conclude that there is no truth property. A bit less standardly, **minimalists** hold that there is a truth property, but it has no nature, or least none that is substantial.

Deflationists who restrict their conclusions to the concept TRUTH, and allow a distinct philosophical inquiry (in which they typically do not officially engage) concerning truth's property, further complicate efforts to gain a clear understanding of the ground-level importance each side attaches to its own position vis-à-vis the other.

For one thing, on this way of carving up the issues, if a certain variety of correspondence concerns only an account of the truth property, it isn't in conflict with this style of deflationism. This is not to say that all versions of correspondence are neutral with respect to truth's concept. In chapter 2 I emphasized a version that involves truth's concept no less than its property. Nevertheless, some correspondence theorists, including Goldman (1999), Armstrong (1997), and Alston (2001a), appear willing to accept, along with those concessive deflationists, this division of the issues. In itself, this need not be regrettable. A convergence of opinion between apparently disparate views, reducing their differences to terminological ones, could indicate that both parties are onto something. However, it does obscure what deflationists have put forth as a sharp break with traditional theories in this area. Despite that, this convergence is only a secondary theme for us. We are primarily concerned with correspondence theorists who believe that their theories are implicit in our concept, and, yet more important, our focus is on deflationists who purport to draw larger anti-metaphysical consequences from their accounts. If deflationists allow correspondence's metaphysical consequences to enter by way of truth's property, that not only emasculates the anti-metaphysical implications of (3), but it seems to compromise seriously the advantages of economy for which deflationism is touted.

Second, a leading tenet of traditional deflationism has been that truth is not a property, or is at most a purely formal one. The minimalist version under discussion scraps that bold declaration. Although it is simple enough to modify the deflationist claim to read "*if* truth is a property, its propertyhood doesn't enter an account of its concept," this view skirts, rather than engages, the metaphysical issue of truth theory, and it is only of minor interest in our pursuit of a viable correspondence theory. (That is, its interest is limited to the question whether the articles of correspondence can be counted as part of the conceptual wherewithal of our TRUTH concept.) Moreover, while it is vulnerable to the other charges I bring against standard deflationism in the next chapter, it invites additional difficulties (as we shall see in sections 5.3 and 5.4) that its more traditional compatriots may not share.

Labels such as 'redundancy' and 'disappearance theory' may make it seem as if SARS is not so much a theory of truth as the renunciation of one. But its proponents do claim to deliver sufficient conditions for a truth concept and, with the exceptions just mentioned, for a truth property. In any event, it is important to distinguish deflationism from the nihilism described earlier. The latter is the doctrine that truth is so fundamental to our thought that no account of it, including a deflationist one, is possible. Frege (1999) and Davidson (1996, in his most recent incarnation) hold this view. In contrast to nihilism, deflationism supplies what its claimants take as a satisfactory account of the subject, grounded in ($\mathcal{R}$) or ($\mathcal{D}$). Strictly speaking, a nihilist may also accept one of those two formulas as a sine qua non of any truth theory, but remain a nihilist by denying that such bits of information are sufficient for an understanding of truth.

We now seem to have enough before us to examine critically certain significant differences between traditional deflationism and minimalism. Sections 5.3 and 5.4 are devoted to that task. (In the next chapter, after having attained a reasonably clear fix on deflationism's commitments, we can avoid further exegetical questions and concentrate on a corporate position.) But first I want to consider, albeit briefly, some strategies that may appear to undermine the foregoing description of the orthodox deflationist line.

5.2 "Is True," Ascribing, and Demonstrating

I have maintained that the general line of argument laid down for deflationism holds, to a greater or lesser degree, for every prominent version of it defended in print. Now let us look at a few doctrines that some may take to establish deflationism independent of going through a distinctively deflationist reading of one of our equivalences. Showing how even those views must rely on the equivalences so understood helps to establish my claim about their foundation beyond serious question.

We have already seen that deflationists typically hold that 'is true' earns its keep in indirect contexts. But what does it do in direct ones? Some deflationary thinkers have given, roughly, performative or speech act analyses of the role of 'is true' or 'that is true' for direct cases, utterances in which the proposition of which 'is true' is predicated is present (or assumed to be in the context). One apparent virtue of those accounts is that on occasion they appear (whether intentionally is questionable) to stand on their own, without the support of our equivalences or the theses into which I have decomposed them. Of course, these theorists may make use of the equivalences as an additional reason for preferring their own account to the one given in the correspondence project. But the positive account is occasionally put forth as if it is an independent reason for supporting their view. Thus, that account of these occurrences of 'true' might be supposed to be an independent argument for deflationism. In this section I want to show that such alternative accounts don't add anything polemically to the arguments of the last section. Or, put more precisely: first, such augmentations add nothing to the case against correspondence not already contained in arguments based on the equivalences. And, second, despite presentations of the positive views as independently strong alternatives to traditional theories, as deflationary articles they ultimately rely on standard arguments from the equivalences to give them whatever force they may have as replacements for correspondence. In short, they amount to no more than proposals to fill an explanatory gap left by the destructive work of traditional deflationism.

The views in question are distinguished by their alternative accounts of 'is true' (or 'it is true that', hereafter understood), in which that phrase doesn't play its apparent property ascribing role. We may illustrate this with two deflationary proposals. First, on ascriptivist accounts 'is true' does no more than endorse, concede, underwrite, etc. a prior utterance occurring (or presupposed) in a particular discourse (Strawson 1949; Kraut 1993). Second, recall the prosententialist theory mentioned in chapter 1 (Grover 1992; Grover et al. 1992). It treats the phrase 'that is true' as an unanalyzable *proform*, akin to a pronoun, merely reiterating another utterance. The entire sentence, not just the familiar occurrence of 'that', is interpreted as a demonstrative. Other constructions with truth vocabulary are then modeled on this one. At first both views might be taken to obviate the need for ($\mathcal{R}$)'s support of the claim that truth isn't a property. They appear to argue directly that their alternative proposals for understanding 'is true' are sufficient (in each case) to defeat any correspondence project.

Because this is not the place for a close examination of such views I ignore various internal difficulties with each. (For more on ascriptivism, see Kirkham 1992. For a detailed critique of prosententialism, see Wilson 1990.) Here I draw attention only to the fact that any pressure the two proposals place on correspondence is drawn from classical deflationism, and not from their suggestion that 'is true' has a function other than ascribing a property. I begin with the second view, prosententialism. Grover et al. set out their proposal as follows:

> In the spirit of Ramsey, our claim is that all truth talk can be viewed as involving *only* prosentential uses of 'That is true'. (1990, 89; emphasis added)

Suppose we grant the possibility and naturalness of prosententialist interpretations in individual cases: they are cases in which we may take it that phrases such as 'that is true' are behaving toward antecedent (or imagined antecedent) uttered sentences just as pronouns of laziness behave toward their antecedents. That is, they are merely shorthand and less stilted ways of reiterating what has already been said. If Maud says "The class has been canceled" and Fred says "That's true," on prosententialism this is merely Fred's way of repeating Maud's claim (and indicating that it has already been said). What evidence beyond the bare possibility of such an interpretation could there be for this positive thesis? I don't find considerations other than procedural ones (viz., relative simplicity) in the relevant texts. That aside, any evidence to this end has its limits: it hasn't the slightest tendency to show that it is the only way, as the passage just quoted has it, to construe such talk. How does it drive out an alternative reading—in the present case, correspondence? Indeed, it hasn't any tendency even to show that whatever grounds there may be for viewing truth as a property aren't at least equally strong. Evidence for an incompatible inflationary construal will include, but not be exhausted by, the obvious fact that "that is true" at least has the grammatical form of a predication.

It is not unusual to have alternative glosses of a single, unambiguous idiom. Only in such a circumstance could there be competing accounts of standardly unambiguous expressions, and there are numerous examples of just such competing accounts. Moreover, prosententialists wouldn't be arguing, as they do, for the superiority of their own view if there weren't a competing, natural way to construe "that's true" (viz., as a predication of something demonstrated). Thus, the word 'only' in the passage quoted from Grover et al. doesn't merely exaggerate the strength of their evidence; it is also curiously out of place in an exposition designed to show nothing more than that their proposal is a natural, perhaps even the most natural, way to construe their favored idioms. Nothing in this even purports to show that it is the only way to construe those phrases. To what then does the authors' claim that all truth talk can be viewed only in their way owe its eligibility? Strictly, it appears, in their acceptance of the standard charge of the redundancy (or, as they prefer, "repetitiousness") of 'is true'. Their proposal does add one element to the deflationist case, namely that their positive view explains why the deflationist criticisms don't leave us without an alternative construal of the predicate. But even that presupposes the standard deflationist criticisms. No additional reasons have opened a new front to reinforce the objections already in the deflationist's arsenal.

Similar remarks apply to ascriptivism. It is obvious on its face that endorsing, conceding, underwriting, and such other noncognitive functions as ascriptivists mention are compatible with a predicate expression also stating something about its subject (cf. Warnock 1954, 57–58). Indeed, it is notorious that even some predicates whose primary task is taken to be to express norms—such as 'is industrious' or 'is rude'—do so only by way of certain thick non-normative content. Thus, once again, being construable as doing a job other than the one correspondence allots to 'is true' is no argument for supposing that nothing makes propositions true. When such claims are made, tacit support from the deflationary critique always lurks in the background.

The foregoing remarks are as applicable to standard deflationist treatments of indirect occurrences as it is to the positive theses just reviewed. The use of 'is true' to enable us to state certain generalizations or logical laws, and to complete descriptive phrases is compatible with that predicate also expressing a property. Indeed, it is tempting to argue that it can do the former only by way of doing the latter. It is the deflationary reading of (1) and (2), the one leading them ineluctably to (3), which is responsible for the treatment of indirect occurrences being relevant. For given (3), the deflationary line countenances a distinctive role for 'is true' in indirect occurrences. It thereby relieves its proponents of the need to modify their earlier conclusion about truth's (lack of) propertyhood in light of such cases.

Of course, even if such positive theses aren't further evidence against correspondence, they do contribute something to the larger deflationist outlook. SARS's blunt rejection of a correspondence explanation of the occurrences of 'is true', without anything to offer in its place, would be counterintuitive enough seriously to damage the view's credibility. After all, the word 'true' doesn't seem altogether idle in such contexts. To make their conclusions palatable deflationists may propose an alternative, non-property-ascribing role played by this (real or apparent) predicate: that account may turn out to be ascriptivist or prosentantialist. Each could fill the lacuna perceived to be left once a correspondence explanation is disqualified. However, although ascriptivism or prosententialism may be construed as an alternative to central implications of correspondence, it cannot be construed as a critique of the latter: the problem is that its replacement interpretation or function is compatible with truth having a nature, expressing a property, or whatnot. Consequently it adds not a whit to the deflationist's direct objections to correspondence. For our limited purposes we are concerned only with the substance of that attack.

5.3 Deflationism Plus a Truth Property?

What price does a deflationist pay for admitting that 'is true' expresses a property? Although, as we have seen, some deflationists restrict their purview to a concept, and allow that a separate inquiry might discover a truth property, it is more usual for them to declare that truth isn't a property, period! Some have even denied that 'is true' is a predicate (Ayer 1946, 1963; Grover et al. 1992; Stoutland 1999), presumably observing the rule that all predicates express properties. We may conveniently, if unrigorously, sum this up with the schema

'P' is a predicate → P is a property.

Deflationists who deny that 'is true' is a predicate may be employing *modus tollens*—from the fact that truth isn't a property to the conclusion that 'is true' isn't a predicate. But we have seen that another sort of deflationist, the minimalist, declares that truth is a property. On this second option deflationists claim to have discovered that truth's propertyhood is less than metaphysically significant. They may say that it is a property without a nature (M. Williams 1986, 240; Horwich 1998a, 5), or with no substantial conditions of application beyond those for its assertibility (viz., no worldly truth conditions). Horwich's view is a *locus classicus* of this combination. At times it seems as if this brand of deflationist is reasoning as follows: there is nothing more to a predicate than its grammatical appearance, a property is whatever is expressed by its correlative predicate, therefore truth is a property. For example, Horwich claims that having a predicate is "a conclusive criterion" for expressing a property (1998a, 37).

In a coda on the subject, Horwich writes that "every term that functions logically as a predicate stands for a property" (1998a, 141–142). Presumably, what this implies for our case is that where x is (identical with) the proposition *that p*, we can infer from "*x* is true" to "the proposition *that p* is true." Truth's robust role in this reasoning is what Horwich seems to mean by its "function[ing] logically as a predicate." But this has the following untoward consequence: it shows that any term which has ever appeared in predicate position "stands for a property." For we can imagine inferences of a relevantly similar kind for any predicate term. (E.g., x exists, x = y, therefore y exists. If you believe that existence is a property, run through the argument with a predicate for your favorite *ersatz* property.) In any event, however intimately related a predicate and its correlative property, they aren't the same thing. Nor is the distinction between them obliterated by qualifying a predicate, pretty vacuously as we have just seen, as logical (or as functioning logically). So the move from a predicate to a property is still an inference, or requires something like the promiscuous principle of propertyhood just cited. Be that as it may, this is all there is to truth's propertyhood on Horwich's account, and on accounts of various other minimalists. In this section I shall examine why it is that such thinkers believe we cannot thicken truth's propertyhood. In the next section I explore whether this sense of being a property is at all plausible.

First, a few brief clarifications. If one accepts the view that truth is a property, however thin its propertyhood, it requires two minor qualifications to our previous account. First, we can no longer state (3), the metaphysical claim, in the first of the ways listed there: namely, as the view that 'is true' doesn't express a property. This still leaves a host of other avenues for capturing SARS's impact. Second, the account of propertyhood for truth that Horwich adopts rules out an earlier deflationist concession—the possibility that the property of truth has a substantive nature, to be revealed by a further inquiry. The claim under review doesn't restrict itself to the concept of truth; it also maintains that the conceptual inquiry yields all that can be said about truth as a property. Thus, it is incompatible with views, such as that offered by Soames, in which there is room for a further inquiry into truth that might reveal its substantive character.

How do minimalists determine that truth is a property without a metaphysically significant nature? To appreciate more fully Horwich's reasoning, consider the following comparison. The paradigmatic property among naturalistically inclined philosophers is a natural kind, such as *gold, zirconium*, or *water*. Given the normal limits of workaday concerns, there are commonplace ways to detect their instances, or even to determine their extensions.

But such properties have deeper natures discoverable only by a further empirical inquiry that goes beyond casual encounters with instances. Thus, having atomic weight 79 is a feature of the nature of gold, just as having atomic weight 40 is a feature of zirconium's nature, and H_2O constitutes that of water. There is no such further inquiry for *truth*. Its nature, if it has one, must be unearthed through a distinctively philosophical type of, loosely stated, *conceptual* and *a priori* inquiry. As noted, both some correspondentists and the rare deflationist leave room for this sort of a division of conceptual labor. Horwich's official position, from which he slips on occasion (see below), is that any such distinction is untenable. I agree. But his reasons for rejecting a further conceptual investigation here are questionable. They seem based on a set of unduly restrictive adequacy conditions for conceptual inquiry. Let us briefly explore those.

One of Horwich's adequacy conditions for successful analysis is that it respect "the usual canons of explanatory priority" (1998a, 50–51). These declare that the "relatively complex" be replaced by the "relatively simple." Certainly correspondence doesn't aspire to anything of that sort. Although it has been called 'reductive' by some, there is no generally recognized hierarchy of concepts such that the correspondence analysis of truth attempts to traffic in notions simpler than truth itself. The thought-world relations and worldly items proposed on it are at roughly the same ontological and epistemological level as the notion they seek to explain. No doubt some broadly Tarskian versions may impose specific requirements that, say, the semantic be grounded nonsemantically. But this is not a desideratum of correspondence theory per se. Rather the requirement arises from the view that semantic relations somehow stand in need of legitimation. It is not a commitment that follows merely from adherence to a correspondence theory. Indeed, it seems that in his own work Horwich sidesteps central concerns—say, involving naturalism—that typically underlie this misgiving (ibid., 41–42).

Furthermore, Horwich's simplicity requirement is dubious: it is not well enough understood to implement confidently, at least not if relative simplicity must first be understood independent of sample accounts. The notions of simplicity and complexity have always proved protean enough to fit just about any account that supporters find otherwise attractive. Notice also how very different the narrow construction of conceptual analysis offered here is from the one countenanced in chapter 2, and which is closer to the one I suspect the largest body of correspondence theorists would acknowledge. In that earlier brief gloss I mentioned that one legitimate goal of conceptual inquiry is to make explicit what is merely implicit in our adequate-for-ordinary-purposes grasp of a concept. Such features are revealed not only by what we are (or should be) willing to offer verbally and spontaneously as implications of the concept, but also by the direction in which we are willing to rectify particular uses in light of new information, by those circumstances for which we feel we must take responsibility, and by our reactions to previously unencountered types of situations. All these seem to fall within the ambit of a concept, and are central features of conceptual mastery even for those who think such mastery has something to do with *use*.

Also, Horwich's daunting requirement states that analyses take biconditional form. This implies that the analysans (the product of the analysis) be a sufficient condition for the analysandum (the concept being analyzed). That is, analyses will take the form, schematically, "P is a truth if and only if condition A obtains," which implies "If A obtains, then P is a truth." But, as Wright's platitudes quoted in chapter 4 make plain, not all conceptual discoveries need supply sufficient conditions for truth. Wright nicely clarifies the point as follows:

. . . skepticism [about the analysis of TRUTH] has been driven largely by the traditional notion that success in this project would have to consist in the provision of a satisfactory necessary-and-sufficient conditions analysis of the concept, and there is clearly some scope for relaxation of that model. . . . Why should not other such claims—even if not biconditional or identity claims—provide illumination of essentially the same kind? To be sure, if one wants *a priori* conceptual clarity about what truth—or beauty, or goodness, etc.—is, then the natural target is an identity (or a biconditional). But perhaps the sought-for reflective illumination can be equally well—if less directly—provided by the assembly of a body of conceptual truths that, without providing any reductive account, nevertheless collectively constrain and locate the target concept and sufficiently characterize some of its relations with other concepts and its role and purposes. (2001, 759)

Taking the traditional notion a step farther, it is also customary to require that the conditions yield meaning-equivalents. But there is no pressure on a correspondentist to hold that "the proposition that x is F is true" be equivalent in meaning to "the proposition that x is F corresponds to x being F." For example, we recently encountered ascriptivist analyses in which it is the office of "is true" to endorse, underwrite, etc. a proposition. Nothing debars a correspondence theorist from acknowledging this as a part of our concept of truth, although it is not, on a correspondentist account, a feature of truth's property. On this expanded view, if one is wholly unaware of that function of the predicate, it may be sensible to withhold from her credit for the concept TRUTH, or at least for a mature version of it. So there is a mismatch between the aspirations of a correspondence theory and the requirement that a traditional analysis yield a meaning-equivalence. Given the room for conceptual insight as stated by Wright, it seems clear that what should be scrapped in a case of conflict is the requirement that one supply a sufficient condition, not the theory. That former demand goes beyond anything that is or has been the immediate, and legitimate, concern of a correspondence theory. Since it doesn't mark the boundaries of all conceptual discovery, it is inadvisable to impose it.

In any event, the requirement of biconditionality for an analysis is strangely beside the point for the deflationist attack on correspondence. Recall that the attack homes in on thesis (3) of deflationism. That thesis, and it alone, is incompatible with truth being a property possessing metaphysical clout. Suppose, in defiance of SARS, it can be shown that our concept of TRUTH demands that propositions be made true by their relationship to worldly states. It is then of no moment whether this is a sufficient condition for a truth concept, or whether additional conditions—e.g., being the most general goal of inquiry—are needed for an adequate, self-standing concept. Thus, where A may be "P corresponds to the facts," the present indictment of correspondence is irrelevant to its capacity to satisfy the condition that if A obtains, then P is a truth. A correspondence clause in any (broader) account of truth would be enough to overturn deflationist thesis (3). Indeed, we could accept the requirement of biconditionality for a successful analysis *and* admit that we are unable to get a biconditional analysis of TRUTH, and it would still be the case that a correspondence clause refutes (3). The interest of Horwich's brand of minimalism can only be in what it does to rule out correspondence as a requirement of TRUTH or of *truth*.

As I mentioned earlier, Horwich appears to waffle on the issue, and, I believe, for cause. But in the end he clearly fails to acknowledge the possibility he, very properly, raises. Let me explain.

While Horwich continues to characterize correspondence as an "explicit definition or reductive analysis of truth" (1998a, 120–201), either of which clearly requires that the definiens/analysans be sufficient for the definiendum/analysandum, he also interjects what seems to be a concession in light of the fact that "almost no concepts are susceptible to exact reductive analysis (not even 'table' or 'house')" (ibid., 121n). To this he quickly responds that as far as truth goes "there is nothing to be said—not even very roughly speaking—about what it consists in" (ibid.). That aside, this relaxation of adequacy conditions is wholly forgotten later when the issue of truth's nature comes to a head. He makes this plain when explicating the division of labor between the semanticist, who examines a concept, and the scientist or metaphysician, who would examine the property expressed by that concept. He illustrates the point with the concept WATER. Whatever our definition of the concept, the property *water* is H_2O. But the moral he then draws from the analogy is telling. Suppose that this account amounts to a reduction of water to its chemical composition (ibid., 135). Horwich then generalizes that any similar information about the nature of a property will also be a reduction (ibid., 138). However, that lesson doesn't follow from the point of the illustration. Suppose all we knew, or even all we could know, is that a necessary condition for being water was containing oxygen (viz., no oxygen, no water). Although that is clearly insufficient for being water, it would just as effectively illustrate the relevant division of labor. Thus, appealing to the fact that we know more than this, enough in fact for water's complete chemical composition, does nothing to enhance this explanation of the division of explanatory labor. More important, it is powerless to install his requirement that the analysans be a reduction in order to draw the distinction.

To this Horwich adds that the equivalence axioms for truth "are *conceptually* basic and *a priori*" (ibid., 138). The claim that they are conceptually basic is in effect a negative existential, an exceptionally difficult claim to make a case for. Even so, it is hard to find anything in Horwich's exposition that so much as purports to supply evidence for that pronouncement. In addition, he again demands at that place that any account be a "reductive analysis." He leaves no opening for the sorts of platitudes Wright mentions, although, if any of them were successful, could they be other than conceptual elements of truth?

5.4 Further Tensions

We have come across two openings for there being a property of truth within deflationism. First, there is the declaration that although truth is a property, it is one without a nature, or is a lightweight property (Wright

1992). Second a deflationist may distinguish accounts of truth's concept and property. The concept doesn't require any inflationary articles, but leaves open the possibility that a separate philosophical inquiry will favor one or another of the familiar substantive accounts of the truth property. The prime feature of this second strategy is that questions about truth's concept and its property can be fairly sharply separated. Let's consider each option, beginning with the former.

This view is familiar from the discussion of our last section. Let us first observe something about properties in general. For a property of any kind—thinness, lacking a nature, degree of levity, all aside—one of the following three circumstances must obtain: either everything (or, everything in its categorial range) has it, or nothing has it, or some things have it and others don't. This is the least we should demand of whatever counts as a property. It is highly unlikely that any minimalist would claim that everything is true. Of course, it is possible to predicate 'is true' of every proposition, but then it is also possible to predicate 'is blue' of every object. That would no more make propositions true than it would make objects blue. More important, it would entail the contradiction that, for all propositions p, both p and $\sim p$ were true. It may seem more in step with deflationism to say that *nothing* is true. Since truth has no nature, it lacks conditions of application, and so couldn't be possessed by anything. However, this entails the absurd consequence that the conditions presented on the right-hand sides of instances of our two equivalences never obtain. As we might expect, Horwich sensibly rejects the *no truths* option outright: " . . . the claim that truth is not a complex or naturalistic property . . . must not be confused with the idea that truths are unreal, or, in other words, that no sentence, statement, or belief is ever true" (1998a, 52–53), and again "there are truths beyond the reach of even an ideal investigation" (ibid., 61). And no other deflationist to the best of my knowledge holds either that everything is true or that nothing is.

The one remaining option is the natural one; namely, some candidates have the property, others lack it. (Horwich (1998a, 129): " . . . on the face of it, propositions exist, some of them (presumably, half) are true. . . .") But then what does this difference consist in? The only sense I can make of the view that the property has no nature (or, of the metaphor of its being a lightweight property) is that the difference doesn't consist in anything. If the difference between propositions which have the property and those which lack it consisted in something, that something would be a substantial truth condition; put otherwise, it would constitute the nature of truth. But this is precisely what minimalists deny that truth possesses. Notice that we need not say that the difference consists in something explicable but yet to be made explicit, something which we can give an independent or a novel account of. What the difference consists in could, for all we have said, be primitive and not further analyzable. But that claim is the province of the nihilist, not the deflationist. The minimalist, on the other hand, seems forced to admit that some propositions have this property, but their having it doesn't amount to anything. How could this distinguish having the property from lacking it?

It must be emphasized that the minimalist can't elude this problem by claiming that I have somehow misconstrued or fattened his *sense* of the word 'property', thereby in effect supplanting it with my own, substantial, one. Of course, one can stipulate senses of any term one pleases. But, as Horwich himself acknowledges, the stipulation must be to a purpose: if one wants to remain a party to the discussion, one can't simply take 'property', say, to mean *buffalo*. As mentioned earlier, however intimate one thinks the relation between *being a property* and *being a predicate* is, there is still a clear distinction between the one and the other. (If for no other reason, the distinction is made unavoidable by the fact they attach to different classes of subjects, the latter being attributable only to expressions.) And it is not easy to see how that difference is nullified by attaching the qualification *logical* to predication. Thus, the points made in the preceding paragraphs aren't a matter of one or another sense of 'property' being chosen, but a consequence that is as common a ground to any concept of a property as is the connection with predication. None of this conflicts with the view that there may be different concepts of a property, and in particular of the property of truth. The points above rely only on a prerequisite for making sense of anyone's claim that something is a property. The minimalist can't evade this responsibility by a declaration that this misunderstands something intelligibly called "the minimal conception of a property."

A recent attempt to reach this conclusion by a different route is, unfortunately, a failure. Crispin Wright, although not taken in by the previous mistake, suggests that despite some misleading formulations in print, all deflationists, not just those heretofore regarded as minimalists, should admit that truth is a property—"once the currency of the concept of truth is granted, it ought to be allowed that all truths have at least the following property in common: the property of falling under this concept" (2001, 753). Thus, the property of truth turns out (at least) to be *falling under the concept truth*. This doctrine is questionable. Even if all truths *have* this property, it doesn't follow that truth *is* this property. Moreover, this is merely a specification of a sort of property that every property has: namely, the property F has the property of falling under the concept F. Despite this, there is little inclination to declare that for ordinary properties this reveals what that property *is* (that is, to fall under its concept). Why should this be different for truth? Is it only because there is nothing else to say about this property? That is a poor excuse. A similar claim made on behalf of this kind of information, *mutatis mutandis*, about uncontroversial properties would be clearly inadequate to count as a component in the identification of those properties. Is it at all plausible to say that the property of being mammalian consists (in part) in falling under the concept mammal? (I am not claiming that Wright maintains this is all there is to say, but relying simply on his implied suggestion that the deflationist can get away with thinking so.)

But this isn't the heart of the matter. To get back on track, let us ask which propositions have the property of falling under the truth concept. Is it restricted to actual truths? Once again, how is the deflationist to make this distinction? Wright elaborates, in a footnote, that it involves "the property of having 'true' *correctly* predicable of them" (2001, 783n5; my emphasis). He adds that this is "presumably what Horwich has in mind when he says that truth denotes a property in the sense in which 'every term that functions logically as a predicate stands for a property'" (ibid., and quoting Horwich (1998a, 141–142)). Because Wright claims that this holds generally for deflationism, if we accept this as a gloss of what Horwich has in mind when he states that truth denotes a property, he has failed to distinguish minimalism from more traditional forms of deflationism. But that interpretive difficulty isn't the main sticking point either. Rather, we are confronted by what to make of "correctly" as Wright uses it to qualify "predicable." Does it mean *truly* predicable? If so, that reintroduces the problem of truth conditions. Could it then mean *justifiably* predicable? Isn't that to claim that truth conditions collapse into justification conditions for this predicate? That would be metaphysical antirealism about truth. Not only do deflationists generally deny that this is a consequence of their view, but it is just the sort of metaphysical involvement they are especially concerned to disclaim. Thus far we have yet to see what sense can be made of the notion, for minimalists or deflationists generally given their other commitments, that truth is a property.

On the other hand, we are stumped by a similar consideration if we try to understand truth's property in terms of the function that deflationists allow it. Take, for example, its function of giving us the means to assert generalizations. It allows us to say things such as "Every proposition or its negation is true." That's certainly an acceptable use of 'is true', and it may implicitly yield conditions of the predicate's application. But then 'is true' is equally useful for stating the generalization "Every proposition and its negation is true." Strictly, just as a matter of serving this function, the second example can't be inferior to the first: if the first manifests the conditions for the correct application of 'is true', so does the second. So the function of asserting generalizations doesn't tell us what difference is made by the fact that some propositions are true and others not. To do that we must find a way to distinguish these two uses, both of which serve that function, in some further way. If we follow Wright's strategy, how are we to avoid distinguishing them by saying, circularly, that the first application is a *true* one, or, inadequately, that it is a justified one?

Perhaps this is sufficient at least to raise a healthy suspicion that the first minimalist strategy will inevitably run into difficulties when pressed to explain what sense there is to the claim that truth is a property without a nature.

Let us then turn to the second opening for truth's status as a property: the doctrine that deflationism concerns only truth's concept and remains neutral about its status as a property. We may find something like this in the writings of Soames (1998) and, when defending his *Übersinn* for truth, in those of Wright (1992). Both at least hint that the account of the concept is neutral rather than deflationary with regard to the metaphysical involvement of truth. Remarkably, even Horwich may be an unwitting ally here. Recall his official position that "'is true' should not be expected to participate in some deep theory ... that articulates general conditions for its application" (1998a, 2). In a rather unclear elaboration of this hard line, Horwich remarks:

> No doubt one may formulate some interesting, plausible schemata that relate the concepts of truth, fact, and correspondence. But the conjunction of such schematic principles is best viewed as yielding a legitimate extension of our theory of truth; it does not provide a tempting alternative. (ibid., 108)

Since there are no relevant empirical facts to uncover here, the extension to which he is alluding must be *a priori*, or broadly conceptual. What could it be other than a further examination of the truth predicate? But this puzzlement aside, is admitting the elaboration outside an account of the concept a viable option for a deflationist?

As has recently been noted, there is some basis for a sharp distinction between components of a concept and its property's metaphysical character with respect to other predicates. Promising candidates for such a distinction are natural phenomena such as water and heat. Back to water once more, it may be held that H$_2$O yields the metaphysical essence of that property, although this can be established only empirically. On the other hand, it is also true that *being H$_2$O* is not a part of our common water concept. Without probing deeply into what our common concept might be, we may note that it is what we share with contemporaries who are ignorant of chemistry, and with ancestors who lived before there was such a science. Thus we can understand Shakespeare and Hume when they write about what they called water, with no more effort or indirection than we can understand our contemporary interlocutors when they use the term. Of course, truth is neither a natural nor an artificial kind, so there is no prospect for a division on similar grounds. There is no conceivable empirical science that could uncover the metaphysical or scientific essence of truth in way in which we might set out to discover, as a student exercise, the constitution of (much less the chemical formula for) magnesium. But the model does show that it is possible to separate questions concerning a concept from those about its correlative property, and that may lend credibility to the second option.

Any inquiry into an analogous metaphysical essence of *truth* must be *a priori*.[4] But how will we distinguish the conclusions of an inquiry conducted at this level from an analysis of truth's concept? Perhaps the following comparison helps us initially to understand some such distinction. The truths of arithmetic are exemplary *a priori* propositions, but, holism aside, it is absurd to suppose that our concept of 3 implicitly contains $652^2 - 425,101$. That last article of knowledge, even once acquired, does not appear to go into any-

---

4. I am ignoring a line of attack that says that the inquiry is empirical because correspondence is contingent, and it is contingent because it begins with ($\mathcal{D}$), which is contingent because it is a contingent, empirical fact that a sentence has its actual meaning. The line doesn't affect the issues now under consideration.

one's possession condition for the concept 3. Again holism aside, conceptual content isn't closed under logical implication. Similarly, it may be held, there is the theoretical possibility of a completed concept of TRUTH, and an additional *a priori* disclosure of the application conditions of its predicate. But the system of rules that make feasible this divided status in mathematics is not in place for the ordinary run of our nonmathematical, non-settheoretic, nonlogical concepts. Here we surely must make use of semantic information for transforming propositions and predicates. Thus, a more compelling case is made for discounting options (for discovery of the predicate's conditions of application) that lie outside or beyond what can be elicited from the concept. This is no ironclad proof that there is no longer space for a correspondence doctrine in addition to (rather than within) its concept, but it puts pressure on this generous form of minimalism, which acknowledges the possibility of a viable correspondence account, to locate the different space in which that possibility can be realized.

But, again, supposing that truth is a property, it is hard to resist the conclusion that an account of its concept omitting this bit of information is incomplete. Consider any concept other than truth. Imagine it not being a bit of conceptually relevant information that it is the concept of a property. That seems highly improbable. And once that much is included in the concept, could we stop there? Is it possible to have a rudimentary mastery of TRUTH which includes knowing that truth is a property, but allows us to possess no further information about *which* property it is? However fuzzy the notion of a concept, thus far we haven't approached any credible boundaries. We don't need detailed knowledge, but it is implausible that once having gone as far as to admit as conceptual knowledge of truth that it is a property, conceptual wherewithal won't also include at least the general structural features of that property. Jackson et al. (1994, 295) put it as follows:

... there is no natural stopping point in analyzing a concept short of finding an analysis that captures the whole network of the central, equally appealing platitudes surrounding the concept that we are trying to analyze—provided, of course, that they really are central, and that they can all be satisfied. For to stop short of capturing all of the platitudes is to make an arbitrary distinction between platitudes; it is to decide, for no reason, that certain platitudes are, and certain platitudes are not, central for elucidating the concept that is up for analysis.

Jackson et al. are using "platitude" colloquially, not in anything like Wright's sense, in which a platitude can have no original metaphysical implications. As in Wright, these platitudes are trivial knowledge for anyone possessing the concept, but, pace Wright, they need not be barren of metaphysical commitment. If this is so, it is difficult to see how anyone could sever the connection between what goes into the concept of truth and the general outlines of its correlative property. What would such a cognizer possess? Perhaps an inference ticket to take us from "S's statement is true" to "p" (assuming that to be S's statement). But if that is included, then surely we cannot omit the knowledge that were the worldly circumstances different in specific ways, so would be the evaluation of the statement. And that makes the connection of statement to world quite indispensable.

Other untoward implications of counting truth as a property under deflationism are explored in the next chapter. Still, we have seen enough to conclude that theorists who want to wed truth's status as a property to their deflationism seem to have acquired in its wake pernicious consequences for that view.

Conclusion

Early in this chapter the main objective was to lay out faithfully the main articles of deflationism. To obtain a corporate view we have had to take a breezy approach to certain aspects of the theory. But this is sufficient for our evaluative purposes. Where a specific version has been pursued in greater detail, it has only been to search out potential remedies for maladies inflicting the view generically. Roughly the second half of the chapter, while still in the business of improving our understanding of the view, supplemented the exposition with a critical examination of a currently popular variety, minimalism. Together with the results of chapter 4, serious troubles for the deflationist outlook have been exposed. However, I don't believe we have yet got to the root of the matter. The problems we have discussed have resulted from particular additions made to the deflationist view. When we return to the simple, Brand X, version, the position seems to me to sink even further into a morass. The next chapter is devoted to making out that charge through an examination of commitments central to standard forms of deflationism.

6 The Perils of Deflationism

6.1 The Indictment

We could devise a continuum with precisely articulated tenets at one end, general outlooks at the other, and a vast middle ground of views more or less tending toward one of these poles. General outlooks have gone by various titles in the literature, among them "(manifest or scientific) image" (Sellars), "paradigm" (Kuhn), and "*Übersicht*" (Wittgenstein). Deflationism, as such, is a general outlook. The fact that it has a number of varieties should put to rest any doubts about its belonging there. This helps to explain the further fact that while deflationism is nowadays a highly controversial view, it has by no means been eclipsed. While some objections to it have sought to undermine its basis, much of the most prominent and effective criticism has been aimed at one or another specific formulation. In this chapter I shall be interested in the sorts of objections that, once allowed, would discourage rather than stimulate efforts at recovering it through reformulation.

The attack on deflationary attempts to accommodate "because" counterparts of the biconditionals in chapter 4 was a start toward showing that deflationism lacks the capacity to secure its own subject matter. Of course, the objections there relied on the assumption that replacing "iff" in the equivalents with "because" is part of its charge. A rather different sort of problem ensues if one rejects that assumption. (The issue is reopened in section 6.5.) In this chapter I want to concentrate on further difficulties. I have in mind three in particular. They may be summarized as follows. First, the method by which deflationism achieves its results works on the questionable assumption that everything there is to be known about the truth property is determinable from a scrutiny of its predicate. Second, it exaggerates what can be gleaned from ($\mathcal{R}$) and ($\mathcal{D}$). Third, it implies (sometimes in spite of itself) doctrines about truth's dependence, or lack of it, although these are insupportable on a strict construal. In sum, deflationists generate a distorted picture of the point of traditional theories they reject and their defenses make use of claims that violate their own austere restrictions. I highlight these points because they don't seem to have gained the prominence that they deserve, even among deflationism's more vociferous critics.

But before commencing the advertised attack, I want to examine a different sort of criticism, one that faults deflationism for assuming bivalence. Bivalence is the view that every proposition has one of the two classical truth-values—it is true or it is false. Nothing falls in the middle or has a third truth-value. Universal bivalence is at least a controversial doctrine. Therefore, it would add to the burden of deflationism if the accusation were true. But I think the objection is at a minimum indecisive. Let's examine the matter more closely

6.2 The Bivalence Flap

Consider equivalence ($\mathcal{R}$), between "$\langle p \rangle$ is true" and "p." If there is a third truth-value, or instances of a proposition not having any truth-value—say, because it is vague or its subject-term lacks a reference—an instance of p occupying the right-hand side of the equivalence would be neither true nor false. In short, there would be two ways for p to fail to be true, either by being false or by being neither-true-nor-false. Suppose p fails to be true for the second reason. Then "$\langle p \rangle$ is true" is false because it says that p has a certain truth-value that in fact it lacks. Thus, while (the proposition expressed by) "p" is neither true nor false, "$\langle p \rangle$ is true" is false. But instances of "$\langle p \rangle$ is true iff p" are true only if the two sides have the same truth-values, which they do not when "p" is neither true nor false. Therefore, ($\mathcal{R}$) depends on propositions each taking one of the two determinate truth-values. There is good reason to suppose that strict bivalence fails for workaday empirical discourse, and *eo ipso* good reason to suppose that our deflationist formulas are themselves not true. This is the sense in which it is supposed that deflationism must fail if it presupposes bivalence, and given the character of the equivalences it certainly seems to do so.

This appears to create a problem for deflationism on several fronts. For one thing, if ($\mathcal{R}$)'s instances aren't all true, how can the view even get off the ground? For another, deflationists regularly hold that instances of their schema are all that people need grasp to acquire a concept of truth. The lack of truth, perhaps even the falsity, of some instances either undermines that claim about our grasp of the concept, or, worse yet, installs at the very center of our concept a misguided quasi-generalization. A third, yet more severe problem is introduced presently.

There have been a few proposals for solving the problem. One is to deny the gap. As I noted in chapter 3, syntacticalists, including recent minimalists, have declared that truth-aptitude belongs to any proposition passing certain trivial syntactic tests. This may raise difficulties of a different order. (See also chapter 9.) But it doesn't address the current problem because the issue is truth-value, not truth-aptitude. The difficulty arises because even some members of a class of truth-apt propositions may lack truth-value. Minimalists may want to deny this too, but the evidence for it is too robust to be dismissed on the mere strength of syntactic criteria for truth-aptitude.

Another response (Kirkham 1992, 176–167) is that, if we assume that "iff" can be translated by "≡" and adopt the standard definition of biconditionality, then

⟨p⟩ is true ≡ p

is not false where p lacks a traditional truth-value: it is indeterminate (that is, has the same "indefinite" truth-value as "p"). Normally someone who holds a theory is committed to the truth of all its logical consequences. But, Kirkham (although he isn't a deflationist) maintains, "I have no steady intuitions on whether the normal rule should apply in a context where it is being assumed (for the sake of argument at least) that bivalence doesn't hold. . . . I do not find it inconceivable that where bivalence doesn't hold, one who embraces (R) is committed only to the nonfalsity of [its] implications, not to their truth" (177). (I'm not certain what Kirkham would say if all its implications were nontrue nonfalsehoods.)

If 'iff' is a truth-functional connective, instances of (R) in which the substituend for 'p' is neither true nor false will be indeterminate on this view rather than false. Although it is hard to shake the conviction that having untrue (even if nonfalse) implications decreases any view's attraction, suppose we provisionally grant that deflationism can live with that result. But none of this addresses the deflationist's more serious difficulty, which is that the two sides of (R)'s instances have *different* truth-values, and thus different truth conditions. This in isolation is damaging enough to any view that maintains that adding the predicate 'is true' states exactly the same thing (both logically and semantically) as that very proposition unadorned. Indeed, it is not the truth of instances of the schema, but the equivalence of the two sides that deflationists emphasize. Thus, Ramsey maintains that the left-hand instance "means no more than" the right-hand one (1960, 142), and even for ineliminable cases in which we understand 'He is always right' as 'For all p, if he asserts p, p is true' Ramsey avers that this shows "that the propositional function p is true is simply the same as p, as e.g. its value" (143). Thus, the thrust of the instances is to highlight that the difference between the two sides is at most, as Ramsey puts it, "stylistic." How, then, could the addition of 'the proposition that . . . is true' turn what is indeterminate into a falsehood? This certainly demonstrates that the deflationist's claim of universal equivalence is mistaken. That result is damaging notwithstanding an acceptance of indeterminate equivalences.

Perhaps this difficulty too can be overcome, but only by a significantly different maneuver. Suppose certain predicates are partially defined in the sense that, however the definition came about (e.g., stipulation, custom), there are sufficient conditions for being Fs and sufficient conditions for being non-Fs, but no sufficient *and necessary* conditions for being Fs (or non-Fs).[1] The one restriction on this is that Fs and non-Fs be mutually exclusive, nothing is both. This opens the possibility, indeed a very real one, that both 'F' and 'non-F' are inapplicable to some things. Thus, for such a case concerning a subject x neither of the following is acceptable:

(a) x is F

(b) x is non-F.

Call the application of F in both cases *ungrounded*.

An imagined example may help. Suppose the legislature (a stipulator for our purposes) passes a law designating anyone twenty-one years of age or older as an adult, and anyone a teenager or younger as a non-adult.[2] Vagueness and inappropriate categories (e.g., ascriptions of adulthood or its opposite to light bulbs or sandstorms) aside, clear cases of twenty-year-olds

---

1. The notion of a partially defined predicate closely follows Soames's (1998) account of it, though he introduces it for a different purpose.

2. If you think this example is too silly to be realistic, consider that an Ohio legislature once passed a law requiring that when two trains meet at a crossing neither shall proceed until the other has passed.

will be neither adults nor non-adults. Ascription to them of this property or its complement is ungrounded. But then the ascription of either truth or falsity (or even untruth) to the proposition that twenty-year-olds are adults will be equally ungrounded. When applied to an ungrounded predication, it will be a mistake to say that the proposition (or utterance) is true, is false, or that it is not true. It will also be ungrounded to say that it is true, false, or not true that the proposition or utterance is true, false, or not true. 'True' and 'false', or 'not true', needn't be partially defined themselves. But when applied to an ungrounded predicate, they can themselves be ungrounded predications. A predicate may be ungrounded because it is partially defined, but it is at least an admissible hypothesis that it can also be ungrounded because its instance is vague, or because it is predicated of an item of the wrong category. It does not matter which of these we admit; the crucial point is that the class of ungrounded predicates will be the source of putative counterexamples to (*R*). If truth or untruth predications of them are eliminated as ungrounded, the bivalence objection to (*R*) will have been effectively rebutted.

If both "F" and "non-F" are inapplicable, we may suppose that both "(a) is true" and "(a) is not true" are unacceptable. Thus, we should refrain from granting that it is false, since "is true" is inapplicable to the sentence "*x* is F" as "F" is to the term "*x*." Call such propositions *truth gappy*.

On the customary Frege-Strawson treatment of indeterminacy it is possible to say of truth-gappy propositions that they are *not true*. I take it that Kirkham accepts this orthodoxy. But on the present revision it is equally inappropriate to say of truth-gappy propositions that they are *not true*, or even that they are *neither true nor not true*. The truth-predicate is ungrounded in this no man's land, and therefore any attempt to sum up that situation with *truth* or its opposite is equally ruled out. Instances of (*R*) for truth-gappy propositions will simply be disqualified from the outset, and, unlike those considered in reply to Kirkham, the two sides of the biconditionals will not have different truth-values. The question of the two sides of the equivalences differing in truth-value disappears. If the right-hand side of the biconditional lacks a truth-value, it will be because it contains a partially defined predicate which, in this instance, falls between its extension and anti-extension. But then that will also be so for the left-hand side, the would-be predication of truth making no difference to its lack of a truth-value. Nor need we say that the biconditional itself is indeterminate, or nontrue in any other way. Given the ungroundedness of the predicate in at least one of its components, the compound may also be regarded as ungrounded.

Of course, this works only if all instances of propositions that are neither true nor false are treated in this way. It seems quite possible that while partiality of definition is a good explanation of why some propositions lack truth-value, another explanation works for other truth-gappy cases (e.g., propositions about the future, or those with empty names). And perhaps at least some truth-gappy instances of the equivalences fall in the latter class. But until someone either provides a case for treating truth-gappy instances in more than one way, or for rejecting the partial definition solution altogether, it is difficult to see how to press this popular objection to deflationism.

Whatever we think of this defense, deflationism doesn't fare as well against the other objections mentioned earlier. Let us now turn to those.

6.3 Overworking the Predicate

A first problem concerns a procedure employed by deflationists and (many) nondeflationists alike. It begins from the assumption that there is nothing to be said about the property if it is not contained in a thorough examination of its predicate. The procedure in question then takes what can be extracted by close attention to the predicate's function as a whole account of its property. Here I concentrate on the problem it raises only for deflationists, though it may have wider implications for linguistically oriented methodologies in philosophy.

Deflationism's point of departure is an examination of the truth predicate. Once it is determined that adding 'is true' to a stated proposition doesn't change that proposition's truth conditions, the deflationist draws conclusions about the nature of both the concept TRUTH and property *truth* from whatever can be culled from an examination of the use (or utility, hereafter understood) of the predicate. Given that direct occurrences of 'true' have no assertoric or descriptive function, the whole of its assertoric character is then summed up by way of its indirect occurrences. Roughly, it is declared to enable us to perform certain logical operations, such as stating the law of excluded middle or making inferences. Thus, Stephen Leeds (1978), after showing how 'is true' is eliminable even in indirect cases, save for some noncognitive uses, concludes that "the *notion* of truth is theoretically dispensable—it does the work that could be done by allowing infinite conjunctions and disjunctions in our language" (128n10, my emphasis). In effect, what can be discerned in our use of the predicate exhausts what there is to be said about the concept and property.

While other deflationists forthrightly proclaim a distinction between a predicate and a property, subsequent practice belies their acknowledgment. For example, Horwich (1998a, 36–37) distinguishes a theory of truth from a theory of the word 'true', but he draws his conclusions about the former from the way the predicate 'is true' operates in instances of (R) and from the functions that such predications generate. (For a further example, see section 7.3.) It would be a different matter if this sort of procedure were appropriate only because of a peculiarity of the predicate at hand. But then the peculiarity should independently justify the procedure, and no such justification is cited. However, if this is regarded as just one instance of a method applicable to any predicate-property pair, and the peculiarity of 'true' is displayed rather as a *result* of applying this general method (the likely drift of the argument), it is assumed, rather than argued, that knowledge obtained through a careful study of the use of truth's predicate must exhaust its nature. This is a precarious way to initiate an inquiry. We may gain some insight into why this is so by looking first at what we may consider to be the default position for the introduction of predicates.

In general, whether there is a predicate 'X' depends on the resources of language (and resourcefulness of its users), while whether there is a property X normally depends on the architecture of reality. We devise a predicate for certain aspects of reality, whose presence doesn't hang on our having an expression for it, when we want to discourse, perhaps even think or think more effectively, about that aspect.[3] If truth had this sort of precedence, that would sabotage any presumption to the effect that whatever there is to be said about a property must be recoverable from an inquiry exclusively into the utility of its predicate.[4] Deflationists regularly take the

---

3. These remarks are intended as neutral between competing nominalisms and realisms about properties, or about the prospects for reductions.
4. For natural kinds and various other empirical properties there is broad agreement that we can discover empirically things about the property's metaphysical nature that cannot be gathered only through a close examination of its predicate. As noted earlier, this partition of inquiries is inapplicable to *truth*. Thus, if there is information about *truth* not discoverable via an investigation of the use of its predicate, minimalists are hard pressed to claim that this information falls outside its concept.

fact that adding the predicate to a proposition doesn't change the latter's truth conditions to show that nothing remains to be said about the property. But to employ the former as grounds for thinking that whatever there is to truth can be discovered only in the use of 'is true' is contentious. This is especially so in light of the fact that the correspondence theorist has a competing explanation for that similarity of truth conditions—namely, that the propositions displayed on both sides are made true or false by the same state of affairs.

At this point one may be inclined to object that my description of the default position begs the question. After all, there are various approaches to the study of language that do not build into them such realist assumptions about word-world connections. For example, a use theory of meaning may propose a procedure similar to the deflationist's for all predicates. We may concede the alternative procedures without further ado: nothing here need be construed as ruling them out. However, the complaint is off target. The deflationist as such isn't maintaining that *truth* isn't a substantial property only because nothing is; that is, because there are no substantial properties. Truth is exhibited as a special case, differentiated from other predicate expressions by the singular opportunities exposed in the equivalence schema. If the argument were rather that truth has no inner nature, is not a property, because *being water, cylindricality, equineness,* and so on aren't properties, deflationism would take on a very different cast. Confining our attention to this issue alone, it would be a huge concession to substantive theories to grant that 'is true' is no worse off in this regard than any other predicate, that its situation is not singular. In vetting deflationism as a corporate view we shouldn't rely on this generic anti-representationalism. Thus, we can provisionally adopt the foregoing description of the default position. Antirealists about properties, those who claim that predicates in general have no conditions of application beyond the use to which we put them, may wish to place their own different interpretation on what I have been calling the default position. Their description of the default will look very different from mine. But unless they preserve the view that the special features of the equivalences differentiate truth from the general run of predicates and properties, and do so by means like these (on their own reinterpretation of the default, of course), there is not much to said on behalf of deflationary theories of truth. And, in particular, their view will not be, as they almost universally take it to be, compatible with realism on virtually all other matters in the philosophy of science.

Returning, then, to the deflationist animus, I am not claiming that once we have a predicate it is a mistake to examine it for information about its correlative concept. On the contrary, this seems the best first place to look, and certainly the great clarifying power displayed by the philosophical study of language has earned that approach the right to its primacy. However, the supposition that investigating the use of the predicate 'is true' must be its only source of information is not a well-grounded verity but a premature plunge. It commits one, without reason, to the view that 'is true' wasn't introduced normally, in accord with the default procedure, therefore that there could be nothing to say about a truth property other than what is revealed from a study limited to the use of its predicate.

However, it is easier to warn against this danger than to explain how to avert it. I suggest we begin by examining truth conditions directly rather than via the utility of occurrences of 'is true'. But that is no guarantee: as shown in section 6.6, truth conditions can be deflated by a related procedure. So how do we get beyond labial homage in doing this: that is, how do we genuinely honor the predicate/property distinction? One way is to supplement our inquiries into the truth predicate (and operator) with situations in which truth plays a role although its vocabulary isn't on the scene. First, we might recognize that *truth*, in Frank Jackson's apt phrase (1998, 53), effects a partition among possible worldly states of affairs. Second, we also note that because we recognize the first point our use of propositions engages us in a cluster of practices which centrally involve attempts to approximate this partition. We do this even when 'is true' isn't used—that is, when we are considering the general run of propositions suited for appearance on the right-hand side of ($\mathcal{R}$) or ($\mathcal{D}$). Put otherwise, statements made with sentences that need not contain the relevant predicates—viz., 'is true' and 'is false'—are still sorted into the true and false ones, and this sorting is recognizably different from that into the justified and the unjustified. Moreover, it cannot be relegated to an indiscriminate acceptable/unacceptable distinction, or any other distinction exhausted by our actual practice. For we can admit we might have been mistaken about any proposition's classification in this respect without any change either in the proposition's acceptability in other dimensions or in its identity. That is the point of the intelligibility of remarks (usually made by clever detectives in mystery novels) such as "I know all the evidence points to it, but it may not be true."

It is difficult to see what the deflationist can make of such a partitioning. It cannot be just another aspect of our practice, for it is introduced at a level that seeks to account for that practice. Without it we cannot explain why the practice is itself not just random, or why we should take any care to determine its extension in one way rather than any other. However inept we may be at approximating such a partition, we understand it as truth's executive role. If someone is not aware of that much, it is difficult to see how we are entitled to ascribe to her anything like a grasp of what we ordinarily consider truth. Furthermore, anything that is supposed to result in this sort of a partition of possible worldly states must have substantial conditions of application. This circumstance is not disclosed just through an examination of the conversational utility of a predicate. We need not insist that a possessor of the concept have a very refined or thorough knowledge of the extensions of the partitioned propositions, or even know how the extensions are formed in complicated cases, but our common concept requires that one has a general understanding of what the difference amounts to.

In this connection, consider briefly the notorious Austin-Strawson dispute about truth. Strawson at the time proposed a combination of deflationism plus a performative account of 'true.' Against that view, and in defense of his own correspondence view, Austin remarked that there are cases in which "I *say* nothing but *'look and see'* that your statement is true" (1961, 101). Strawson (1971b, 207) responded that the case not only failed to support Austin's thesis, but lent itself to deflationism. We needn't reconstruct Strawson's argument in its entirety here, but the way he sets up this response reveals just how his deflationism depends on the possibility of a truth predicate. He begins by comparing two *statements*: (i) "Y's statement is true" and (ii) "X sees that Y's statement is true." Strawson's original doctrine was about statements for which (i) might serve as a paradigm, but his response is that his deflationary thesis can be extended to cover (ii) as well. However, we may very well ask how it is that Austin's scenario becomes a comparison between two utterances in which 'is true' is predicated, when his point was to compare one utterance—say, of form (i)—with a wholly nonlinguistic exercise of our concept of truth, an exercise whose significance is that the predicate doesn't figure in it. Recall that Austin began "I *say* nothing."

This doesn't show that Strawson isn't within his rights to reconstrue the case as he does, although he certainly owes readers more of a defense for revising the original case. Rather the case illustrates just how deeply deflationary theory is driven by the need for a truth predicate (or operator) in order to draw its moral. Strawson's reply *needs* to rework Austin's point as one about the occurrence of a predicate. It is difficult to see how he can fold into the deflationary thesis such irreducibly nonlinguistic applications of our concept of truth.

We must be careful to distinguish the partition in question from the epistemic point that one must know the grounds on which such judgments are made. Even if that point is also well taken, it is a different one. Although we scarcely put it to ourselves in these terms, our distinction focuses on what we aim to achieve by engaging in the epistemic practice. As Wright puts it, "The concept of truth is a concept of a way a proposition may or may not be in good standing which precisely *contrasts* with its justificatory status at any particular time" (1999, 214), a point about truth he notes that "the deflationist clearly *cannot* allow" (1999, 212). There is a difference between a proposition having this property (more precise, standing in this relation) and lacking it: no one with a conversational mastery of truth can lack this much understanding. Some propositions just are true, others, say, false (or so we believe). Even minimalists don't maintain that the difference reduces to an epistemic one—say, between justifiable (or ideally justifiable, or superassertible) and unjustifiable, etc., instances. But if there is such a difference, and it is not an epistemic one, how can it be possible that it be made by anything other than (something including) *truth*? And, if that is so, how can *truth* be an insubstantial property?

There are various reasons why a feature of a property might be invisible to an inspection of its predicate. For example, with natural kinds or natural features there is room for a further empirical inquiry: and it would be pointless, not to say counterproductive, to build those results into the conceptual wherewithal of the predicate's normal users. Another reason might be a pre-existing, pervasive utilization of the property that doesn't require the use of the predicate. This utilization might be too obvious to bother incorporating explicitly into the predicate. These or other situations may provide a rationale for examining truth conditions without the artificiality of viewing them exclusively through the use to which one puts a truth predicate.

The foregoing point about partitioning should not be confused with a claim, briefly raised early in chapter 1, that correspondence truth is needed to explain the normal success of our behavior or of our theories. It has been argued that because, say, behavior is the (partial) product of belief, true belief is needed to account for its normal success. This defense has been challenged by critics who produce candidates for competing explanations of successful behavior, and even of successful belief (M. Williams 1986). The present point concerns information, not belief. Taking truth to partition possible states of affairs is crucial to any efforts we ordinarily undertake to gather information. The practice of gathering such information no doubt involves an epistemic component to supply grounds for making the division. But without a certain grasp of what the distinction consists in, even if only a spotty and incomplete one, it is hard to see the point of the enterprise of gaining information on which to base a belief. This partitioning is not only rendered unaccountable on all forms of deflationism, its rejection is actually implied by those deflationists who declare that truth has no nature.

We may also detect the importance of distinguishing the truth property from what can be read off the surface of its predicate or its use in the following way.

Possession of a concept occasionally demands an ability to recognize instances. That is, we wouldn't allow that someone had a certain concept C if she was not sensorily incapacitated but was a miserable failure at recognizing instances (and recognizing non-instances as well). This isn't so for concepts requiring special expertise (e.g. MIDDLE C, MESON, BEECH TREE); but we generally think it essential for a certain range of nonspecialist concepts. It is also widely agreed that some of those concepts can be exercised without having a language in which they are incorporated: that is, they are language-independent concepts. Accordingly, it is plausible that some nonlinguistic animals and prelinguistic infants have color concepts, such as RED, embodied in their ability to recognize things by their colors. The same sorts of abilities can be exercised by linguistic creatures; but whereas language certainly enables us to refine those skills in ways that would be unthinkable without it, the basis of the ability is still nonlinguistic. If we come to acknowledge the existence of a correlative property, our doing so can be seen as accomplished independent of a corresponding predicate. And this is so whether or not we credit the possessor with possession of that predicate.

Now consider TRUTH. Is the ability associated with its possession basically linguistic or not? For the sake of simplicity, I restrict the discussion to the truth of statements and/or sentences. No capital is being made of the fact that nonlinguistic creatures might have true or false beliefs. Even so, truth seems to be one of those concepts tied to an ability to recognize straightforward instances. Again, if someone simply couldn't recognize instances of it, was wayward in her truth recognitional abilities in an unsystematic way, we wouldn't credit her with possession of the concept. The core of this ability is as nonlinguistic as our basic color concepts, despite the fact that the subjects of attributions of truth and falsehood are themselves linguistic and quasi-linguistic items. Of course, our case is complicated by the fact that our restriction to language users suggests that anyone who does recognize instances will likely be in possession of a truth predicate. (We needn't consider stripped down versions of a language, say, that is just like English except for the absence of a truth vocabulary.) But we must divorce our consideration from an understanding of that predicate if we are to discover the basis for concept possession in this case. The implied ability is recognitional, not the ability to wield a predicate. And while some of this may be *mis*recognition, no one can be credited with the concept of truth who is, once again, wholly wayward and random in her practice of detecting instances.

Clearly, some quite ordinary truths are not recognitional, others altogether recognition transcendent. It is our use of language that enables us to extend our notion of truth thusly. This is part of the initial package we receive when acquiring the concept. Nevertheless, we can still ask whether the ability to partition statements on the basis of their truth is at bottom linguistic. Where at least some truth is recognitional, it is hard to see how the ability itself could be linguistic, even if language is wholly responsible for its further development. Nor does recognizability imply infallibility. But certainly one can recognize, though not infallibly, the truth of a statement that a pear is on the table in front of one.

Once again, the recognition in question is not that of grasping what it is to be *justified* in accepting a statement. Among other things, this is shown by the fact that the set of factors that would undo my justification is a different, if overlapping, set from that which would undo the statement's truth. Furthermore, it is difficult to see how this feature of our conceptual lives can be merely one between contrasting predicates. Indeed, just as our possession of the concept RED seems independent of and conceptually anterior to our acquisition of a term for it—the likely commonplace view would be that the ability largely accounts for our having the term 'red'—so also the ability to apprehend the distinction between truth and falsehood seems anterior to our acquisition of terms used to describe it. Thus, TRUTH will involve at least some elements that cannot be elicited from reflection on features of its predication in instances of (R) or elsewhere. That is not surprising once we recognize that, initially at least, the ability supports the predicate rather than the other way around.

But we should also be mindful that truth and falsity play a less significant role in ordinary deliberations than narrowly focused philosophical pursuits make it appear. We are often more interested in exactitude, exaggeration, vagueness, misleadingness, and the like than bald truth or falsity. Moreover, the boundaries of truth may shift pragmatically with the needs and conventions of a given discourse or investigation. Still, once the target has been located we have a glimmer of a distinction between those propositions that hit reality's target and those that miss it. And it is part of this conceptual constellation that these hits and misses can occur independent of our grounds for believing them to occur. Context may set the target, but once defined it is not up to us whether it is hit or not. This notion of a kind of partitioning of possibilities also accounts for our fashioning the predicates 'is true' and 'is false'. I am not arguing that it is right for us to make such enormous commitments. After all, the mere possession of a concept doesn't guarantee that its property has instances. But it is difficult to see how the ability to draw such a distinction, one independent of our use of its expressions, can be wholly absent from our concept of truth. All of which is orthogonal to whether this feature shows up in an examination of its predicate. And that, once again, is why I claim that it is rash to assume that what escapes us when concentrating only on the truth predicate and its uses is thereby absent from its concept. This point converges in a satisfactory way with the Variability insight of chapter 2, which will elude any investigation confining itself solely to an examination of what can be read off from isolated occurrences of 'is true'.

6.4 Explanatory Adequacy

It is customary among deflationists to claim that the equivalences contain virtually all that is required to *explain* our truth concept. Of course, if the equivalences are understood differently some inflationists (e.g., Tarski,

Alston, McGinn) may agree. But here I am particularly interested in getting at what a deflationist could mean by this, and whether, on her principles, the equivalences can do the explanatory work advertised for them.

First, a preliminary point. The explanatory adequacy of the equivalences doesn't follow just from their status as definitory, *a priori*, or conceptually basic. Quine (1990, 84) writes that "disquotation is loosely definitive of truth," Soames (1999, 231) notes that "the leading idea behind deflationism about truth" is that the equivalence of '⟨S⟩ is true' and 'S' "is in some sense definitional of the notion of truth," and Horwich adds "our knowledge of [the meaning of 'is true'] . . . consists in the fact that the explanatorily basic regularity in our use of it is the inclination to accept instantiations of [(ℛ)]" (1998a, 35) and "the truth schemata are the explanatory basis of our overall use of the truth predicate" (ibid., 126n). However, inflationists of almost every stripe can accept (ℛ) as definitional of truth (see, e.g., Gupta 1999, 298), and this has nothing to do with its thin or thick interpretation. The main point is that definitional status doesn't preclude a principle from being only part of the story. *Being married* is definitional of the notion of *wife*, though it is incomplete. Indeed, an inflationist needn't reject any article of deflationism other than its conclusion that the equivalence of the two sides, interpreted in a certain way, is all there is to the explanation of truth. Thus, unless the earlier remarks take "being definitional" to imply "being explanatorily adequate for its concept," (ℛ)'s status as definitional does not advance the case for deflationism.

What, then, of the extent to which the equivalence explains truth? In one obvious respect, whose effect has been surprisingly minimized, biconditionality should be a puzzle here. What I have in mind is not the issue raised in chapter 4, in which the sticking point was how to understand dependence, but rather a concern about the intended force of the explanation. However strong a biconditionality we adopt, it conveys nothing more than covariation. Unidirectionality is tidier. While biconditionality is compatible with each covariant being explained by the other, it is also available when both are explained by a third thing. For example, the correspondence theorist may reason that '⟨p⟩ is true' and 'p' covary because both have the same substantial truth condition: that is, both have the same state of affairs or fact as constitutive of their truth. It is difficult to see how the covariation in (ℛ) favors a deflationist explanation. The position must be supplemented by, among other things, the supposition that there is nothing more to be said. And that is not attained just by dwelling on the importance of the equivalences. Thus, instances of ($\mathcal{R}$), and the triviality of the equivalences they contain, don't yet disclose what does the explanatory work.

This may look like a standoff. Whereas there is no compelling reason to prefer an asymmetry, in which the left-hand side is understood in terms of the right-hand one, there is also none to prefer an interpretation on which both sides are dependent on a common source (say, a state of affairs or fact). However, the failure of a deflationary understanding to yield an explanation of truth may ultimately provide grounds for motivating a correspondence reading of formulas such as ($\mathcal{R}$). The remainder of this section is devoted to developing an argument to support that conclusion. But before setting out on that mission, a brief comment on its significance is in order.

Deflationists emphasize that our inclination to accept instances such as "the proposition that snow is white is true iff snow is white, the proposition that coal is black is true iff coal is black, . . . etc." *explains* our concept of truth. According to Soames, no better explanation of 'is true' is in the offing. And Horwich adds: "the meaning-constituting fact is this: that the explanatorily basic fact about our use of the truth predicate is our tendency to infer instances of 'The proposition *that p* is true' from corresponding instances of '*p*' and vice versa. . . ." (1998a, 126) Even a nondeflationist such as Tarski (1949, 64), though a rich resource for deflationists, chimes in that the analogous T-sentences "provide satisfactory explanations" of the term 'true'. There is a crucial ambiguity in such claims. Is the explanatory adequacy of the equivalences intended for ordinary users of the concept or primarily for its theorists? If the former, then the claim is (roughly) tantamount to the view that virtually everything users need know about truth is summed up in their inclination to accept the instances of the equivalence. If the latter, although rank and file users may lack this knowledge, or need it supplemented, a survey of the uses of 'is true' can be accounted for (or explained) by the equivalence and its instances. Of course, both claims in tandem are possible. But the ambiguity is nonetheless a standing threat. Because the two ways of taking the claim aren't clearly distinguished when its implications are drawn, it is obscure whether particular arguments and examples are appropriate to the thesis being supported. But the claims are importantly different, and if we are to get to the bottom of this issue, they must be sharply distinguished.

Let's deal with these interpretations in reverse order. Although the adequacy of the equivalences for a theorist of truth seems the less likely construal of the explanation claims, the textual evidence doesn't rule out that this is at least sometimes what deflationists have in mind. But what could it mean? It appears that it can amount to nothing more than the claim that deflationism is correct. It is not a defense of the deflationist doctrine, citing additional evidence for it, but a restatement of it. As such, no explanatory power is accorded to the equivalences other than what may be supplied by further arguments on their behalf. Moreover, it is no assurance against counterevidence, such as the Variability precept of chapter 2. According to Variability, a proposition's truth-value would have been altered if a certain state of the world had been changed. I have claimed that if one isn't cognizant of this, one hasn't grasped TRUTH. In the absence of this understanding, truth hasn't been explained. Given that admission, the deflationist's task is to show how Variability is a consequence of, and thereby part of the explanation contained in, its equivalences. While I can foresee no overarching argument to rule out this possibility, neither is there a shred of evidence that this bit of data can be explained via the equivalences. Moreover, there is some evidence that it cannot, given the ineliminability of Variability's quite robust appeal to a state of the world. Let us then turn to the other sense in which it might be said that ($\mathcal{R}$) or ($\mathcal{D}$) explains truth.

Consider the explanation of TRUTH in question as summarizing what we grasp when deploying this concept (that is, as an account of what an ordinary user and her informed audience must understand, at least implicitly). This brings onto the scene a relativity to one or another audience, a consideration it would be convenient to suppress in a discussion of this nature. But it can't be suppressed altogether because audiences come into explanatory situations with certain capacities and backgrounds. If the point made in the earlier quoted statements is to be at all plausible, we must remain mindful of that. Insofar as Soames or Horwich construes the foregoing as an argument for ($\mathcal{R}$) being an adequate account of our concept, the only way I find to read it is that it is due to the fact that the whole of the content of 'is true', together with rules for its further implementation, is laid bare by the contents of the explanation. That is, they must be assuming that our inclination to produce the instantiations of ($\mathcal{R}$) is not due to certain background knowledge about 'is true', knowledge that allows one to generate these instances. Let's assume, *pro tem*, that the assumption is correct, but it is no argument for the negative existential implied by the conclusion simply to point out that we have such an inclination.

Indeed, it is difficult to see how anyone could acquire a truth concept merely by ingesting the equivalence, the rules for its instances, together with the rules of inference to take us in and out of formulas in which 'is true' is predicated. Indeed, if we are to be consistently strict in carrying out the procedure, indirect cases aside, anyone who didn't know better could draw from it that the predicate 'is true' is no more than a piece of extra verbiage, on a par with meaningless interjections we find in ordinary conversation. Why shouldn't we take this sort of instruction the way we would expect someone to take it if we were explaining the workings of semantically zero-valued colloquial interjections such as "I mean" or (in hipster slang) "like, man"? "I mean, *p*" and "*p*," or "like, man, *p*" and "*p*" appear to convey cognitively equivalent contents. How is one to distinguish these latter pairs from sorts of explanations embodied in the T-sentences that deflationists claim to be explanatory? Nevertheless, it is a typical deflationist claim that "the content of the claim that a putative truth bearer is true is equivalent to that of the truth-bearer itself" (Soames 1998, 229; cf. Field 1994, 251).

In fact, although Horwich *rejects* the view that the right- and left–hand sides of ($\mathcal{R}$) have the same content, his commitment to the explanatory exhaustiveness of that equivalence is at odds with his intent. He claims that because 'true' expresses a property, the left-hand side of an instance of ($\mathcal{R}$) will always contain some content absent from its right-hand side: and this despite the fact that in those instances predications of 'is true' "have no great value: we could easily do without them" (1998a, 39)]. The denial of synonymy is a significant aspect of Horwich's minimalism: it constitutes much of what he takes to be his divergence from classical redundancy. But let us then ask, "What does 'true' contribute to defeating synonymy?" Horwich wrote: " . . . the explanatorily basic fact about our use of the truth predicate is our tendency to infer instances of 'The proposition that *p* is true' from corresponding instances of '*p*' and vice versa. . . ." (1998, 126) However, this isn't incompatible with the two sides meaning the same thing. In fact, if the inference is brought off here only by a meaning postulate, that would be precisely tantamount to claiming that the two have the same meaning. And why not regard ($\mathcal{R}$) as a meaning postulate?

What other role could it be playing if the implication and its ilk deliver the whole explanation of our ability to use 'true'? Thus, it is unclear just how we are expected to understand the claim that there isn't an equivalence of content of the two sides in ($\mathcal{R}$). But if they have the same content, how can we escape the conclusion that the truth predicate has a null semantic value?

We still have the option of accepting the remainder of Horwich's view while abandoning the part stating that the two sides differ in meaning. In fact, abandoning the nonsynonymy would strengthen the case for the explanatory adequacy of instances of ($\mathcal{R}$). But it wouldn't put to rest earlier doubts about its having an explanatory pulse. That is, we still have grounds for a strong suspicion that if the explanations succeed in explaining a truth predicate, they do so only because the audience is capable of construing them properly against a sizable dividend of background information. Put negatively, our inclination to accept instances of ($\mathcal{R}$) doesn't result from the fact that its manifests the whole content of our concept. I shall try to reinforce the case for that claim.

Before getting to that, a brief side note. Soames has admonished us that "the content of the truth predicate is given by the *totality* of . . . instances of these truth schemata" (231, my emphasis). Nothing in the present objection relies on our having ignored that advice. All versions of the criticisms offered here concentrate on what is missing from each instance, and not on the unavailability of a completed series of instances.

Here is another way to indicate the explanatory deficiency of the equivalences, one that sets in relief why it is that adding instances won't improve the deflationist's explanation. Consider the schema

($\mathcal{R}$*) $\langle p \rangle$ is D iff p.

If all instances of ($\mathcal{R}$*) are *a priori* and trivial, the natural conclusion for the deflationist to draw is that 'is D' is a truth predicate. By stipulation, it is not. It is a conjunctive predicate, creating 'p and p' from 'p' wherever one encounters 'is D': that is, it is the predicate "and . . . " in which the blank is to be filled by whatever '*is $\mathcal{D}$*' is predicated of. Or think of it as a function that takes a proposition as argument into a conjunction as value, each of whose conjuncts is (a token of) that argument. Call this the doubling schema. Because '$p \leftrightarrow (p\ p)$' is a sound rule, each instantiation of the doubling schema will be a theorem, whatever the strength of the conditional.

($\mathcal{R}^*$) is as good (or as woeful) an explanation of the predicate 'is D' as '⟨p⟩ is true iff p' is of the truth predicate. If someone merely understands the propositional schema at the abstract level which the deflationist takes as sufficient to explain TRUTH, how is she to determine that the explanation is one of 'is D' rather than 'is true'? In both cases we know only that it has, and will always have, the same truth condition as *p*. If this is sufficient for grasping the concept TRUTH in '*p* is true,' it is sufficient for grasping the concept D in '*p* is D'. We may even replicate the dispute between deflationists over cognitive equivalence: there is a case to be made for the two sides being cognitively equivalent (the conjuncts on the left-hand side contain nothing not already in the content of the right-hand side) or as meaning something different despite their equivalence (the conjunction sign has a use in other contexts).

Elsewhere, Soames (1998) appears to appreciate the general point. Although his remarks concern our grasp of the property truth, the application to its concept is obvious. He states that our grasp "is not exhausted by our dispositions to accept [instances of ($\mathcal{R}$)]" (247). He continues, with respect to indirect cases, that we find some predications of truth "fully acceptable," and others "puzzling and pathological [and even] arbitrary. These reactions are not arbitrary. There is something about our grasp of the notion of truth that guides them. No account that leaves this out can be complete" (247). The suggestion is that there is a thicker concept to be explained than can be gleaned from the surface features of instances of ($\mathcal{R}$). And this in turn suggests that only a (shared) background enables audiences to take the explanations in the right way. The contents of the explicit explanations are merely partial, pointing toward something that generates the instances. This is inconsistent with using the explanatory value of instances as an argument for deflationism. If Soames wants both, perhaps he can find a way to pry apart our grasp of the property just explained from our grasp of the concept. But even if one acknowledges some such distinction, this would seem to be a poor place at which to draw it. For here we are only talking about what a *grasp* of the property must consist in, and that, like the discovery of the Liar Paradox, is achieved by pure *a priori* reflection on *truth*.

Those complications aside, regarding the equivalences as a full explanation of truth is a deflationist staple. However, even the exposure of the explanation's insufficiency shows only that something else is required for the concept of truth, not what else is needed. Nevertheless, once it is acknowledged that we are forced to go beyond deflationism, it is difficult to see where this takes us other than to the familiar metaphysical (or epistemic) competitors—to see what faint outlines, if any, we may find traced in the concept, outlines that may point us in the direction of a more adequate concept of truth. If this is right, it challenges the deflationist once again to show that, say, correspondence, if a possible philosophical position, falls outside our truth concept. That isn't how deflationists typically view the debating positions. For example, Field (1986, 59) has remarked that to get "a clear positive characterization of what a correspondence ... notion of truth is, we would need to first get clear on what if any point there might be to having a notion of truth that goes beyond the disquotational." (Cf. Lewis 2001a.) And Field seems to require nothing less than such "a clear positive characterization" to move us away from deflationism. I am not sure what counts as a clear positive characterization, though I'm confident that nothing produced thus far in this essay would be regarded by him as one. However, the foregoing line of argument indicates that if this is the recipe for replacing deflationism with correspondence, it is certainly not mandatory. Thus, we have arrived at the sort of position I described earlier. Correspondence hasn't been interjected into the discussion by showing what its point is, but by showing how the deflationists' own formulas fall short of being understood as required. I say 'required' because this is how they must be taken if, as they maintain, we can make do with fewer commitments than those in inflationary theories. If this is enough to reinstate the correspondence project, that is sufficient to overthrow deflationism.

I have come up empty in my search to find a plausible defense of the claim that the equivalences, or their instances, convey a complete explanation of truth. Quite the contrary, my miniature experiment with 'is D' convinces me that the claim is a nonstarter. But even *qua* critic I am uneasy about this state of affairs: the deflationist claim, as I have understood it, seems weak enough to engender doubts that her point has been properly understood. I don't deny that users of the concept would need to acknowledge many simple instances like "⟨snow is white⟩ is true iff snow is white." But that is a far cry from saying that this acknowledgment *explains*, much less explains *fully*, what users understand by being true. And it is difficult to see how the argument might be fleshed out plausibly. Of course, there is the possibility of switching senses here and seeing the explanatory conclusion not as pertaining to ordinary masters of the truth concept, but to those who are seeking a theory of truth: for them, perhaps it will be maintained, ($\mathcal{R}$) or ($\mathcal{D}$) is a complete explanation. However, once again this is a circumlocuous way of saying that deflationism is correct. So this is the conundrum I have finally settled into. As an explanation of the wherewithal of concept employers, appeal to the equivalences looks like an utter failure. It can be salvaged by serving not as an additional argument for, or even a corollary of, deflationism, but merely as a way of restating it. I invite readers to find a better interpretation.

6.5   Oddly Paired Interpretations

Consider, once again, ($\mathcal{R}$): "$\langle p \rangle$ is true iff p." A natural way of viewing this construction may be labeled for convenience *the first perspective*. From it we pay heed only to propositions flanking a connective. On this understanding the formula is a suitable candidate for displaying logical relations such as *equivalence* between the two sides. Moreover, ($\mathcal{R}$), considered only as a (compound) proposition, statement, or sentence, could be *a priori* and *trivially true*. Even if one rejects all these claims, each of them makes sense: none is literal nonsense. Broadly, because both sides of the biconditional are semantically evaluable items, they are the right sorts of subjects for these varieties of properties and relations. Soames (e.g., 238) holds that ($\mathcal{R}$) displays all three features. Thus, when we speak of the propositions in ($\mathcal{R}$), or those comprising the two sides of ($\mathcal{D}$), as equivalences (Horwich 1998a, 7; Wright 1992, 50), we are contemplating only the vehicle or the content of its two sides. To repeat, this makes perfectly good sense when we are dealing with propositions, sentences, or statements.

We may approach a *second perspective*, and at least equally natural, reading by noting that the right-hand side can also be taken as a rather unextraordinary case of synecdoche. This would be an implicit, abbreviated way of saying, roughly, that a worldly situation of this description obtains. This too, as I explain below, doesn't prevent any equivalence allowed by the first perspective, but it is significant for de-emphasizing the role of the actual descriptive vehicle on the right-hand side. Consider "Many big names attended the conference." No one with a mastery of English idiom would construe this as saying that proper nouns, as distinct from those named, were at the conference. On this perspective, so to speak, we "look straight through" the medium and its content on the right-hand side, and focus on what that proposition might be said to pick out, express, denote, designate, or so on. It doesn't encourage us, as the first perspective has encouraged deflationists, to stop with the right-hand sentence itself and regard only its syntactic and verbal resemblance to the one on the left. What it picks out will be something worldly. For convenience let us term the relation the right-hand proposition has to the worldly item *signification* and say that what is signified is a *fact*. These titles are chosen only to simplify the discussion: by using 'fact' I certainly want to make clear that it is normally non-intentional, but other than that my choice of terms is meant to be neutral between outstanding issues about the make-up of facts. 'Fact' here is a placeholder for any non-intentional truthmaker one deems to be the best candidate for the job, even if one thinks no proposal along these lines finally succeeds. I also leave wholly underdescribed what the relation between a proposition and its correlative truth-making fact might be, and there are no further restrictions on the sorts of worldly items that determine truth.

The second perspective is important in the present context because it enables correspondence theorists to see ($\mathcal{R}$) as saying in part what is said by

⟨p⟩ is true iff the signified (would-be) fact obtains.

The only difference is that this last formula doesn't explicitly identify the fact making ⟨p⟩ true, although it can be recovered from the formula by those familiar with the drill. The vehicle that states the fact in ($\mathcal{R}$), even the vehicle's semantic content as such, is secondary: what gets stated by that vehicle with that content is central. Now on this understanding the left-hand side of the biconditional certainly can't bear a logical or linguistic relation of equivalence to what the right-hand side signifies: on its face the logical or material equivalence of a proposition and a fact doesn't make any more sense than talk about the color of fortitude. Nor does it make sense to suppose that the combination consisting of the left-hand side, the biconditional, and what is signified by the right-hand side is a candidate for being *a priori* or trivial. These aren't properties that can be attributed to combinations of such categorially mixed items. Thus, it is only when read as presenting us with two propositions, statements, or linguistic entities, as happens on the first perspective, that the triviality or the apriority of the formula, or the equivalence claim, makes any sense.[5]

Of course, as promised the second perspective reading doesn't eliminate any equivalence that the first perspective allows. Synecdoche here demands only that 'p' abbreviates some other form of words such as 'the fact that p obtains'. And it makes equal sense to claim that the last clause is equivalent to '⟨p⟩ is true' as it does with the earlier pair. Moreover, it is arguable that it is *a priori* and that the resulting formula is trivial in some sense. However, this is not a deflationary-friendly reading. The central point of a deflationist reading of ($\mathcal{R}$) or ($\mathcal{D}$) is that once we remove 'is true', together with syntactical accompaniments which make that predication possible ('the proposition that . . . ' or the quotation marks, respectively), we are left with only the unadorned proposition/sentence whose truth was ascribed on the other side of the biconditional. "The fact that p obtains" does not deflate the left-hand side; rather, it specifies a hardy condition that side must meet to satisfy "is true." If the deflationist required a second perspective reading for any purpose, she would be undermining her most potent source of support. (Of course, this must always be *modulo* irreducibility to one of her favorite equivalences. But that caveat applies to just about anything one holds in philosophy.)

Thus far I haven't introduced any reason for the deflationist to construe ($\mathcal{R}$) or ($\mathcal{D}$) in accord with a perspective other than the first one. That is the more natural way to regard these formulas when viewed simply as stating an equivalence. It is precisely in elaborating these sorts of properties of the biconditionals as a whole and the relationships between the left- and right-hand sides that minimalists draw the deflationary lesson of their treatment. The serpent invades this paradise only when deflationists rely on claims that incorporate both perspectives in a single construal. For a single, unambiguous form of words can't both be and not be synecdochal. And rely on them they must. For the claims deflationists wish to make for these equiv-

---

5. I ignore the view that a proposition may be identified with a set of possible worlds. Ultimately, this seems only to defer the main point, not change it, since sets and possibilities are themselves abstract objects. Moreover, it is not appropriate here to speculate about whether deflationists are willing to commit themselves either to realism about possible worlds or to the truth-constitutive potency such worlds may have. Other than that, we may remain open about the account of propositions.

alences require them to appeal to notions that can be made out only on a second perspective reading.

Deflationists declare that they deliver what truth "consists in" (e.g., Soames 1998, 23, 230, and passim), or that equivalences ($\mathcal{R}$) and/or ($\mathcal{D}$) "explain truth," or that 'p' is true *because of* p (Horwich 1998a, 105; Wright 1992, 26–27). Idioms of this sort promise more than equivalence alone can bear. These notions strongly suggest dependence—that $\langle p \rangle$ is true in virtue of p, or, (the converse of that relation) that p makes $\langle p \rangle$ true, or that this constitutes the truth of $\langle p \rangle$. Nor is this suggestion incidental to the impact minimalists proclaim for their theories. They may want to deny that there are any heavy duty conditions for the constitution of truth, but they can scarcely deny that they have provided whatever it is that truth *consists in*, however lightweight that may be. This is merely to take seriously SARS, the claim foisted upon us by the Metaphysical Thesis, condition (3), of chapter 5.

In saying that this portends more than ($\mathcal{R}$) or ($\mathcal{D}$) can supply, I am not relying on the fact, noted in chapter 4 and the preceding section, that biconditionality is symmetrical (or, commutative) and therefore can't capture the asymmetry of explanation that deflationists intend between '$\langle p \rangle$ is true' and 'p'. Rather I am drawing attention to the right-hand side, considering it merely as a propositional vehicle (and not in terms of what it signifies). As such it is not a remotely plausible candidate for what p's truth consists in. The point to notice is that at best only a tiny fraction of truths are made true by propositions, and that only when the subject matter of a proposition is itself a proposition. If in general a proposition's truth consists in anything, it is its relation to a fact (in our current, tolerant sense). It is strikingly beyond the pale of serious theory to claim that, say, the truth of the proposition that Fido has fleas is explained, made so, consists in, or is so because of the proposition that Fido has fleas, or even because of the *proposition* that the fact that Fido has fleas obtains (rather than saying simply that the fact that Fido has fleas explains, etc. this truth, which—though not illuminating—at least makes sense). No deflationist to my knowledge has ventured so irresponsible a claim.

The catch is the inability to bridge the gap between the claim that deflationism doesn't supply substantial truth conditions, on which deflationists and inflationists can agree, and the claim that there are none. To satisfy a commitment to deflationism, a theorist first wants to confine her reading of

($\mathcal{R}$) to the first perspective. The claim is that deflationism on this perspective achieves all there is to be done on the subject, even if it falls short of satisfying the truth-constitution expectations promised by traditional theories. But it is the equivalence that shows this: it is only on the first perspective that the appeal to the equivalence of the two sides or the triviality of the formula makes sense. Thus, it sums up what we are entitled to know about truth's *constitution*, even if it is a paltry something. But this must also count as an explanation; and that language, if it is to carry any authority, opens the door to the other formulations of the right-hand sentence. It, or what it signifies, is the only competitive truthmaker, however thin it may be. But we are immediately confronted with the fact that propositions are not good general stand-ins for truthmakers. For that we need to appeal to the second perspective. However, doctrinally cleaving to the first perspective, deflationists seem incapable of providing truth conditions. It is not that the truth conditions they put forth are thin, but that they don't satisfy whatever rudimentary understanding one may have of what such things are. What choice has the deflationist to protect this latter claim but to run together readings from the two perspectives? And this seems to be a typical enough conflation.

The threat of mixing of idioms when treating this topic is not confined to deflationists. For example, McGinn (2000) supports what he calls "thick disquotationalism," on which he rejects a deflationary reading of ($\mathcal{R}$). The key to his own view is that "truth is that (unique) property of a proposition from which one can *deduce* the fact stated by the proposition" (97, my emphasis) Now there may be notions of implication on which a proposition and a fact could enter an implicational relationship (e.g., propositions as sets of possible worlds). But this would require either an assimilation of propositions to (possible) facts, or facts to intentional contents. McGinn's way of describing the relationship indicates that he favors neither. For he also calls his facts "extra-propositional" (97), regards the relationship as representational (96n), and construes propositions as intentional items (87–88) in a way that at least actual facts are not. Rather, it appears that he has bought at least this much of the deflationary view: namely, that we can shift back and forth between first and second perspective readings of the equivalences without a shift in our interpretation of their terms. (The point applies although McGinn accepts only the "only if" portion of ($\mathcal{R}$).)

Returning to the deflationary muddle, a countercheck might be to deflate the dependency vocabulary that goes with deflated truth. This would also involve deflating the correspondence restatement I supplied from the second perspective. We examine just such a proposal in the next section with respect to truth conditions. But for the present I merely indicate, in general terms, the weighty commitments incurred by that approach. Let us begin by asking "How broadly are we to deflate dependency vocabulary? Do we deflate it for every topic or just for *truth's* dependence?" Unless there is a motivation to apply this method selectively to truth, wouldn't the deflationist be committed to extending that account to the constitutive conditions of every property? Moreover, are we to do this across the board for all dependency vocabulary—including 'consists in', 'because', 'has as a truth condition', 'is made true (or constituted) by'—or just for one or another of these idioms? And if we deflate dependency for properties generally, not just for truth, how are we to avoid being committed to the implication that nothing robustly depends on anything? Of course, rabid antirealists (or, quietists, if there can be such fauna as rabid quietists) may be content with this consequence, but should it follow just from the local internal demands of a deflationary theory of truth? At any rate, we would require a viable deflationary scheme, and the two detailed attempts in this direction examined earlier, those of Horwich and Wright, were shown in section 4.3 to have failed. So in lieu of a workable procedure and a good reason for confining the maneuver to the issue at hand (viz. that of truth), we may simply note that deflationists don't account for the dependencies on their preferred reading of (R). Whereas they highlight readings on the first perspective to emphasize the lack of serious metaphysical consequences, in the absence of a further deflation they require a metaphysically charged second reading in order to support their claim to have shown that in which truth *consists* (or *consists in nothing more than*).

In light of such problems, why shouldn't deflationists just scrap all aspiration to show what truth consists in? Isn't it enough to claim that TRUTH is entirely summarized by the trivial equivalences, without drawing consequences for *truth's* constitution? A deflationist taking that route would seem to be committed either to the view that nothing constitutes truth or to the view that deflationism can remain neutral on that issue. I examine each outcome in turn.

Although some deflationists have written as if nothing constitutes truth, a fairer, if less provocative, reading of their view seems to be that nothing *other than their account* constitutes truth. They do insist that their accounts are complete, nothing further remains to be said on that particular subject. Thus, the rather superficial features that their claims uncover are intended, in some sense, to expose the whole of that in which truth consists. However, it has been the point of the foregoing discussion to establish that those claims can't be taken seriously without mixing perspectives. On the other hand, to say in all seriousness that nothing makes the proposition (or sentence) true is not merely a comment about the left-hand sides of our equivalences, but comments on their right-hand sides as well. So bold a claim would put deflationism in a much less attractive light.

Turning to the other option, what if the theory purports to display everything needed for a concept of truth while remaining neutral on what *truth* consists in? That view forfeits any claim to completeness. Moreover, it leaves unguarded just the territory that many correspondence theorists and other inflationists will want to occupy. What then becomes of the deflationists' Ur-motive to replace, rather than stand alongside, traditional truth theories? Still, not every correspondence theorist will be satisfied with such crumbs. Some will claim (for example, I do) that their traditional views are implicit in truth's concept. And here there will still be an opposition to be worked through. But that isn't the central point. The problem is that the deflationist who takes the path of neutrality about truth's constitution will have conceded enough to traditional theories to go a long way toward rendering his claims much less significant than deflationist rhetoric promises. For remarks to the effect that truth has no nature, or that if it has one, that nature is lightweight, are hallmarks of deflationary discourses. And if a property's nature isn't connected with conditions for its satisfaction, it is difficult to know what such claims amount to.

The outlook here for deflationism seems to me pretty bleak. Propositions are simply not standard truthmakers. But without a pronouncement from the second perspective, which invokes truthmakers, the deflationist is in no position to tell us that there are *no* metaphysical conditions for the application of 'is true'. Of course, the deflationist can retreat to the concept-property distinction of its most concessive version to defend the irrelevancy of metaphysical theories. But once it is granted that there may be something that the truth of a proposition consists in, but that the deflationary side of the account is silent on the matter, the view is seriously compromised as an account of TRUTH. That alone would confirm the objection that deflationism is at best incomplete. Perhaps the only avenue left to this position is to try to negotiate the minefield of retaining a dependency claim while deflating the vocabulary in which the dependency is couched. I now turn to the only detailed attempt to do this with which I am familiar. It focuses on the dependency notion of a truth condition.

6.6 Are Truth Conditions Deflationary?

The recent problem with deflationism, or so I have argued, is that its interpretation of the equivalences prevents it from discharging its commitment to disclose what truth consists in. This has to do not with the claim that truth has a nature, but rather with the allegation that the deflationist account is complete. I have argued that to get around that difficulty deflationists seem lured into drawing from incompatible readings of the equivalences. Taking the dependency idioms seriously succeeds in stating what the property of truth depends on, but it undermines the claim that truth has no nature, or is metaphysically lightweight. Now I want to review the "no nature" claim from another angle. Because it is difficult (for me, at any rate) to understand the claim that truth, or anything else for that matter, is a property without a nature, suppose the claim is restated as follows: there are no truth conditions for something's being true. The lack of truth conditions seems to assure the absence of a nature. However, it also reopens the difficulty of understanding what it means to say that truth is a property (beyond acknowledging that 'is true' is a grammatical predicate), as recent deflationists such as Horwich and Soames want to maintain. So I shall try a different maneuver. Perhaps even this view can be salvaged if what has already been done for *truth* can be done for *truth conditions*: that is, deflate them. Then it will be possible to see how true propositions can have truth conditions without raising the specter of a substantial account. So let's examine the possibility that the deflationist can add to his repertoire an account of deflated truth conditions.

Hartry Field (1994) has suggested a way to achieve this. (Because his preferred equivalence is ($\mathcal{D}$) rather than ($\mathcal{R}$), these are called 'disquotational' truth and truth conditions.) He writes:

... the cognitive equivalence of "'Snow is white' is true" and "Snow is white" will lead to the (more or less indefeasible) acceptance of the biconditional "'Snow is white' is true iff snow is white"; and a natural way to put this (more or less indefeasible) acceptance is to say "'Snow is white' has the truth conditions that snow is white." A pure disquotational notion of truth gives rise to a purely disquotational way of talking about truth conditions. (1994, 251)

Before we return to the reasoning in this passage, some preliminary points are in order.

First, Field (255n9) discourages talk of two kinds of truth conditions—deflationary ones and heavy duty ones. He thinks there is no way to make sense of a distinction of this sort. If that is right, and he can make out the case for disquotational truth conditions, all truth conditions are really disquotational. The seeming difference between types of truth conditions turns out, he claims, to amount only to different ways of relating the one kind of truth condition to language. I agree that a distinction of this sort between different kinds of truth conditions doesn't pan out. But I also fail to see how whatever appearance there is to the contrary can resolve itself into one between different ways of relating truth conditions to language. This isn't a mere quibble; it concerns Field's explanation of how there can appear to be heavy duty truth conditions despite the fact there aren't any. The only way I have found of making sense of his subsequent discussion of the issue is that what is being discussed is indeed different kinds of truth conditions. I will try to stay uncommitted on this issue as long as I can. However, *caveat lector*: as will soon become evident, my efforts are quickly frustrated.

In section 6.5 I cast in an unfavorable light views whose grounds were so broad that they committed one to deflating truth conditions for every property. Presumably Field accepts just the view criticized there. His disquotational account of truth conditions for truth is not a selective treatment. It is an aspect of a more general discussion of theories of content and meaning for sentences. Although the tone is exploratory (Field calls himself at most a "methodological deflationist"), the relevant point is that no appeal to explanatory truth conditions is required for the sorts of semantic theories being entertained. We can, if we like, introduce truth conditions into even the most austere of such accounts, but because they need be no more than disquotational they will not explain meaning. For the truth predicate in particular, their sole function will be to get us from "'p' is true" to "p" and back. (They also function as devices to formulate infinite conjunctions. But this is a matter of logic, which, Field maintains, should be distinguished from semantics.)

Before we come to grips with Field's view, two further problems remain in relating it to our issue. First, our concern is with a predicate, but he offers a theory of the meanings or contents of whole sentences. Second, to say that inflationary truth conditions don't figure in accounts of the meanings of sentences/predicates is not tantamount to claiming that sentences/predicates don't have them. They may have them even if they fall outside the limits of semantic accounts.

The first point is easily resolved. Field himself extends his view to "the set or property that my term 'rabbit' stands for" (260). Even without this endorsement we can apply his view to an account of any open sentence '*x* is a rabbit'. There is no difficulty in extending the view explicitly to cover characteristic subsentential elements.

The second point leads us onto a thornier path. Even if there is no *property* of truth expressed by 'is true', I assume Field doesn't hold that *nothing* is a property. This shouldn't be taken to raise the issue of nominalism (for which Field has shown proclivities elsewhere). The failure of other predicates to express properties on nominalistic grounds will be very different from the specialized deflationist grounds for rejecting a truth property. Given this, choose your favorite paradigm of a property—say, an empirical one. Since it is already in the example bin, I choose *being a rabbit*. Then suppose that our preferred account of the meaning of '___ is a rabbit' doesn't invoke inflationary truth conditions. Still can we seriously suppose that *being a rabbit* doesn't have inflationary truth conditions, even if they play no role in its predicate's meaning? That would take us from a methodology governing semantic theory to one governing the very nature of philosophy in general, and metaphysics in particular. That is a quantum leap. We can no longer claim the protection of solicitously modest theorizing about language. Instead we have been catapulted into the rarefied air of a view concerning the limits of language about, and knowledge of, the world, an atmosphere which doesn't seem to be preordained by tenets about the thinness of our semantics. Can such semantic commitments be used as a basis for rejecting inflationary truth conditions for predications in general? At most, such a theory would appear to warrant only that the semantic accounts of such predicates by themselves, however far those extend, aren't the source of our commitment to inflationary ones. But there is more. It may seem at first as if it is at least a consistent combination to cordon off strictly semantic accounts from any extra commitments one may have to inflationary conditions. But that position quickly generates problems of its own. For it is difficult to resist the conclusion that when a predicate expresses a property, this must be reflected in its account. What grounds could there be for halting in an attempt to give a satisfactory account of a concept without mentioning the predications' inflationary truth conditions? The obvious facts seem out of step with such limits on the semantic package.

It may appear that I am not in any position to make this sort of complaint after having agreed with Field that there aren't two kinds of truth condition? I haven't defected: the only kind of truth conditions I acknowledge are the heavy duty ones. The deflationary ones, once it is seen that they play no role, are superfluous. The functions of deflationary truth conditions cited by Field are merely compatible with instances of the equivalence, (D) in this case. Since the equivalences are as compatible with correspondence as with deflationism, this provides no support for preferring one rather than the other kind of truth condition.

However, perhaps it is possible to deny that there are inflationary truth conditions for any predicates. This seems to be Field's tactic for avoiding that problem. (On the other hand, a deflationist of Soames's cast of mind, who leaves open the possibility of a remaining philosophical issue about the property *truth* independent of his deflationary resolution of the conceptual issue, is thereby allowing room for inflationary truth conditions that have no role in the semantic account. That is not an option on Field's view.) A natural objection to this, implicit in my earlier remarks, is that without inflationary truth conditions for any predicates, language would be disconnected from the world.

Field responds that this last objection is "based on misunderstandings" (1994, 270). He presents as an example the following T-sentence:

"There are gravitational waves" is true iff there are gravitational waves.

The deflationist can block the objection by establishing a connection between the quoted sentence and actual gravitational waves, "independent of the truth schema." Field then argues that deflationism can admit facts about uses of this sentence other than disquotational ones. They would relate the sentence to actual gravitational waves, thereby putting to rest the objector's worries. "For instance, the laws of physics are such that gravitational waves, if they exist, will cause pulses in a quadropole antenna, and such pulses are one of the things that would increase our confidence in the sentence. . . ." (Field 1994, 271) However, this proposal, treating a *constitutional* problem with a *causal* solution, seems to me to be "based on misunderstandings" about the character of the concern prompting the objection.

If the sentence inside the earlier quotes were the only one whose truth conditions were disquotational, there would be no difficulty. But we also have

"There are pulses in a quadropole antenna" is true iff there are pulses in a quadropole antenna.

In addition, we have

"Gravitational waves caused pulses in a quadropole antenna" is true iff gravitational waves caused pulses in a quadropole antenna.

In brief, it is the entire causal sequence that is "cut off" from the world, not just one sentence among others. The only way I can see around that dire consequence is to show that *being a gravitational wave*, *being a pulse in a quadropole antenna*, and *causing something* consist in something. For this reason it is hopeless to say that their being caused by something else can be a satisfactory substitute for their having a constitution. But if, say, being a gravitational wave consists in something (even if that something is not more illuminating than *being a gravitational wave*), isn't this constitution the inflationary truth condition of any predication to the effect that *x* is a gravitational wave? The deflationist needs a reply that is consistently constitutional. A causal claim by itself cannot rescue the thesis from this objection.

The objection has limited scope. It doesn't stem from deflationism as such, but from an extreme form of it requiring not only that non-disquotational truth conditions be eradicated from our accounts of the meanings or contents of expressions, but that the actual applications of such conditions have no place in our speech and thought. A more muted version eludes the specific objection by admitting inflationist truth conditions for predicates other than 'is true', or, if, as in Field's case, generic semantic deflationism is on offer, by admitting that predicates have inflationary truth conditions lying outside accounts of their meanings. But this is only a temporary respite, because such hybrids quickly give rise to a different set of problems—viz., showing how such a selective exclusion of inflationist truth conditions can be justified and/or explaining how the inflationist truth conditions of standard predicates can be kept out of their semantics.

Still, Field has offered a deflationary account of truth conditions, which we must confront directly. Otherwise, we may find ourselves in the position simply of having to choose between two different sets of unpalatable consequences. Let's begin by examining more closely the first passage quoted from Field (in the second paragraph of this section).

Recall that early in the passage Field mentions "the cognitive equivalence" of the two sides. This is a relation that, in the context, only sentences that is, contentful entities) could bear to each other. But he concludes the passage with mention of the sentence having "the truth conditions that snow is white." However, in the relation "*x* having the truth condition *y*" only the first term standardly mentions a semantically evaluable (= contentful) item. Exceptions in which what the second term signifies is semantically evaluable occur only when the sentence in the first slot is specifically about a sentence, an expression, or the like. Field's position conflicts with this generalization. Where does his narrative go astray?

Among other things, Field's way of stating the truth condition neglects a point emphasized in the discussion of Horwich's position in chapter 4: the truth condition for "Snow is white" is not

(i)   that snow is white

but rather

(ii) snow being white.

Of course it is easy to overlook the difference between these, and when nothing hangs on it, it is harmless enough to take (i) as a way of conveying (ii), although (i) is strictly inaccurate in the setting. Indeed (i)'s serving this role asymmetrically depends on its being substitutable for (ii). From the point of view of truth conditions alone one doesn't concede any plausibility by claiming that (ii) yields the truth condition of 'Snow is white', but that (i) does not. However, it is quite another matter (again, from the exclusive point of view of truth conditions) to claim that (i) but not (ii) expresses that sentence's truth condition. (i) standing alone, without the possibility of being glossed, in a pinch, by (ii), seems bereft of force. Once (ii) has been granted this pride of place, notice next that *snow being white* is not a sentence. It is a nominal phrase suitable for denoting something when properly embedded in a sentential context. What might it there denote? Nothing, it seems, other than a state of affairs, or another kind of complex in that ballpark. This is a crucial difference between our two phrases. Field's introduction of deflationary (disquotational) truth conditions succeeds only if we suppose that (i) and (ii) are on a par as specifications of a truth condition. My claim is that they are not.

This is not to deny that some "grammatical adjustments" (see Field 1994, 279) are insignificant. For example, Field cites the need to convert 'don't' to 'doesn't'—say, when we shift from a first to third person sentence—as a mere grammatical adjustment that it is only fair to allow the disquotationalist. But such minimizing of differences won't work in the case of (i) and (ii). It may seem a small difference, given that 'being' is merely a nominalization of 'is'. But the difference between a noun and a verb form is not incidental here. It marks the distinction between a sentence and a denoting phrase. Sentences as such do not denote, so we must take greater care with such devices. On reflection, this is not on the same scale as a shift of person, or tense, or mood. The unguarded neglect of their differences works, as it does in most contexts, only when nothing hangs on them. Similarly, I can speak of the sun setting without being committed to geocentrism. But in the present case, because of the important connections noted (and differences cited in the next paragraph), this will have no tendency to show that (i) is a truth condition, rather than loosely and inaccurately (albeit conveniently) substituting for one.

In this connection it may be helpful to bear in mind that the force of the deflationist position is that what appears on the right-hand side of an equivalence is supposed to be precisely the same thing, or at least a translation of it into a metalanguage, without being enclosed in the larger context "the proposition that . . . is true" or "' . . . ' is true." That is, the right-hand side is itself supposed to be a proposition or a sentence. But how could a proposition or a sentence standardly be a truth condition for another proposition or sentence if we retain the core idea—common it would seem to any sensible notion of truth condition—that satisfying a truth condition makes something true?

I have maintained that neglect of the crucial distinction between (i) and (ii) is explicable in part by the similarities in their colloquial uses. But it is also aided by overlooking another distinction that is equally easy to miss and equally important—that between the relation expressed by

(a)   ___ is the truth condition of ___

and the sentential connective (or operator) expressed by

(b)   ___ has the same truth condition as ___.

Provisionally setting the earlier difference aside, we are frequently able to phrase (a) and (b) with indistinguishable substitutions in both places. Thus, it may seem as if there is no significant difference between them. The first identifies a truth condition, the second doesn't even purport to do so.

In part this is disguised by the fact that in (b) legitimate candidates for the first slot are phrased so that their formulations largely overlap with the phrasing of the first terms in (a). But in those cases the overlap is incidental to what (b) reports. Making out the distinction is also complicated by the fact that what it is to identify anything is a tricky, frequently context-dependent, business. Nevertheless, there is a difference between identifying something and giving any old description of it. If there weren't, and the differences between (a) and (b) collapsed, then for any instance of the proposition P, we could give as its truth condition a uniformly substituted instance of "Any omniscient being knows that P." That condition will be true whenever P is. But I trust that we needn't take seriously the possibility that my fanciful replacement identifies the truth condition for any but the most arcane instances of P. If so, we have no choice but to acknowledge that presenting something that has the same truth condition as P is not tantamount to showing what the truth condition of P is, any more, say, than claiming that Jack and Jill have the same model car identifies what model car that is.

I believe the work of synecdoche is at play here too, though in a different role from its earlier appearance. If we provisionally put aside the differences just noted between (i) and (ii), a sentence such as "Snow is white" could fill the first blank in (a) as well as the first (or second) blank in (b). But paying no price other than that of being long-winded, I could also insert "That snow is white obtains" in the first blank of (a). Thus, when plain "snow is white" is serving, that appears due to our typical breath-saving practice of synecdoche. However, "That snow is white obtains" is, at best, an awkward candidate for either blank in (b). Not that "'snow being white' obtains" doesn't have the same truth condition as "'Snow is white' is true," but it is too close to the sentence "Snow is white" to display what is wanted when we affirm the sameness of truth conditions. At best, there is a Gricean infelicity about it. In any event, this is made clear by the fact that "snow being white" is a direct specification of the truth condition of "'snow is white' is true," although the former is not a substituend for either position in (b). If a function of (b) were to identify truth conditions for a sentence of which "is true" is predicated, how could it fail this baldly to accommodate so direct a specification of that condition?

Soames writes that "*'s'* is true iff *s* will provide information about the meaning of *s* by (implicitly) providing information about the truth conditions of the proposition it expresses" (1998, 254). And the locus of the implicit information about "'s' is true" is no doubt the right-hand side of the schema. Here again one sentence provides truth conditions for another. This may seem to overturn the distinction I have just been at pains to legitimate. On closer inspection it can be seen that my point is compatible with Soames's remark. The reason the latter passes muster is that if Q's information is more accessible than P's, we may use Q to supply an (implicit) understanding of the truth conditions of P. And in this case Q is more accessible just by being a sentence of the metalanguage that, unlike "'P' is true," doesn't mention anything in another language (viz., the object language). But method (b), as such, doesn't disclose what the truth of either sentence consists in or what constitutes it, though it may happen to mention it incidentally. Of course, the deflationist may want to contend that truth doesn't consist in anything. But then it is difficult to see why the deflationist should be concerned with truth conditions in the first place. For, despite the deflationist's best efforts, to say that "P" is the truth condition for "'P' is true" (or, for "the proposition that P is true") doesn't state what is required of it. If two things have the same truth conditions, that suggests *prima facie*, though it may not strictly imply, that each has a thing called a truth condition. The onus is then on the truth-conditional deflationist to show how we can stop at (b) without admitting the legitimacy of (a). Then when one says that P and Q have the same truth conditions, and that this is all there is to the matter, one seems committed to the implication that the truth of the one sentence is the truthmaker of another one, or else to tell us why, in this particular case, that implication is canceled. This may be disguised by the fact that we can take Q, when uttered in a certain tone—that is, as a deliberate attempt to specify not an equivalent sentence but the worldly situation which that specification is brought in to signify—as a truth condition.[6] But, once again, that is a second perspective reading of Q. And the deflationist cannot admit an unreduced reading from the second perspective.

The result is that this rescue of Field's notion of a deflationary truth condition (whether or not he would approve of it) rests on a double conflation

6. Compare the fact that I may believe, say, that the sentence "La neige est blanche" is true, without believing that snow is white. Confining ourselves to the sentence needn't take us to a belief in the proposition it expresses, just as concentrating on the propositional vehicle won't take us to truth conditions. (This is not meant to suggest that the reasons for the failure in the two cases are also similar.)

between a sentence and a state of affairs, on the one hand, and between a relation and a sentential connective on the other. Thus, it fails to preserve the deflationist's entitlement to draw conclusions about what truth depends on from its interpretation of the equivalences.

Conclusion

Given deflationism's own terms of engagement, its failure to provide an account of truth has a stunning consequence. Consider each of the following theses:

1. Among inflationary (= substantive) theories of truth, correspondence is the front-runner.
2. Epistemological theories of truth are not promising.
3. Revisionary theories of truth are not under consideration.
4. There are no hitherto unsuspected promising theories in the wings other than those before us.

I believe deflationists generally would accept each of these. (1) may be inferred from their practice in taking correspondence as the lone serious competitor to their own view. They are certainly trying to capture a current notion, and their claims to being at least neutral with regard to realism are founded on rejecting epistemic truth. Moreover, their own claims to adequacy as a conception of truth indicate that they are committed to the view that they haven't overlooked promising competitors.

To these articles let us add a typical critique leveled against correspondence:

5. We are in no position to provide further details of the correspondence theory past the crude formulations offered earlier. (See, e.g., Horwich 1998a, 121; M. Williams 2001, 140.)

Perhaps any further details are cognitively closed to creatures with our makeup. Whatever the explanation, let us suppose that no further details of correspondence are available. This too is commonly assumed in deflationist narratives, but, at any rate, it is here a concession for argument's sake rather than a thesis I am inclined to defend. The question I want to raise is "What lesson are we to draw from the situation described in these five theses when combined with the clear failure of deflationism?" The answers into which we seem forced are either nihilism or a generic form of correspondence. But nihilism, it seems, won't suffice if we still admit, as correct as far as they go, the sketchy versions of correspondence cited in section 4.1. We can still regard such a sketchy version as a project rather than a full-fledged theory, but it is the only direction left standing in light of (1). How could anything less be open to us once it has been accepted that this sketch of correspondence must be included in any complete theory of truth's constitution?

However, we need not rest here. There is a prospect of saying more about the character of the embattled correspondence relation. But before that, I shall turn to some exegetical matters concerning early forerunners of deflationism. They affect the interpretation of popular versions, and so are worth examining before departing permanently from the topic of the deflationist challenge. After that we can explore the prospect for fleshing out the notions indigenous to a correspondence theory.

7 An Interlude on Progenitors

7.1 Exhuming Ancestors

Contemporary deflationists cite a number of early predecessors who cleared a path for their efforts. Frank Ramsey is a celebrated example, and many have found inspiration in the work of Frege and Tarski. Although neither of the latter two is a deflationist,[1] each has undoubtedly supplied that view with potent matériel. Here, however, I want to concentrate on two looming figures who have dominated much of twentieth-century philosophy: Ludwig Wittgenstein and Willard Van Orman Quine. Each has been a deflationary beacon, although their influences have been felt in rather different ways. Deflationists have regarded their comments, though indirect (Wittgenstein) or highly telescoped (Quine), as models for their own doctrines. My own view, to be spelled out in this chapter, is that neither is a card-carrying deflationist: Wittgenstein is a nihilist, Quine—zut alors!—a sort of correspondence theorist. However, this is dangerous turf. So much has been written and said about each of them that any commentary lands one in a thickly seeded minefield of scholarly controversy. Worse yet, I claim no expertise as an interpreter of either philosopher. Nevertheless, I can't shake the conviction that careful attention to the relevant, and frequently cited, passages used to support these deflationist interpretations reveals serious doubts about conclusions mainstream commentators have drawn from them.

1. And even Ramsey (2001, 439) writes: "Although we have not yet used the word 'correspondence' [our view] will probably be called a Correspondence Theory of Truth." He nowhere declines the title, warning only against compound facts for compound truths (quite a common warning among correspondentists) and against the assumption that there is a "simple relation of correspondence applicable to all cases" (ibid.). So this alleged father of the view is no redundancy theorist after all!

Although my examination here will be brief and very selective, I shall attempt to set the record straight by looking at those passages with a fresh (or perhaps just a differently tainted) eye.

Of course, it does not follow that, just because deflationists misinterpreted the passages from which they derived their own insights, their own deflationist proposals are flawed. Nevertheless, getting an accurate historical record isn't irrelevant to clarifying our main issues. For one thing, a more adequate and nuanced interpretation may reveal how far someone can incorporate the insights of ($\mathcal{R}$) (Wittgenstein) and ($\mathcal{D}$) (Quine) without being committed to deflationism. Also, we may uncover something valuable when we ponder why claims that have sounded deflationary to others didn't lead these thinkers to take the plunge. And, perhaps most important, it is more than remotely possible that it is crucial to the orthodox deflationary interpreters of both Wittgenstein and Quine that they overstated points, ignored something central, or took missteps closely mirroring moves made by that view's current defenders. Interpretations of others are mentioned only in passing. But a review of some key passages in Wittgenstein and Quine afford us an opportunity to revisit critical junctures in the arguments for deflationism.

A brief warning: In the case of each philosopher, more than a single part of his work may have inspired deflationary interpreters and followers. My concern is limited to those passages in which the main concern is most explicitly *truth* or true propositions. They are typical of those most frequently cited in deflationary interpretations. My minimal claim is that if either writer is a deflationist, this has not been made out in the passages customarily employed as evidence for it. My more ambitious claim is that contrary evidence indicates that a deflationary interpretation doesn't suit either figure.

7.2 Wittgenstein

As previously noted, I believe Wittgenstein is best viewed as a nihilist. Occasionally the same view, as ascribed to Wittgenstein, is called quietism. Reflection on Wittgenstein's general posture toward philosophical explanation would normally be sufficient to show that he can't be a deflationist; deflationists claim to have provided a complete and satisfactory explanation of truth, and Wittgenstein, to understate the case, isn't an ardent

Interlude on Progenitors 193

promoter of that form of explanation. However, there are passages in which Wittgenstein may appear to be chanting a redundancy mantra. And it is just such passages on which those who interpret him as a deflationist rely. So before building the case for Wittgenstein's nihilism, we must consider what to make of those pronouncements.

In *Remarks on the Foundation of Mathematics* (1978, appendix III, §6), Wittgenstein writes:

For what does a proposition's *'being true'* mean? *'p'* is true = p. (That is the answer).

And the formula '"p" is true = p' occurs elsewhere in his elucidations (e.g., 1958, I§136; 1974, 123). It is no wonder that many commentators take these for expressions of redundancy (Bolton 1979, 159–160; Dummett 1978, xxxiv; Baker and Hacker 1980, 317; Kripke 1982, 86; R. Read 2000, 75), and that a considerable number of deflationists regard Wittgenstein as anticipating them on this score. The quote from *Remarks*, with its parenthetical gloss on the formula, looks like an unmistakable instance of deflationism.

Perhaps it is worth noting at the outset something that may strike those familiar with this text as a problem for my use of this passage. The broader discussion in which the quoted material is embedded is concerned with Russell's (and Whitehead's) notion of a proposition as set out in *Principia Mathematica*. The passage quoted from *Remarks* (1978, appendix III, §5) is introduced as follows:

Are there true propositions in Russell's system, which cannot be proved in his system?—What is called a true proposition in Russell's system?

It might seem natural to conclude from this that Wittgenstein's remark applies only to a narrow class of propositions in a certain formal system. We shall return to that topic below, but it seems appropriate to insert the following four preliminary points. First, Wittgenstein's interest in Russell's sense of 'proposition' concerns features that Wittgenstein was inclined to believe that the Russellian notion shared with propositions in general. I do not mean by this that Wittgenstein believed that all propositions belonged to axiomatic systems, but he did seem to believe that all propositions belonged to practices that determined, more or less loosely, permissible moves. Second, while the focus of appendix III of the *Remarks* is Russell's view, Wittgenstein also makes a number of general observations that are not confined to the system of *Principia*, although they bear upon it. The equivalence quoted earlier is one clear instance. Third, although Russell isn't explicitly mentioned in a comparable passage quoted below from *Philosophical Investigations*, similarities between Wittgenstein's discussions in those two places make it quite likely that the target is largely the same. Finally, discounting this passage as influential for the popularity of redundancy interpretations, although I believe it is unwise for the reasons given, would do no harm to my case. My contention is that Wittgenstein doesn't display approval for deflationism in any of the passages cited for a redundancy interpretation. The objection under review merely suggests removing one piece of evidence that it is natural to use on behalf of that interpretation.

Before returning to the passage from *Remarks*, let me set the stage for further discussion by examining other passages cited for this interpretation.

In I §136 of 1958a, Wittgenstein is writing of an attempt to summarize the general structure of a proposition:

... instead of "This is how things are" I could have said "This is true." (Or again "This is false.") But we have
'*p*' is true = *p*
'*p*' is false = not-*p*.

A first warning that things may not be as they seem is that the term whose definition is in question in this passage, as in the one from *Remarks*, is not 'true', but rather 'proposition'. (The German word *Satz*, used regularly in this context, is sometimes best translated as 'proposition', though its closest standard English equivalent is 'sentence'. As we shall see, this ambiguity also troubled Wittgenstein.)

Wittgenstein first broaches the topic in the *Investigations* at §134: "Let us examine the proposition: 'This is how things are.'—How can I say that this is the general form of propositions?—It is first and foremost *itself* a proposition [*Satz*], an English sentence [*Satz*]. ... " Briefly, he first determines that generality won't give us what we want, the general form of a proposition. He begins §134 by quoting the very sentence from the *Tractatus* —"This is how things stand" (1922, §4.5) ["*Es verhält sich so und so*"] that he there displayed as the general form of a proposition. In the search for something better he entertains the possibility that we can explain what a proposition is in terms of truth. The interjection of truth in this matter is not irrelevant to the Tractarian characterization just quoted, for he says in a remark leading up to that one that "a proposition is an expression of agreement with truth-possibilities of elementary propositions" (1922, §4.4). But this too comes to grief. Shortly after the passage from the *Investigations* quoted earlier (§134), he adds:

And to say that a proposition is whatever can be true or false amounts to saying: we call something a proposition when in our language we apply the calculus of truth functions to it. (1958, I, §136)

Before continuing the narrative, it is worth briefly taking a step back to compare this with *Remarks*, appendix III, §2, where Wittgenstein writes:

And—you say—these sentences are true or false. Or, as I might also say, the game of truth-functions is played with them.

These remarks lead up to the passage (appendix III, §6, quoted earlier) in which Wittgenstein states the crucial equivalence. The similarity in the two cases is telling. I shall have more to say about its significance below.

Let us resume our examination of the upshot of *Philosophical Investigations* §136. One lesson drawn from the failure earlier to capture the form of a proposition is that *being a proposition* and *having a truth-value* are too closely related for the latter to enter as an independent signifier. Thus, truth cannot throw the needed light on propositionality. However, nothing in this implies that when a proposition is true it is not made true by something. No doubt, post-1930 to say otherwise would be an uncharacteristic observation: it is not something on which Wittgenstein is likely to dwell. Nevertheless, he does give signs of accepting the almost universal assumption that something makes true propositions true. Thus, when writing casually about the subject, he remarks: "A wish seems already to know what will or would satisfy it; a proposition, a thought, what makes it true—even when that thing is not there at all! Whence this *determining* of what is not yet there?" (1958a, §437) Wittgenstein is certainly posing a problem, but it has nothing to do with doubts over whether something worldly satisfies wishes or makes propositions true. Rather, he is reflecting on how such conditions could be present in thought even before they obtain in the world, or even if they never do obtain. This might have been a feature to puzzle over were we considering truth-conditional theories of meaning. But it tends to presuppose, not deny, that truth has constitutive conditions. When we explore the limits of this and other dismissive sentiments, there is no reason to read more into them than is demanded by the concerns he is treating.

To see just how misleading the deflationary reading can be, consider more closely Wittgenstein's further discussion of propositionality at §137 of the *Investigations*. This summarizes the brief discussion in which the apparent redundancy equivalence occurs (§136). There Wittgenstein takes up the question of "fit" between a proposition and truth:

> . . . a child might be taught to distinguish between propositions and other expressions by being told "Ask yourself if you can say 'is true' after it. If these words fit, it's a proposition."

And he adds a similar proviso for putting the words '*This* is how things are' in front of the proposition.

If 'fit' were to be understood as we have been understanding 'correspond', Wittgenstein's comment might look like additional fuel for deflationism. And in isolation that is a natural way to understand the quoted remark. But it is clear that this is not the sort of *fit* he has in mind at this place. Rather, he is using the key term here to explain what is *fitting* or *appropriate*, what concepts go with what other concepts. Indeed, he introduces the point in the same paragraph by mentioning a subject's fitting a question. It is apt that a term like 'true' goes with a term like 'proposition', just as it is apt that a term like 'tasty' goes with 'pudding', but inapt (save as an awkward metaphor) that a term like 'tasty' goes with a term like 'promontory'. So, it is fitting that certain sorts of appraisals ('true', 'false') should go with propositions, and that the question of truth or falsity should come up naturally when a (stated) proposition is the subject. (See §225: The use of 'proposition' and the use of 'true' "are interwoven.") In sum, a certain variety of appraisal goes with a certain sort of subject, and this connection is intimate enough to render it useless to try to explain the subject simply by pointing to the fact that this sort of appraisal is suitable for that sort of subject. But Wittgenstein is no more attempting to tell us what the conditions for the correct application or the complete understanding of those appraisals are than that the congruity of 'tasty' with 'pudding' tells us what it is for a pudding to be tasty.

One might object to my comparison as follows: whereas we cannot understand truth and propositionality independent of each other, pudding and tasty are independent notions. However, that the two cases are different in this respect isn't relevant here. Wittgenstein gives us two ways in which one concept may be involved with another (1958, §136): first as a *constituent part*, in which the connection is secured by the syntactical rules (e.g., rules for sentence formation); second, as *fitting*, in which the relation comes about by being an integral move in the practice (viz., language game) in which each concept occurs. He doesn't deny that truth and falsity may also be constituent parts of the concept of a proposition, but as such they *belong* to the concept (viz., are its constituent parts) rather than fitting it. Thus, the interdependence of the notions has to do with the constituency requirement which Wittgenstein is putting to one side here. Truth fits propositions or vice-versa only as used in the language game for propositions—that is, the language game of stating. In this sense, tasty also fits pudding in the just the same way—as a pre-prepared possibility for coupling in the practice involving both notions.

In this connection we might consider another passage in which Wittgenstein appeals to the equivalence, again to discourage using truth to understand the notion of a proposition. In *Philosophical Grammar*—composed just before dictating *The Blue Book* (1932-34), although not published until 1974—he writes (1974, §79, 123):

. . . if we speak of what makes a proposition a proposition, we are inclined to mean the truth functions . . .
"p" is true = p
"p" is false = ~p.

But shortly thereafter, in the same number, he raises and answers his own question:

Does "'p' is true" state anything about the sign "p" then? "Yes, it says that 'p' agrees with reality."

As it turns out, Wittgenstein believes this is unhelpful for the problem at hand, that of understanding propositionality. I did not reproduce this last remark to show that it represents Wittgenstein's position here—clearly the quotation marks he places around it indicate that it doesn't—much less that it is his view by the time the relevant parts of the *Investigations* are composed. What is striking about it is only that it shows that Wittgenstein isn't inferring that accepting "'*p*' is true = *p*" *by itself* forecloses on the on the fact that "*p*" is true says that "*p*" agrees with reality. Thus, for him an argument from the equivalence directly to a deflationary moral is, at the very least, unlicensed. While Wittgenstein does proceed to say some things that throw into doubt the utility of this response, nothing in those remarks overturns the point that this response, even if ultimately unsuccessful, is not ruled out by the equivalence of "*p*" and "'*p*' is true." In fact, in §134, after rejecting "This is how things are" as an account of propositionality, he writes: "But though it [i.e., 'This is how things are'] is a proposition, it still gets employed as a propositional variable. To say that this proposition agrees (or does not agree) with reality would be obvious nonsense." To emphasize the fact that it would be "obvious nonsense" to say of a propositional variable, or what functions as one, that it agrees or doesn't agree with reality would be a strange, and ultimately ineffective, way for Wittgenstein to bring out this proposal's shortcoming if he held that saying *of anything* that it agreed with reality was nonsense.

Perhaps there is a temptation to dismiss these remarks because Wittgenstein could deflate phrases about "agreement with reality" as easily as his admirers deflate "is true." If that were so, Wittgenstein would end up saying something tantamount to

'p' is true = p = 'p' agrees with reality.

However, we cannot merely assume such a reduction of the last term on the basis of Wittgenstein's attitude concerning the futility of such appeals as attempts to understand propositions. Granted that he doesn't approve of saying "'p' is true" states something about the sign 'p' (in particular, it doesn't state about 'p' that it "agrees with reality"). But the reasons he gives for this are orthogonal to disputes over correspondence. They don't indicate that he rejects the correctness of these correspondence-sounding sentiments. Rather, the problems he notes are twofold.

First (a point he probably considered less central, although I believe it has more profound implications down the road), Wittgenstein observes that placing 'p' within quotes makes it "a mere ink mark." How can an ink mark be true "in the way in which it's black and curved"? He sees a muddle in this way of transcribing the point. (However, he says only that once 'p' is understood as a propositional sign, the quotes are "superfluous"—which is an odd way to sum things up, given the seriousness of the problem.) I don't know that he ever found a satisfactory solution. He continues to use the same formula in the *Investigations* and *Remarks*. But for us, all that matters is that this predicament concerns only the bearer of truth, not the problematic nature of the bearer (whatever it may be) agreeing with reality.

Next, the central problem, once we regard 'p' as *more than* an ink mark, can it be *less than* a proposition? But if it is already a certified proposition, we have presupposed propositionality before we can come to understand what it to have 'is true' sensibly predicated of it. Once again, although by a very different route, "true" has no role to play in the constitution, and therefore in the explanation, of propositions. But, just as in the preceding case, the point being made doesn't bear on whether or not agreeing with reality (sometimes or always) makes a proposition true. Wittgenstein's point is rather that what makes a proposition true and what makes it a proposition *must* be different matters. This is compatible with nothing, something, or everything making a proposition true and/or making something a proposition. One cannot derive redundancy from this way of dividing those two issues.

What weight, then, shall we accord the equivalence? To the extent that these passages are transparent, Wittgenstein is simply admonishing us against the use of truth, or better yet the predicate 'is true', to cast light on various of our logical practices. Truth is so thoroughly implicated with those practices that we can't imagine them without truth: they belong, as he characteristically puts it, to the same language game.

A similar explanation applies in other passages in which Wittgenstein appeals to the equivalence. For example, at *Remarks* I§5, probably written late in 1937, he is considering the inexorability of logical inference as a model for that of mathematical rules, and his alter ego asks "But isn't there a truth corresponding to logical inference? Isn't it *true* that this follows from that?" To this Wittgenstein's mentorial self replies: "The proposition 'It is true that this follows from that' means simply: this follows from that." The point here is not that truth is superfluous, but that it is hopeless to use it to explain a practice such as logical inference. This is a constant theme in Wittgenstein. It is futile to interject truth to explain our logical practices, either our dealings with propositions or inference. (Of course, that does not imply, conversely, that if truth were altogether deleted from our understanding of logical inference, we could still make roughly similar sense of the latter practice.)

Let us, then, return to our first passage from the *Remarks*, appendix III, §6: "For what does a proposition's *'being true'* mean? *'p' is true = p*. (That is the answer)." In its context, the comment is the culmination of a train of reasoning having to with a problem created for Russell's notion by Gödel's first theorem. What can it mean for Russell's system of logic to contain propositions that (i) are true, but (ii) cannot be proved in the system? Wittgenstein's point is that *'p'* is true = *p*, taken innocently, at most sets the stage for the problem in that context. For in Russell's system—that is, for

Wittgenstein, at least one of the language games in which propositions are asserted—a proposition enters only as the conclusion of a proof or as a fundamental law. Wittgenstein adds shortly thereafter, "[a] proposition which cannot be proved in Russell's system is 'true' or 'false' in a different sense from a proposition of *Principia Mathematica*" (1978, appendix III, §7). We can call either a fundamental law or the last line of a proof in that system true if we like, but there is no other place for the consideration of the truth of a proposition. Thus, in that system the combination (i) and (ii) can find no home.

Does the narrow concern with Russell's system disqualify this appearance of the equivalence as evidence for the redundancy interpretation. It would advance my case if it did, but I don't see that it does. For one thing, as mentioned earlier, Wittgenstein intersperses his discussion with comments about propositionality in general (e.g., appendix III, §2), and, in any event, it is quite clear that in the passage under review Wittgenstein means propositions generally, not propositions as they occur in Russell's system. Although he does earlier consider the difficulty of regarding arithmetic formulas as propositions of any kind (appendix III, §4), it is clear from the very next section on that he adopts, at least as an assumption of the discussion, that the issues concern *propositions*, and not something less than them. As for the differences between propositions in a formal system and "ordinary" ones, that distinction needn't detain us here. It is true that the rules governing Russell's system are more rigorous than any restrictions that might be applicable for casual, largely empirical, talk about the world; but both are instances for Wittgenstein of practices in which "the game of truth-functions is played." It is the playing of that game, not the particular way that it is played, that gives rise to such problems.

The passage recently excerpted from appendix III, §2 of *Remarks* is of present interest for yet another reason. Whitehead and Russell (1927, 92) distinguish a proposition from its assertion as Wittgenstein does not. The latter writes:

And—you say—these sentences are true or false. Or, as I might also say, the game of truth-functions is played with them. For assertion is not something that gets added to the proposition, but an essential feature of the game we play with it. (1978, appendix III, §2)

The argument here seems to proceed as follows: "sentences/propositions (of sort S) have truth-values" amounts to "we play the game of truth functions with S," which implies, in turn, that "we assert (deny) the members of S" because "asserting (denying) S is an essential feature of playing the game of truth functions with S." Of course, we may want to inspect each step of the argument with greater care, but it seems clear that Wittgenstein is supposing that we think of propositions and the paraphernalia that go with them (e.g., truth-values) functionally. Thus, if we are willing on this basis to conclude the equivalence of "p" with "'p' is true," shouldn't we, on similar evidence (*mutatis mutandis*) attribute to him the following?

p = "p" is asserted (or, assertible).

Admittedly, this is a highly implausible result—precisely my reason for displaying it. It affirms a simplistic assertibility-condition account of truth. (As we saw in chapter 1, it is typical for deflationists adamantly to oppose epistemologized theories of truth.) It is arguable that Wittgenstein can avoid this result because he is only thinking of certain uses of propositions, their role in a limited context, and not propositions abstracted from all employment. This is a plausible defense: I accept it. But the point to be emphasized here is that the same might be said of the equivalence of "p" with "'p' is true" as it occurs in the *Remarks*. It is "true's" involvement in the language game of truth-valuation, and nothing else, that Wittgenstein gives as grounds for the equivalence of 'p' and "'p' is true." Recall that the first step in the argument goes from "propositions of sort S have truth-values" to "we play the game of truth functions with S." If the replacement of "being a (dispositional) property of a proposition" by "being a property of the use we make of the proposition" is enough to scotch the argument for the equation of "p" with "'p' is assertible," it is enough to overthrow the one for the equation of "p" with "'p' is true." The moral: It is premature to cite passages such as those beginning appendix III, §6 as support for a redundancy interpretation.

No doubt, a broader interpretation of Wittgenstein's later philosophy might yield a basis for regarding these passages as minor skirmishes in a wider war against representationalism. A small point—one that I doubt will deter any commentator of that cast of mind—is that this would be quite untypical for Ludwig post-1932. No twentieth century thinker is more emblematic of a bottom-up rather than a top-down approach. But, beyond that, the striking similarities of all these to the earlier passage in which Russell's theory of propositions is certainly the target strongly suggests that the results apply only to attempts to define propositionality. The use of a wholesale anti-representational outlook to reinstate the deflationary orthodoxy will have to overcome these, among other, indicators pointing in the contrary direction.

My disagreement with the redundancy interpretation should not be taken to suggest that (the later) Wittgenstein might be a correspondence theorist, not even timid or reluctant one. In *On Certainty* (1969, §199) he wrote, in an entry probably from 1949 or 1950, that the notion of a proposition or hypothesis "agreeing" or "tallying" with the facts or reality gets us nowhere. (See also §§191, 200 and 215.) (While there are grounds for suspecting that in *On Certainty* Wittgenstein had further radicalized some of the views in the later canon, as represented by the *Investigations*, there is at least circumstantial evidence that the remarks alluded to here encapsulate some of the original thinking behind his renunciation of his earlier Tractarian flirtation with correspondence.) He certainly wasn't willing to accede to any such notion without a view comparable in detail to the one put out for serious consideration in the *Tractatus*. Wittgenstein is neither a reluctant correspondentist nor a deflationist, nor is there evidence for imposing yet another inflationary theory of truth on him. But could there also be positive evidence, evidence other than the difficulty of pigeonholing him elsewhere, for regarding him as a nihilist?

For starters, it is highly unlikely that Wittgenstein believed truth admitted any general explanation. This is in line with the approach that he brings to a host of subjects: namely, that "[a]t some point one has to pass from explanation to mere description" (1969, §189). We learn by concrete instances, not by grasping a generalization about a rule; logic cannot be described; well-founded belief rests on belief that is not founded (well or poorly); and so on. As early as *The Blue Book* (pp. 17ff.) Wittgenstein expressed fundamental disagreement with what he called "our craving for generality," and this theme, if not that catch phrase, is constant throughout his subsequent writings:

> . . . we must not advance any kind of theory. There must not be anything hypothetical in our considerations. We must do away with all *explanation*, and description alone must take its place. (1958a, §109)

Such pronouncements may play only a regulative, or procedural, role in Wittgenstein's approach to philosophical topics. But there is no indication that Wittgenstein has strayed from them when tackling our subject. This does not mean that he should also have repudiated the equivalences he displays. A nihilist can allow us some (perhaps trivial) information about truth, as long as he doesn't hold that this takes us very far toward an understanding of that notion (or property), or, as in Wittgenstein's case, does hold that the would-be explanation is in a broad sense circular.

Nor am I relying on an equivocation here. It is not implausible to hold that, despite passages such as that cited in §109 of 1958a, Wittgenstein did not turn his back on all forms of what *we* might call explanation. Explanation is a sprawling topic, and Wittgenstein had something relatively narrow in mind when he insisted that we abandon it for description. His elucidations are explanations in the sense that (assuming their success) they clear things up, advance our understanding. That is a perfectly good sense of 'explaining'. However, it is too broad for the sorts of explanations that deflationism purports to deliver. Deflationists offer what they take to be a theory of truth, and although on standard versions it officially eschews truth's metaphysical implications, it is supposed to have implications for metaphysical implications, which is one way of taking a nonrealist stance with respect to this particular concept. Deflationism is a view about the reach of truth, not about the reach of philosophizing (or even just speaking) about truth. While it is possible to ascribe the latter view to Wittgenstein, the former would be the sort of metaphysical immersion against which he repeatedly warns us.

Earlier I stated that Wittgenstein's attitude is evident even in *The Blue Book*, but it is present in embryonic form as early as the *Tractatus*. A theory of the character of the world is impossible for us because it would require us to occupy a vantage point outside logic, and therefore outside the world we sought to explain. But there is no cosmic exile, the lack of which renders attempts to arrive at that sort of explanation futile. Contrary to customary opinion about the comparison between Wittgenstein's two philosophically fertile periods, I would say that the later one is the more philosophically optimistic. For there he seems to offer something of a foothold in the issues. We are still unable to get outside our situation and see the world in its entirety, but we can probe matters from the inside. To take but one example, that of language games, whatever else they are useful for, they allow us to explore, typically through simplification, the boundaries of our practices. They achieve this by making manifest where the sensical begins to chafe up against nonsense. The procedure enables us to see what can or can't be removed or added to our practices as a condition of preserving them. No doubt, Wittgenstein takes us even further: his method enables us to see complications in the very notion of "having the same practice." The facts may, frequently do, run out before a decision about preservation can be achieved. Nevertheless, while the relationships in question, such as those between propositions and the world, may be genuine, we couldn't encompass them in our theories and/or explanations of our practices because of our inescapable position within those practices. However, this is not to deny that the relationships toward which our explanations strive do not hold (though it is misplaced emphasis to dwell on this aspect), but rather that their comprehension, even their sensible formulation, demands that we occupy an impossible vantage point. This is the point, noted earlier, of the distinction between the limitations on the properties captured by our concepts and the limits of our ability to construct theories or explanations concerning them.

Now, insofar as Wittgenstein believed that this holds generally of philosophically charged concepts, it applies to TRUTH as well. If Wittgenstein were a deflationist—redundancy theorist or otherwise—that would be a wholesale departure from his general line, one that would stick out prominently. To construe him as a proto-deflationist we would need to suppose that he regarded himself as having a satisfactory general explanation of the nature of TRUTH. But he warned against just these sorts of aspirations in general, and the practice of his later philosophy exemplifies this approach to virtually all the subjects he treats. Taking, for example, our semantic competence, we *show*, say, a rule for color ascriptions by pointing to cases, or to our training with them. There is nothing more than this in a situation in which a learner acquires the rule, and there is no further explanation of what it is that she has grasped when she masters the rule. In fact, Wittgenstein applies this method directly to propositions:

Asked what a proposition is . . . we shall give examples and these will include what one may call inductively defined series of propositions. This is the kind of way in which we have such a concept as 'proposition'. (Compare the concept of a proposition with the concept of number.) (*Philosophical Investigations* I, §135)

Such an explanation needs no traffic with the notion of truth at all. Moreover, we could scarcely expect him to give a different sort of answer if asked what truth is.

A last gasp! Mightn't a deflationist claim that Wittgenstein's appeal to the particular case matches her own view—that it is not ($\mathcal{R}$) or ($\mathcal{D}$) as such, but its instances that yield the explanation of truth? The problem with this comparison is that Wittgenstein did not regard the appeal to instances as an approximation to an inductive definition, or a consolation prize we get for being unable to frame such a generalization. They do not achieve piecemeal what a general explanation sought to achieve whole hog. Rather, Wittgensteinian reminders replace that sort of effort with a different kind of approach to the topic. While they are the only tools we have at our disposal for imparting a concept, Wittgenstein would certainly regard it as wrongheaded to suppose that they were in the same line of business as those who sought definitions, inductive or otherwise.

I have not attempted to offer anything like a full account of Wittgenstein's attitude to philosophical explanation, and I have tried to make my remarks as compatible as I am able with the various prominent competing interpretations. But I hope enough has been said about the general outlines of Wittgenstein's view to make it exceedingly unlikely that he would have accepted deflationism's cardinal claims.

7.3 Quine

Quine is a source of defining ideas for disquotionalism. Not only did he coin the term, but his work is the *locus classicus* for the device. And as he plainly put it, "Truth is disquotation" (1990, 80). Moreover, it is Quine (1970) who explicitly noted that the prime utility of the truth predicate is to enable us to generalize over sentences (or propositions for that matter) that are not before us. "[T]o gain our desired generality, we . . . talk about sentences: 'Every *sentence* of the form '*p* or not *p*' is *true*'" (1970, 12). All this sounds supremely deflationary, and it would only be natural to expect him to then draw the deflationist's signature conclusion "regarding the *underlying nature* of the property of truth . . . it almost certainly does not have one" (Horwich 1998a, 107). Moreover, this is not the only source commentators cite for Quine's rejection of substantive truth theories. We also have his views on radical interpretation and the indeterminacy of translation. Given some prominent disparaging views about meaning—briefly, e.g., that (i) the facts almost always run out before determining meanings of our terms ("the poverty of ultimate data for the identification of meanings" (1987, 7)) and

(ii) there is no principled distinction between the meaning of a term 'X' and ordinary beliefs about Xs)—no room seems left for a correspondence between a sentence and the world. Quine remarks:

> What makes sense is to say not what the objects of a theory are, absolutely speaking, but how one theory of objects is interpretable or reinterpretable in another. (1969, 50)

For correspondence to survive, there must be some relation between language and the extralinguistic world about which we can sensibly theorize. But, on Quine's view, as summarized by Field (1974, 200), "the only interesting correspondence you can get is a correspondence between the words of one theory and the words of another."

However, in the teeth of these indications of anti-correspondentist sympathies, and despite the impressive backlog of conflicting interpretation that follows in its wake, I shall maintain not only that Quine fails to embrace deflationism, but that he frequently states just the opposite, and observes the needed distinctions that enable him to do so plausibly. As it turns out, Quine is a correspondence theorist. I do not claim that he has, or supposes we can get, a detailed correspondence theory, or that he thinks of himself as a correspondence theorist. To cobble together a coherent view from his remarks on the topic—consistently repeated though often as asides—it would need to be a quite general version. However, what he does say on the matter of truth's constitution is such that any attempt to supplement it without distortion could go in only one direction—that of a fleshed-out correspondence theory. Everything else, including deflationism, is ruled out. And that is sufficient to commit him to the correspondence project. No doubt not all commentators consider Quine a deflationist. But by and large even those who think of Quine as a nondeflationist do so not because they believe he is a correspondence theorist, but because they suppose he provides tasks for truth (say, in the theory of interpretation) that take the concept in an altogether different direction.

Any claim that Quine is a correspondentist cries out for a strong defense. I begin with his remarks about the disquotational formulas themselves, and, after establishing that their discussion contains all the elements needed for correspondence, I return to the question whether the other Quinean doctrines to which I have alluded, concerning language and theory-relativity, are incompatible with my reading.

A widely cited source for Quine's views on the nature of truth is a small slice of a chapter of his 1970 *Philosophy of Logic*. He addresses the issue in a number of other places as well, most particularly in chapter 5 of his *Pursuit of Truth* (1990), but the earlier work is frequently cited as the canonical statement of his view on the subject. Undoubtedly much of what concerns him there is a defense of (*D*). But what is seldom noted about the discussion is that, without announcing an intention to do so, he scrupulously adheres to a distinction between (a) the predicate 'is true' (or simply 'true') and (b) truth. Whether by (b) he intends the property truth or its concept is not clarified by the text alone, but we can safely assume from his general views about meaning that it is the property. The point to keep in mind is that he is careful in this exposition not to state or imply that his results regarding the predicate can be extended to the character of truth itself. In the few cases in which he may appear to do otherwise, those appearances evaporate upon closer inspection.

Much of the argument in *Philosophy of Logic* is devoted to showing why sentences rather than propositions, the latter conceived of as either the meaning of or a name for a sentence (or set of sentences), are the bottom-line bearers of truth. The choice of sentences leads to what Quine calls semantic ascent, disquotationalism, and his explanation of the utility of 'is true'. Semantic ascent is the move, say, from talking about the world to talking about talk about the world. But throughout this discussion, he never loses sight that "no sentence is true but reality makes it so" (1970, 10). As a number of supporting passages indicate, this is a persistent theme in his expositions of this and related subjects. The distinction between the predicate and truth, (a) and (b) above, enables him to preserve both (*D*) and an inflationary view without incongruity.

In the preceding chapter deflationists were chastised for not distinguishing sharply enough between truth, the concept or property, and the predicate 'is true'. Even when their prefatory remarks explicitly acknowledged a distinction, it was glossed over in subsequent discussion when they drew conclusions about the entirety of truth's nature directly from what they could discern in the utility of its predicate. Quine too seems to acknowledge the distinction, and his subsequent discussion, unlike those of the deflationists chided there, doesn't reintroduce the confusion by extending points about the utility of the predicate to its property.

Here is a passage in which both notions are employed, but there is no hint that Quine has failed to keep them apart:

> Truth hinges on reality; but to object, on this score, to calling sentences true, is a confusion. Where the truth *predicate* has its utility is just those places where, though still concerned with reality, we are impelled by certain technical complications to mention sentences. Here the truth predicate serves, as it were, to point through the sentence to the reality; it serves as a reminder that though sentences are mentioned, reality is still the whole point. (1970, 11; my emphasis)

Because truth's hinging on reality is, according to Quine, a potential grounds for preferring propositions to sentences, Quine adds the qualifying clause to that claim in the first sentence of the quoted passage. To talk about sentences, as noted, is to shift from talk about the (nonlinguistic) world to talk about language. Quine certainty agrees with the propositionalists' premise—viz., that truth hinges on reality—but rejects the conclusion that they draw from it. He then proceeds to explain just what follows for the predicate 'is true' (not necessarily for the property of truth) when we opt for sentences rather than propositions. Of course, the divide isn't absolute even under Quine's ground rules. He writes that disquotationalism "is a full account: it explicates clearly the truth and falsity of every clear sentence" (1990, 93). Such claims may seem to glide indiscriminately over what I am claiming are the two separate components of Quine's view. (I will have more to say presently—in fact, two paragraphs hence—about how this and other problematic passages may be smoothly incorporated into the present interpretive line.) Nevertheless, it seems clear from the foregoing passage that he is concentrating on the truth predicate, and is at pains to disavow a certain sort of deflating consequence for the truth property that some may see in this. A property/predicate distinction is thereby instituted. Rather than understanding the property via the technical innovations demanded for the use of the predicate, he warns against allowing our use of the predicate to blind us to truth's character. It is only via its connection to the property that "reality is still the whole point." And only if this distinction between (a) and (b) is recognized, even if but implicitly, can we infer that there is more to the predicate than the technical innovations it enables.

I am not claiming that what I have construed as the interpretive orthodoxy on Quine always simply ignores such repeated remarks about reality deciding the case. But its more sophisticated versions don't square the disquotational theses with such remarks, as I have done, by distinguishing tenets about a predicate from those about its property. Instead they give a different twist to the notion of "reality" by seeing it through the prism of Quine's remarks about the theory relativity of sentences. As I shall try to make clear below, this is more convoluted than necessary to make perfectly consistent and plausible sense of Quine's views.

The sort of distinction I have emphasized is not restricted to a certain stage in Quine's career: it is something he seems to have been sensitive to throughout. But it hasn't safeguarded readers against attendant misconstruals. For example, earlier Quine had stated: "Attribution of truth in particular to 'Snow is white', for example, is every bit as clear to us as attribution of whiteness to snow." (1953, 138) Lifting this passage out of its context, and reading into it other things we know about Quine's outlook, especially its later development, this might easily enough be taken to deflate attributions of whiteness to snow as amounting to nothing more than we can get from attributions of truth to "Snow is white." In fact, Donald Davidson, an eminent authority on Quine's thought, seems to have done precisely this (1994, 439). And the lack of a clear distinction between a truth predicate and its property no doubt encourages that reading. Thus, it may look like the disquotational counterpart of the stock claim attributed to Ramsey that 'is true' is simply redundant. But if we return to the beginning of the paragraph in which this passage occurs, we see how remote this is from the point it is intended to impress. In plumping for a Tarskian treatment of reference and truth over those drawn from the theory of meaning, Quine's point is diametrically opposed to the superfluity view. The Tarskian treatment, according to Quine, doesn't reduce truth or reference to the trivialities of deflationism; rather it renders truth (and reference) pellucid. They are now as unmysterious as the attribution of any property in reality to any thing in (nonlinguistic) reality. In other words, Quine assimilates the truth attribution to that of whiteness to snow rather than vice-versa. He is claiming that, unlike the theory of meaning, the Tarskian treatment makes attributions of truth and reference as straightforward as ordinary empirical attribution. This is not to repudiate truthmakers for truth, but rather to show, via Tarski's treatment, how they can be made transparent despite the superficial appearance of abandoning talk about the (nonlinguistic) world for talk about language.

Once this explanation is at hand, we can see why stating that disquotationalism "is a full account" of truth, and that "it explicates clearly the truth and falsity of every clear sentence" is no threat to an interpretation that relies on Quine distinguishing a truth predicate from a truth property. As long as he believed that Tarski's referential approach, as opposed to those emanating from theories of meaning, did not permanently shift the discussion away from the same world that the subject sentence took as its topic, he could hold that it did not bar us from seeing through the predicate to the first-level concerns with truth. The predicate may have its distinctive utility, but that utility is made possible only through the conditions that constituted truth for certain sentences.

Well, then, just what is a truth predicate's utility? For Quine, it is chiefly its ability to frame certain generalizations. Where we want to generalize about persons or bicycles we may employ quantification (or its natural language counterpart). Persons and bicycles are *things*, nameables, and are thereby legitimate values for variables. But when we want to generalize over sentences such as[2] "the rain has stopped or the rain has not stopped," "Jones is guilty or Jones is not guilty," or "Theo won or Theo did not win" by saying something about any sentence or its negation, these straightforward generalizing strategies fail us. We can't generalize with "$(\forall p)(p \vee \sim p)$": sentences are not names, and "this reading is simply incoherent" (1970, 11). To resolve our quandary we say instead that a sentence or its negation is true. That sums up the utility of the truth predicate for him. In this connection it is worth bearing in mind that although Quine is constantly alive to the threat posed by the paradoxes for a universal theory of truth, when he warns against turning the series of Tarski's T-sentences, such as

"Snow is white" is true if and only if snow is white,

into a generalization through the mediation of open sentences such as

"p" is true if and only if p,

the problem he singles out here is not the threat of paradox, nor that of quantifying into quotational contexts, but the fact that "p," encumbered or otherwise, cannot serve as an individual variable. Sentences aren't names, not even compound ones (1970, 12–13).

While this involves us in semantic ascent—so that at first blush we are talking about sentences rather than what the sentences themselves are talk-

---

2. Quine would use eternal sentences. I drop that restriction for ease of exposition. Assume that all sources of ambiguity (lexical, structural, and indexical) are eliminated.

ing about—the detour is minor. Slightly beyond the partial semantic obstruction we see the same reality that the sentences themselves without a truth predicate would be talking about. Semantic ascent does not change the subject. Rather, it is an alternative route to a destination we wanted to arrive at, but were thwarted from approaching more directly by an inability to employ normal devices of quantification. "This ascent to a linguistic plane of reference is only a momentary retreat from the world, for the utility of the truth predicate is precisely the cancellation of linguistic reference" (1970, 12). It is still the case that "The sentence 'Snow is white' is true, as Tarski has taught us, if and only if *real* snow is *really* white" (1970, 10;, my emphases). And, twenty years later, he still writes that "To ascribe truth to the sentence is to ascribe whiteness to snow" (1990, 80). And again, "What is true is the sentence, but its truth consists in the world's being as the sentence says" (1990, 81).

The repeated enunciation of this point is, unfortunately, often minimized or sublimed by those commenting on Quine's view. But these passages are not just sops to popular idiom, otherwise out of step with the general tenor of his outlook. Rather, he is making a point whose consistency is perfectly obvious once we keep in mind the distinction between the property *truth* and its predicate. These persistent reminders about what truth consists in create a clear challenge for anyone who might want to enlist Quine in the deflationist ranks. He never to my knowledge shirks from saying these sorts of things up front, nor does he attempt to deflate all such "reality" talk. One thing that might have made the recognition of this point obvious for Quine (though here I am speculating) is something widely emphasized in print by major contemporaries with whom he may have interacted: namely, there would be true sentences even if there were no such predicate. Any language with assertoric resources will be usable for asserting truths and falsehoods. This in no way depends on or necessitates its having predicates to express truth or falsehood.

The distinction between the property truth and predicate 'is true' rescues Quine from an objectionable feature of deflationism discussed earlier. Horwich (1998a), to return to a prominent exemplar, starts from the fact that a utility of 'is true' is its ability to mediate inferences. He gives three examples (21–23) and concludes: "According to the minimalist thesis, all of the facts whose expression involves the truth predicate may be explained in such a way. . . . ." (23). Of course, from the fact that 'is true' is useful for task

T it doesn't follow that this is all it is useful for. But Horwich is not thereby guilty of a gross non-sequitur: he is resting his case on a canvass of candidates. Presumably (although this isn't made explicit) he rejects other options.[3] The particular instance aside, I am willing to cut some slack for anyone having to argue (at least in part) for a position by way of a canvass, and rejection, of a list of leading alternatives. If one attempts to argue that such-and-such is the sole utility of something or other, perhaps there is simply no better way to show this than by reviewing the various possibilities that one can enumerate. Conclusions based on reviews of promising options are always vulnerable to the possibility that something might turn up, however unlikely, that hadn't been anticipated. Quine's reasons for citing only the ability of 'is true' to state logical generalizations seem to be of this character. We can regard both writers as issuing the following stern challenge: if you think that 'is true' has functions other than these, tell us what they are. We may then see whether the additional proposals pass inspection and, if so, whether they too can be handled consistently with the strictly intralinguistic ones already mentioned.

Trouble begins for Horwich only when it is inferred from these results about a predicate, first, that this yields a complete story about the utility of *truth*, and, second, thereby exhausts its nature. I will concern myself here with only the first step. Horwich's argument is posed as an answer to the following challenge (stated in the title of the section covering the answer described a few paragraphs ago) "It seems unlikely that instances of the equivalence schema could possibly suffice to explain all the great variety of facts about truth" (1998a, 20). But when his account of the utility of a predicate is transformed into an explanation of "all the great variety of facts about truth," the Variation datum discussed in chapter 2 is a clear embarrassment. On it we acknowledge that certain changes in worldly circumstances will result in a change in the truth or falsity to a proposition, and thus in correct ascriptions. Whereas I claim that this is a bedrock principle underlying the property of truth and our concept of it, it is difficult to see how it can be worked into a list of the functions of the predicate 'is true'. After all, the intuition compares changes in the ascription of the predicate

---

3. Interestingly, Horwich doesn't include the function Quine mentions, that of stating certain general principles. This may be, in part, because he is less hostile to substitutional quantification than Quine. However, even were Horwich to have included this example, it would not alter his minimalist/deflationary view.

to a single bearer on distinct possible occasions, and while this doesn't violate anything displayed in the equivalences, it is hard to see how the latter could be invoked to explain that phenomenon. It is not merely something Horwich doesn't account for, unless we grant the assumption that there is no nontrivial distinction between the predicate and its property; it is something he doesn't so much as address. But it is surely a salient feature of the property (and concept) truth. So, when we compare the problem he poses for himself in the title of his section (quoted earlier in this paragraph) with what he achieves, we see clearly that what is claimed for the truth predicate is assumed similarly to be the cardinal achievement of both the property and concept of truth.

The Quine of the present interpretation is not vulnerable to this charge. His views on the utility of 'is true' and on the nature of truth are stored in separate compartments, and to the best of my knowledge he regularly avoids confusing them. But we may inquire, given the programmatic form of correspondence I have attributed to him, how he would handle the Variation intuition? Well, it really doesn't come up in his discussion of a truth predicate because isolated uses of that predicate naturally will not speak to what is basically a comparison between different, and conflicting, potential uses. But his appeals to reality are in perfect concert with the acknowledgment that a difference in reality can make a difference in truth.

Meanwhile, a host of other commentators may find rather different reasons for counting Quine a deflationist. One avenue of support for that conclusion might begin from the admonition, examined in chapter 3, that nothing is gained by talking about "facts" rather than "true sentences" (1960, 247).

Unquestionably, Quine is a critic of the notion of fact. But his objections to it are part of his more direct attack on that of a proposition. He writes that the main utility of facts "seems to be . . . as a reinforcement of the flimsy 'that' of propositional abstraction" (1960, 247). Moreover, facts share the concerns about their conditions for identity that Quine regards as fatal to propositions. He sums up his disdain for the notion when he writes:

The sentences 'Fifth Avenue is six miles long' and 'Fifth Avenue is a hundred feet wide', if we suppose them true, presumably state different facts, yet the only concrete or physical object involved is Fifth Avenue. (1960, 247)

However, despite the loss of FACT, Quine never doubts that something about reality determines truth here:

> Our two sentences . . . are true because of Fifth Avenue, because it is a hundred feet wide and six miles long, because it was planned and made that way, and because of the way we use our words; only indirection results from positing facts, in the image of sentences, as intermediaries. (ibid., 247)

Quine holds that these turns of phrase and the absence of strict identity conditions are devastating for the notion of a fact. I have already had my say about why I believe otherwise. However, we are concerned here with understanding Quine's views, not with their pros and cons. Although truthmaking facts are rejected, there is no indication in Quine's writings that he is willing to extend this disapproval to the whole of truthmaking reality. Quite the contrary, there would be little point in the first two of the three 'because' clauses of the last passage if unadulterated, unexpurgated reality were not a truthmaker of some sort. This theme is repeated throughout his career. Not only is reality crucial to actual truth, but he emphasizes that this is "unlinguistic reality" (1970, 11). Even the ascent to the truth predicate in instances of (*D*) doesn't abolish the concern with such reality; it merely exchanges our direct talk of the world for indirect talk of the world:

> This ascent to a linguistic plane of reference is only a momentary retreat from the world, for the utility of the truth predicate is precisely the cancellation of linguistic reference. The truth predicate is a reminder that, despite a technical ascent to talk of sentences, our eye is on the world. This cancellatory force of the truth predicate is explicit in Tarski's paradigm: 'Snow is white' is true if and only if snow is white. (1970, 12)

Quine doesn't seem anxious to discover another selected class of truthmakers with the specificity of facts to replace 'reality' or 'the world'. Perhaps he didn't think it could be done (and perhaps this is for reasons having to do with his views on language, discussed presently); perhaps he supposed *reality*, and his various views on how it was constituted, was sufficient. But as long as the notion of reality on display in these passages is neither deflated to something linguistic, on a par with sentences, nor epistemologized in the manner of coherence[4] or pragmatism, it suffices for a version of correspondence. It is hard to square this with that hallmark tenet of deflationism, the absence of all metaphysical implications for truth.

4. As Davidson (1990, 298) at one time thought it was.

In making quite clear how the truth predicate acquires a utility through semantic ascent, and in deploying Tarski's methods in the definition of the predicate, Quine has supplied deflationists with ammunition that they can use for their own purposes. None of those extended uses is inappropriate just because Quine himself doesn't pursue them to a deflationist conclusion. But there is a feature underlying Quine's larger view that reinforces the notion that we should be careful about the lessons to be drawn from the devices to which he appeals. When he bluntly states that "truth hinges on reality" (1970, 11), he is firmly rooted in the soil of correspondence. To this he adds "but to object, on this score, to calling sentences [as opposed to propositions] true, is a confusion." This enforces a recognition of more than a nominal distinction between the property *truth* and the predicate 'is true'. He scrupulously avoids claiming that what can be discerned in the predicate 'true' gives us an account, much less an exhaustive account, of its correlative property. Things go rather the other way round. Simply because truth does hinge on reality, we cannot treat the predicate, even when operating as a device of semantic ascent, as not doing indirectly what the sentence of which truth is predicated does directly. In this he seems to show proper care for his subject. He neither claims nor denies that in general we can probe features of a property by examining its predicate, nor does he claim or deny that such an examination will lead to a complete account of the property. In other words, there are no ironclad prescriptions for the methods of inquiry implicit in these remarks. But he is quite clearly declaring that in the case of truth, what holds for the property has little to do with the utility, and perhaps even the definition, of its predicate. This point was emphasized earlier in my criticism of deflationism. It would have averted much unclarity, perhaps even the need for much of the last two chapters, if those who patterned their own work on his start had also observed that distinction.

But doesn't correspondence require at least word-world relations? And how can our understanding of sentences, always relative to a translation manual, be related to the world as such? Recall that in the paragraph introducing this section Quine was quoted as claiming that we can't say (absolutely speaking) what the objects of a theory are, but only "how one theory of objects is interpretable or reinterpretable in another" (1969, 50).

We needn't open a broad discussion of Quine's views on radical translation, the indeterminacy of meaning, the inscrutability of reference, or the rejection of the analytic/synthetic distinction to justify refusing an anticorrespondence construal of these remarks. Thus, for convenience, I grant the standard accounts of the Quinean notions just listed. Still by heeding a few simple reminders we can see why they do not damage the correspondence interpretation I have proposed.

First, to say that we cannot pick out with our terms, absolutely speaking, just what they refer or correspond to is not to say that the determinate reality which we are unable to pick out with a bit of our language doesn't determine the truth or falsity of our sentences. Second, sentences needing interpretation or reinterpretation in terms of one or another theory still belong to, as Quine puts it, theories of *objects*. The connection to the world is not severed just because it is siphoned through an interpretation. To say that we cannot adequately express something is not to say that our remarks have lost their direction of import. I think these two points not only allow us to preserve the correspondence interpretation, but together with that interpretation lock onto a significant aspect of Quine's naturalism. Recall that while Quine thought scientific theories were *underdetermined* by the evidence, he didn't think they were, per se, *indeterminate*: there is a fact of the matter in nature, even if our *theories* can never be sufficiently determinate to encapsulate it fully (1987, 9–10). This is no mark against nature, nor against the notion that nature determines the matter. Of course, because our theories also require formulation in words, in the present case we are assaulted by a double dose of indeterminacy/underdetermination. But this second wave of complexity doesn't overturn our previous judgment. In the end, it is reality that determines the truth both of a scientific theory and of all our truth-apt sentences.

Any broad interpretation of Quine's views is a notoriously complicated and contentious business. Perhaps we should say of him what he once wrote of attributions to Aristotle, that they are "subject to contradiction by scholars, such being the penalty for attributions to Aristotle." But if we may separate his views on these local matters from his larger philosophy, a delicate task at best, it seems that they can appear at only one location on our map of positions. To rank him as other than a correspondence theorist would require a significant reconfiguration of his claims. Undoubtedly he doesn't subscribe to a detailed enough version to be entirely satisfactory. He is certainly isn't a role model for the theory. But his commitments, however far they go, allow no way to extend the remarks I have cited but in a correspondence direction. Those commitments already rule out deflationism, and without a massive infusion of alien doctrines his views can't be developed into a coherence or pragmatist theory of truth (whatever might be said about Quine's relation to pragmatism in other respects). Nor do his remarks about the role of reality allow us to think of him as a nihilist about truth. Quine seems to believe that there is no way to get around the word-world connection for the constitution of truth, and there is nothing in his deliberations about the truth predicate to indicate that he believed truth not to have a constitution.

Conclusion

Perhaps not much is to be gained from this review. The positions held by Wittgenstein and Quine certainly don't commit anyone who hasn't an exaggerated respect for their authority to follow them. But it is worth noting that these two thinkers held views more nuanced and complex than those frequently attributed to them. And if we ponder how it is possible that philosophers who have written so much of what has been taken up as support for deflationism need not themselves have been committed to a version of that view, we may glimpse how it is possible to accommodate much of what deflationists care about without ourselves being committed to the most serious defects of those views.

However, by themselves the deep problems besetting deflationism may not seem to be much consolation for a correspondence theory. Philosophers have grown suspicious, not to say weary, of arguments by elimination because the unexamined view left standing—the one set out to appear as the lone remaining sensible option—might have been cast in a rather different light if we had begun with its examination rather than that of its opposition. It was for this reason that I first tried to fend off other, more direct, objections frequently cited against correspondence. But is that all that we can do? Is there no prospect of gaining some further insight into the actual working machinery of a correspondence relation? In fact, I don't believe that our predicament is quite so dire. There is at least one scheme—which opens the prospect that there may be others as well—that gives us a glimmer of what the correspondence relation and its worldly relata may be like. Let's explore that avenue.

8 Corresponding . . .

Stankevich: . . .Everything now depends on artists and philosophers. Great artists to express what can't be explained, philosophers to explain it! —Tom Stoppard, *The Coast of Utopia*, Part I: "Voyage," Act II

8.1 The Challenge

The word 'correspondence' has been a stumbling block to its theory's assessment.[1] Faced with demands for the details of corresponding, supporters may protest that, strictly speaking, the notion is optional rather than essential to its theory. There is more than a modicum of justice in this reply. Recall that Plato and Aristotle, cited as proto-correspondentists in chapter 1, don't deploy terms resembling (a translation of) 'correspondence', nor do their elaborations appear to invoke it covertly. Nor does the term occur in the last three of the ten epigrammatic summaries of the position quoted early in chapter 4. The correspondence theory requires only that propositions, when true, are made so by virtue of a worldly circumstance selectively relevant to the content of the proposition. After all, the plea may continue, the word 'coherence' doesn't appear in many of the sketchiest summaries of coherence theories, when it does occur it is seldom taken as ultimately explanatory (rather than merely serving as

1. The earliest mention of correspondence in this connection with which I am familiar is Moore's 1901 entry in Baldwin's *Dictionary* (vol. 2, 717). But there he states that the terms 'correspondence' and 'agreement' are already in general use. The OED cites a relevant use of it by Coleridge in 1809 (Wolenski (1999) led me to it), but its occurrence doesn't appear to be part of, or to originate, a tradition.

a cover term for something else),[2] and this scarcely seems to detract from that view.

To this it may be rejoined that although the word 'coherence' may not appear in the theory's fuller statements, the notion is subsequently fleshed out by the evidential relations constituting truth. Similarly, it is not the word 'correspondence', but the relation's details that want explanation. Their absence troubles not only those with competing theories, but also certain of those vaguely sympathetic to correspondence-style theories. For example, as noted earlier, among the latter some endorse a generalized realism about truth while shying away from identifying it as a correspondence theory. And this may be done just because they believe themselves to be unable to supply the details of the relationship. In chapter 4 I tried to dispel the notion that giving further details is a desideratum for holding, or defending, the view, and I stand by that claim. That isn't inconsistent with there being further details, or with such of them as we can uncover being valuable. In the present chapter I chart some progress on this front.

The explication of a truth-constituting correspondence holding between propositions and facts looks, when the project is presented point blank, like a formidable, indeed daunting, task. But much of this appearance is due precisely to regarding the task *point blank*. We begin demystifying the relation by latching onto an intriguing clue provided by J. L. Austin (1961), a clue that leads us to shift our attention elsewhere. No doubt, much of what is to follow deviates from Austin's intentions, and the end product differs significantly from his; but Austin provides a good starting point for seeing our way past a familiar charge of, in effect, hand waving over the correspondence relation. (That objection, in various guises, often emerges in debates over Correspondence.) The key to this solution is showing that we can understand more familiar thought/language relations to the world, and from them correspondentist answers will naturally fall out while disarming the chief concerns voiced by critics. By no means is correspondence then without remaining issues. That would be too much to ask of any large-scale philosophical enterprise. But the remaining questions will be those that philosophy inherits even without the correspondence theory,

2. The views of some absolute idealist-leaning theorists, such as Joachim (see esp. 1906, §26), are exceptions. But those versions have all but disappeared from the literature. I have in mind more recent editions.

and I hope to show they don't represent mortal dangers. The version of correspondence to be presented will not give rise to novel and distinctive challenges.

The advantage I foresaw in Austin's view was its ability to unearth a more basic relation of thought/language to the world, so well entrenched that its credibility couldn't be undermined even by a repeated failure of attempts to analyze it. It is a datum compatible with many different semantical analyses, and it survives the shipwreck of just about any specific semantic program. From it we can then devise the elements from which truth conditions flow, without needing any further appeal to correspondence at the commonly contested levels. That's the direction of the exposition to come. However, before exploring this relation, let's try to get a clearer fix on the relevant issues.

8.2 Understanding the Relation

Some may believe that the question "How can one compare a proposition or thought with an independent nonmental reality?" represents a serious challenge to any correspondence theory. The unbridgeable epistemic gap between the cognizer and the world (or, as a traditional idiom has it, between subject and object) has induced some to embrace coherence (Bradley 1914, 108; Hempel 1935) or an ideal warrant theory (Putnam 1981, 55).[3] But, as many will agree, this concern is quite distinct from issues that theories of the nature of truth need address. Despite that, I did briefly touch on a related issue earlier when we examined the Berkeleyan gambit in section 3.3. Reasoning of that variety has been one source of the perplexity. Past those sketchy remarks I have little to add here. Even if I didn't think it largely a side issue, the underlying assumption of the question conflates concerns and would thereby lead the discussion away from more pressing issues. But, all too briefly and dogmatically, I will add here that the worry seems to be rooted in a theory of knowledge that is not fallibilist and a theory of perception that is not direct realist. Neither view seems attractive on its face, and, indeed, I don't believe either pans out.

3. For further commentary on inducements to coherence theories, see Vision 1996, chapter 6 .

Instead of probing that issue, I concentrate on matters surrounding the constitution of truth. Here too we may begin with perceived difficulties for correspondence. They may be divided into two sorts. First, there are problems about the correspondence relation itself. Second, questions have been raised about the character of potential truthmakers. The division isn't as sharp as we might hope, and, as we shall see, not all the issues of present concern fall neatly into one or the other of these classes. But the classification allows us to organize much of the ensuing discussion proficiently.

Here is how the remainder of the exposition proceeds.

In this section, I state, in the form of a set of provocative questions, misgivings about the correspondence relation itself. In section 8.3, I present a distinction that is crucial to the positive view developed in sections 8.4–8.6. In those sections and in 8.7, I explain how my view handles the initial set of challenges framed by the first set of questions below, (A)–(D). In section 8.8, I put into perspective the widely presumed urgency of that or any other positive detailed view.

Chapter 9 introduces a second set of questions: those concerning problems for truthmakers. In section 9.1, in addition to formulating those questions, I explain the relation of *constitution* in which truthmakers are claimed to stand to true propositions. In sections 9.2–9.5, I address the concerns raised by the questions. In section 9.6, I discuss leftover business concerning related objections not strictly covered by our two categories of questions. Section 9.6 ends with a further reflection on the price to be paid for borrowing some basic notions from correspondence while nevertheless trying to avoid the theory. The final section of chapter 9 concludes this discussion.

Here then is our first set of questions, those challenging our ability to devise or select an appropriate correspondence relation.

(A) Can we discover isomorphisms between constituents of a proposition and those of its correspondent (say, a fact) responsible for the proposition's truth? Perhaps a bit more broadly, but still in the same line of inquiry, what, if any, structural similarities between true propositions and their truthmakers allow the latter to constitute the truth of the former?

(B) Must there be a distinct fact corresponding to a false proposition in addition to that corresponding to a true one?

(C) Do whole propositions refer, in the way, or an extension of the way, that singular terms do? (Can propositions be names? Can facts be named?) If so, what do false propositions refer to?

(D) Given that propositions are related to more than a single worldly circumstance, how are we to identify the right one for our theory? (Why is it "only the fact that *p* that [the proposition] p corresponds to, and not, say, the fact that not-*p*" (McGinn 2000, 90)?) And, following up, if we do choose only one of a proposition's correlates, can we avoid rendering our account viciously circular by choosing it because it is the one that makes the proposition true?

Questions (A) and (C) ask whether such a relation is at all possible; questions (B) and (D) challenge us to select the right one. Although my point of departure is directly relevant to the issue raised by (A), I shall not first run through answers to each question seriatim. Instead I shall lay out what I consider some of the important details of one kind of developed correspondence theory. We may then return to the questions; for with the completed view in front of us we will be able see clearly how the concerns represented by each of them evaporates.

8.3 Correlation or Congruity

As before, I use 'worldly circumstance' to cover states of affairs, facts, situations, individual-property complexes, thick individuals, events, moments, or whatever may figure on the nonpropositional side of the relation. (A), then, is an inquiry about the existence (and character) of an isomorphism between structured propositions and worldly circumstances. George Pitcher's (1964b) classic exposition of the topic initiated a tradition of distinguishing two sorts of understandings of the correspondence relation: correspondence-as-correlation and correspondence-as-congruity. (We may abbreviate them to "correlation" and "congruity," respectively.) That distinction gives us a handle on a crucial assumption underlying (A). Let us begin with correlation.

   Correlation obtains when there is a match—most likely, an isomorphism—between the internal structures of a proposition and a fact. (When we think of propositions in this connection, we cannot but ascribe to them the structures, deep or surface, of the sentences with which we express them.) Attempts by the likes of Wittgenstein (1922, esp. §4.04) and Russell (1985) to find relevant matches have been frustrated by the many problems just below the surface. The procedure may look promising at first: singular terms refer to individuals, predicates denote or express properties. But we quickly run afoul of complications. For example, suppose we ask "What in the fact that the Sears Tower is taller than the Hancock Building does *taller than* stand for?" Is it a type of thing along with its two terms (thereby transforming our proposition into a list of names, with no discernible glue)? Or do worldly facts only contain the individual height properties of the items being compared? If the latter, it would appear that *being taller than* isn't a separate feature of the world beyond the two buildings and their intrinsic heights, thereby dashing any hope of an isomorphism between constituents of proposition and fact. This is but one of countless problem cases.[4] These and similar vexed questions, quite likely without authoritative answers, have impeded efforts to work out correlation solutions. For those and similar reasons, attempts to discover correlations have been largely abandoned. Indeed, although the account to follow makes limited use of relations between some elements in propositions and some aspects of their truthmakers, this type of point-by-point matching falls out of the picture.

In spite of this, certain critics, including Johnston (1993, 111), appear to suppose that spelling out the relation in correlational terms (what Johnston calls a "robust relation of correspondence"), and those of a particular kind, is a desideratum for any correspondence theory. Of course, one can employ the title 'correspondence theory' in various ways. However, in the sequel I propose to show that a view for which it would be quite unnatural to refuse that name can set aside the correlational task.

Let us, then, turn to congruity. As Pitcher notes, the first definition of 'correspond' in the *Oxford English Dictionary* is "To answer to something else in the way of fitness; to agree *with*; be conformable *to*, be congruous or in harmony *with*." Such congruity provides a perfectly good sense of 'correspondence'. The congruity of one complex with another needn't be explained by a structural similarity in the arrangement of their constituents. Even a key will have working features (for grasping, for fitting on

---

4. For extended reviews of the difficulties, see Cartwright 1987 and Urmson 1956.

a key ring) having no counterparts in its lock, although this may have seemed a paradigm with which to explain correlation. There may be fit here, but nothing amounting to complete structural matching.

Whereas correlation provides an explanation for the relation in terms of matching parts, congruity as such offers no account of why *this* goes with *that*. To say that the wholes are congruous, and leaving it there, doesn't remove any initial perplexity. Thus, *qua* explanation, correlation has an attraction that congruity lacks. Nevertheless, there may be good reason for a congruous correspondence. For example, pairings set up by convention (say, by arbitrary stipulation) are likely to be congruities rather than correlations. Moreover, things always do eventually come down to brute relatedness. Even for correlation, we can't go on *ad infinitum* finding smaller structural similarities between correlated elements. Structural similarity must stop explaining a connection somewhere. We hit bedrock with singular referring expressions and predicates. Nominata and their names as such have no interesting similarities, properties can't be said to be similarly structured to their predicates, individual musical notes bear very little interesting resemblance to their scored notations. Furthermore, the range of onomatopoeia in natural languages is slim. If not-thoroughly-decomposable connectedness can work at the level of names, predicates, and the like, what barrier can there be to its working at the level of sentence-size units? The fact that those units are built out of smaller ones may have given rise to the prospect of a correlation of parts in the offing, but it no more forces this conclusion on us than that a property should have features corresponding to the letters used to spell its predicate. What is wanted is a motivation to suppose that the connections are made independent of considerations about correlations of elements. The notion to be developed below supplies a basis for just such an explanation. As a bonus, making out such a relation will dispatch the concern voiced in question (A).

One last warning. The compositionality of language and thought, which I take for granted here, will not revive correlation. There are some systematic connections, say, between whole sentences and their parts. But this is not the same as the relation between parts of sentences and parts of the world, and the kinds of inducements that lead us to acknowledge language's compositionality do not extend support to the view that the relations between sentences, once composed, and worldly states are all computable from relations between their parts. Indeed, the compositionality of language doesn't even support the view that worldly states have parts.

8.4 Austinian Foundations

Recall from section 4.5 that Austin's theory is summarized in the following formula:

A statement is said to be true when the historic state of affairs to which it is correlated by the demonstrative conventions (the one to which it 'refers') is of a type with which the sentence used in making it is correlated by the descriptive conventions. (Austin 1961, 90)

Various notions employed in this view set off alarms for critics. In fact, in the past comments on them have gone off in directions that take us away from the basic idea. That is unfortunate because the account also harbors important insights. After several adjustments I want to concentrate on at least one of those insights. To co-opt potential distractions, I begin with some preliminary clarifications and modifications. I hope that they will at least remove enough of the disquiet to get on with a serious examination of the view's main thrust.

To begin with, Austin's earlier use of the verb "correlated" is not the same as Pitcher's, but is strictly neutral between Pitcher's two senses of "correspondence." Shortly thereafter Austin makes it abundantly clear that he has in mind what Pitcher calls "correspondence-as-congruity" by remarking that "there is no need whatsoever for the words used in making a true statement to 'mirror' in any way, however indirect, any feature whatsoever of the situation or event; a statement no more needs, in order to be true, to reproduce the 'multiplicity,' say, or the 'structure' or 'form' of the reality, than a word needs to be echoic or writing pictographic" (1961, 93). This doesn't preclude a structural relationship, in whole or part, between the constituents of a statement and those of its correspondent, but the discovery of one forms no part of Austin's view. Indeed, a leading virtue of his particular way of setting out the correspondence theory lies in its ability to avoid the need for, without further commentary on, these sorts of point-by-point correlations.

Next, 'convention' is a thoroughly theory-laden term, more controversial than the occasion demands. No doubt, words, and the sentences composed of them, mean what they do as a matter of convention. The facts that 'dog' means *dog* and 'cat' means *cat* are conventional if anything is. But it doesn't follow that once those conventions are in place the relevant correlation between sentences and types of states of affairs must be established by a further convention. It should be noted that Austin's reason for calling these connections conventions has a very different sort of motivation. Given that a relation must be either natural or conventional, and since a sentence needn't—and seldom does—'mirror' the (type) state of affairs to which it is appointed (which would make the relation natural), he supposed that the only alternative is to regard it as conventional: " . . . the truth of statements remains still a matter . . . of the words used being the ones *conventionally appointed* for situations of the type to which that referred to belongs." (1961, 93–94) Austin seems to have had little in mind by this use of conventionality other than to deny that the connections were natural in his sense. Still, all that need be said at this point is that by virtue of these conventions a sentence *describes* a type of state of affairs. We needn't go so far as to say that descriptive conventions bring off, as opposed to underlie, the correlation (or the congruity), any more than that we need to say that the conventions of arithmetic derive a certain theorem from a set of axioms, or that the conventions of trading with currency are responsible for my paying my electricity bill. The implications and implementations of conventional connections need not be themselves conventional in the same sense, and at a minimum it will avoid confusion if we remain uncommitted on the propriety of that label.

On the other hand, for the most part it will not affect the points I want to raise if we employ Austin's original terms. Thus, when convenient I'll use his idiom of descriptive and demonstrative *conventions*. It is easy enough to see how this jargon is eliminable, to be replaced by that of descriptions (describing) and demonstrations (demonstrating). Thus, if we were to go in for circumlocutions we might say simply that a sentence describes a state of affairs, and it does so by means of whatever conventions govern the construction of the sentence. Similarly, if the need arose we could replace talk of demonstrative conventions with talk of demonstrating. The choice in the sequel is dictated only by ease of exposition.

(To be explained presently, as I develop this scheme it allows us to dispense in practice with the demonstrative side of the correspondence. Thus, the only correspondences required between an item which is a semantically evaluable whole utterance and something which need not be semantically evaluable are at the descriptive level. This already reduces by half whatever unclarities or snags are introduced by talk of conventions.)

Finally, Austin confines himself to statements and the sentences used in stating them. However, we want a theory of truth that also covers the contents of belief and other propositional attitudes (even simply the entertainings of propositions). We also want the account to capture propositions occurring in larger compounds, although the former may not be stated (and thus, not be the contents of statements) in those occurrences. We have at hand the ability to extend the account to all propositions, simply by devising for them a distinction analogous to the sentence/statement distinction as explained below. However, actually doing so would be wordy and would involve potentially distracting neologisms. If it is, as I soon claim, simply a matter of including or withholding, roughly, indexical and/or demonstrative elements, we need not even assume that true propositions reflect our familiar sentential structures. But I'll provisionally refrain from generalizing this way so as not to divert us from our main business. Rather, the exposition will proceed in terms of Austin's sentence/statement distinction to explain the relevant points of the relationships. For those interested in seeing how greater generality can be achieved, once the view is succinctly summarized in (V), I illustrate its extension to propositional contents of other sorts with (VP).

We are now ready to turn our attention to oft-neglected strengths of this view.

8.5 Constructing a Correspondence Theory

Austin's formula utilizes both demonstrative and descriptive conventions (viz., demonstrations and descriptions). A key element in my reconstruction is that once the descriptive are in place, demonstration, at the level of sentence-size units, is otiose and its distinctive problems vanish. Not that all the questions that were formerly raised about demonstration are thereby resolved; but those concerning a relation between whole statements and parts of the world disappear. Still, we require representational accounts of terms in recognizably referential positions, and some oppose *any* representationalism in philosophy. But that issue was on the table before we got entangled with correspondence, and the objections to representation in general are less widely or easily held than those brought against the demonstrative function of statements. We needn't go fishing for a new, distinctive, relation, and in standing against thoroughgoing nonrepresentational accounts of language we occupy the high ground. The problems posed for so-called representational theories emerge from positions that are deeply contentious given the current state of the art. However, this isn't an essay on the theory of reference, and it would not serve our main interest to launch into that vast topic as a side issue. The point to be emphasized here is that these problems are not those of generating *ab initio* a new relationship between a statement and a worldly circumstance. Thus, I shall concentrate below on what Austin calls descriptive conventions. Here we can show that these connections between sentences and types of states of affairs are too robust to be easily dismissed.

For Austin (1961, 89–90), descriptive conventions correlate "words (= sentences) with *types* of situation, thing, event, etc., to be found in the world." For many theorists sentences are merely syntactical strings, meaningful marks, or sounds. On such accounts, tokens of a single type sentence might appear in different languages with wholly distinct meanings. But for an Austinian reconstruction it is most convenient to regard sentences as coming with meanings (what he would call "senses"). Nevertheless, qua types their lexical vocabulary is stripped of (many) specifications of individuals,[5] times, and places—any specifics determinable by what we may for convenience call their *deictic* elements, including indexicals (e.g., 'I', 'you', 'here', 'now'), demonstratives (e.g., 'this', 'that'), tense, and context. Once restored, deixis takes us from a sentence to a statement.

We wouldn't need to include context but for the prevalence of ellipsis in humble conversation. For example, the use of a definite description may imply uniqueness, but usually we must look beyond its strict formulation. When Russell's theory of descriptions is in question, this may be regarded as a minor inconvenience, resulting from unguarded talk. But it cannot be so easily finessed when we want to understand how we manage to convey information in day-to-day interchanges. For example, consider an utterance

5. Proper name specifications are an exception because it is customary to assimilate homophonic/homographic names of distinct individuals to ambiguity, rather than treating such names as, say, indefinite descriptions or pronouns (viz., single, unambiguous terms applying to different things on different occasions). Barwise and Perry (1983, e.g. 21) are an exception, lumping proper names with my treatment of deictic elements.

of "the bird was just on the roof." Not only does it pick out the recent past (*via* tense), but in that conversational milieu 'the bird' (or 'the roof') will refer to a particular one, not just any old avian. Which bird may depend on factors that can't be reduced to anything more definite than the miscellany collected under "context." If the foregoing statement occurs in a conversation about your recently escaped parakeet, context indicates that the referent of 'the bird' is that individual. No pigeon which happened to be on the roof, and was not (mistakenly) responsible for the reference will be referred to by this utterance. Indeed, the description is doubly indebted to context, for it certainly shouldn't be taken to imply that only one bird exists! Thus, like indexicality, demonstration, and tense, context (or speaker intention) can provide a type of deixis from which an Austinian sentence is extrapolated.

Deixis, then, is a common route to go from a (type) sentence to a specification of a statement made or makeable with it via its tokening. Not every type of deixis operates in every sentence, and some tokens import none. The latter are known as eternal sentences. However, whenever deixis is present, its actual values are not determiners of the type state of affairs with which the strictly descriptive conventions align the sentence.

Of course, the vehicles of indexicals and demonstratives also have aspects fixed by descriptive conventions. For example, and simplifying a bit, a sentence containing 'I' is used to refer to its utterer, whomever it may be, 'she' is dedicated to indicating females (or, by customary extension to ships, fate, nature, etc.), 'now' to the present,[6] and so on. What is not contained in the descriptive component is the identity of the actual person who happens to be that first person on a certain occasion of utterance, the actual female who is she, etc. Thus, where 'I' is the subject term, and ignoring rare exceptions, that the sentence states something about its utterer is a part of what the sentence conventionally conveys. What is not included will be something determined by particular utterances: say, that it refers to Tony Blair or Kofi Annan.

Similarly for other deictic elements. 'Now' and present tense may indicate the present, but at the type level there will be an indefinitely large number of presents (of *nows*), including yesterday's presents and tomorrow's presents. On this issue I may be departing from Austin in counting types of

---

6. For exceptions, see Vision 1985.

states of affairs. Strawson (1971c, 237) asks whether Austin would consider the following sentences "correlated by descriptive conventions with . . . the same type": 'At least one guest will drink no wine at dinner,' 'This guest is drinking no wine at dinner,' 'That guest drank no wine at dinner.' Strawson believes that Austin would answer affirmatively if the statements made with them were appropriately arranged in time. But if I make my statement before the dinner I would need to use the first of those sentences to express what I want to say. And what that sentence can be used to convey about the future is crucial to the identification of the types with which it is associated. Thus, while these sentences may be used to make the same statement, and the tokens of the appropriate states of affairs may converge on one and the same concrete state of affairs (making them all true by the same worldly circumstance), the different sentences on my reconstruction are not connected with the same types.

Are we then committed to a different type corresponding to every sentence? Probably not. Consider the sentence "Dinner is served." The type of state of affairs described by *dinner being served* no doubt fits it, but also fits "*Diner c'est servi,*" probably fits "Dinner is ready," and, if this can count as a sentence, fits the clanging of the dinner bell. But it is of little moment whether or not types, which are abstract entities, are counted as associated with only a single sentence, *modulo* translation of course. (We should expect, and can live with, fuzziness at the edges because we are attempting to account for a common practice that doesn't have sharp outlines.)

Although the foregoing account is sketchy, it should give a fair idea of sentences as I intend to employ them here. I haven't attempted a complete account of all the factors that take us from sentence to statement, rather I have concentrated on the simplest cases. I purposely ignore certain complications at the level of the interpretation of a meaningful sentence. Various of these factors are summarized in chapter 2 of Barwise and Perry 1983. All of them have to do with information conveyed, and many don't affect the truth or falsity of the resulting proposition. But if some do, that is no flaw in the present sketch. The few factors mentioned here are intended merely as illustrative of the things that take us from a sentence of the right kind to a truth-apt proposition or statement. If more is required, that will not override the function of the factors mentioned here. That set of functions is all we need to understand the constellation of relationships required for this style of correspondence.

The descriptive connection of a sentence to a (type of) state of affairs is as clear and secure a datum as we are likely to get, too much so to abandon for the odd theory. Sentence *types* with certain descriptive contents are designed for expressing certain sorts of situations etc., and are unsuited for expressing others. Unless we have a specially prearranged code (as might be concocted between spies), I know that the English sentence "dinner is served" is suited to a certain type of situation, and thus usable for making certain types of statement. Another English sentence—say, "the earthquake destroyed the village"—is not apt for making the first type of statement. Not only does anyone who speaks English have this sort of information at hand, but whatever one's view about the rationale for having a language, this had better be a central element in it. Even so minimally descriptive a sentence as "it is here" or "she did it" is covered by this aspect of communication. While details of explanations may vary, the datum itself that certain sentences, and not others, can be used to state or express certain kinds of situation is so irresistible that it is virtually unthinkable that a promising theory of language could explain it away. Perhaps the datum won't get a clause in one's linguistic theory—or perhaps it will show up only as a primitive—but when a proposal is incompatible with it, can we really imagine it not reflecting poorly on the proposal rather than on the datum?

Let us dwell a bit further on this consequence. It may seem ridiculous, say, to suppose that a sentence so indefinite as "she did it" is attached to a type of state of affairs.[7] It could refer to redecorating, setting the hotel on fire, a sexual escapade, getting elected, washing the dog, turning on the radio, signing a declaration, tripping on the stairs, and so on. I assume that these various employments of 'to do' aren't the result of polysemy. If there were an ambiguity here, each use would employ a different type sentence, and no threat of absurdity would ensue. Rather, 'do' is a single very broad term embracing each of these diverse kinds of states of affairs, and indefinitely many more. My contention is that there is a single type to which it is conventionally attached, of which each of the manifestations listed can be the correlates of potential tokens. Why isn't this absurd?

Instead of the variety of things that count as a doing, think of the myriad of types of states of affairs that can't be picked out by using this sentence. They include not only all future and present tense episodes, but samples of

---

7. I'm grateful to David Houghton for this sharp formulation of the point.

types that can be picked out by sentences such as "It's raining," "He failed the test," "The brakes failed," "The gods are angry," "If you want to succeed, get a good education." 'To do' may be an elastic verb—a feature exploited by a popular sports shoe manufacturer whose advertisements carry the simple slogan "Do it!"—but the sentence is not so wide that it is not suited selectively to a certain type rather than others. Indeed, the very ability to understand the objection is indirect testimony to being aware of this suitability. For if we didn't recognize the various uses to which it could be put, why would we even think of using it for this spread of activities and non-activities?

This feature of our practice is frequently ignored in accounts of sentential content. There are no doubt reasons for this, one being that it is too obvious to be worth explicit mention. Another may be that the sort of descriptive correlation explained here falls awkwardly between two levels at which semanticists find recognizable tasks. It has been customary since Frege (1892/1960) to distinguish between sense and reference. Not that everyone accepts this dichotomy. But there is at least a discipline-wide tendency among those who reject it to acknowledge doing so, which is enough to certify the distinction's orthodoxy. But the connection under investigation doesn't seem to fit into an investigation of either phenomenon.

For one thing, the sentences employed here are not mere syntactical strings; they are already bearers of sense. It is because of the sense they have that they are associated with one rather than another type of state of affairs. Therefore, it is difficult to argue conversely that they have their sense because of their association with a certain state of affairs. Doing this would require that we find a way to distinguish the varieties of "because" in our two dependences. Were this at all plausible, carrying it out would still be an extracurricular exercise. So, it is, at the very least, incidental (and thereby irrelevant) to the current project to be able to convert this into an account of sentence sense.

On the other hand, because we have abstracted away from the deictic elements of a given sentence, save for proper names, our account clearly disqualifies itself as a theory of reference. So it doesn't figure in typical semantic inquiries or their resultant theories. However, neither does it deserve to be relegated to the only other category—the catch-all of "pragmatics"—provided in standard language-study taxonomies. There is nothing pragmatic about the relation of a sentence to one rather than another state of affairs. Nor does it appear as an offshoot of mainstream semantic theories of either type. Accordingly, while the relationship we have been scouting is unavoidable, there is a good chance of its disappearing from the radar screen for language theorists.

At this stage of inquiry, in which we are deciding *what* requires explaining, worries about correlating constituents of sentences with those of states of affairs, or whether there are two, three, or more constituents in either, are not focal. Doubts may infect particular attempts to explain correspondence-as-congruity, even at this syntactical level, but the failure of a series of promising explanations doesn't dislodge the certitude that particular kinds of sentences are suited for use in, and the expression of, certain types of states of affairs. Of course, while not mandatory, it is worthwhile to seek a further explanation for this phenomenon. However, should we decide (as unlikely as this may be) that this connection is simply inexplicable, perhaps too fundamental to be understood in other terms, I do not see how we can use that as a basis for scrapping the connection. The details, fascinating though they may be, are secondary. And this is quite enough to enable us to utilize this fact in another theory, in particular our theory of truth, without first providing a further theory about why the connections hold.

One reason that this phenomenon is so irresistible is that we can't avoid employing it in the commonest cases in which we use language as an instrument for making assertions. This simple, inescapable fact pulls us up short, giving the lie to any subtle philosophizing that would seek ways around it. It seems to say no more than that different sentences are suitable for stating different things, and equally it is hard to see how saying that implies less than that different sentences are associated with different types of states of affairs. Whereas this datum may seem most readily built upon a semantic theory that derives the meanings of sentences from the worldly circumstances to which they are connected (as in situation semantics), it must also be a staple of theories which are ideational (from Locke (1700) to Frege (1960)) or conceptual role (Block 1986; Field 1977), or just about any sort. Similarly, states of affairs may admit further analysis—say, as set theoretic constructions *à la* Barwise and Perry. Although the datum emphasized here can figure in each of these accounts, it needn't be a working cog in any. And, my best guess is that all attempts to evade it will ultimately be traceable to the mistaken impression that it is tied to one among other competing theories of meaning, rather than being a more primitive datum that any such theory must, at a minimum, accommodate.

No doubt, at this level sentences in the imperative and interrogative moods also correlate to types of states of affairs. Thus, the sentence types "Shut the door" and "Pass the salt" are used for commanding or requesting the bringing about of distinct types of states of affairs. That their token utterances are neither true nor false depends not on this typal connection, but on the fact that their utterances do not anticipate the same sorts of tokenings of those states of affairs that are (customarily) conventionally introduced by sentences in the assertoric (or propounding) mode.

Making this connection central to the theory also averts another difficulty over the correspondence relation. Of course, we haven't yet explained how the account of truth falls out of these devices; but if the sentence/state-of-affairs nexus is the central word/world correspondence being sought, it obviates certain quandaries sometimes encountered by investigators. Those problems arise because it is surmised that the relationship between statements or propositions and tokens of states of affairs can't be explained in terms of anything more basic. Consequently, some thinkers seek out familiar analogies for understanding the case at hand. Is correspondence like the relation of a portrait to its subject? Like that of a map to a territory? Or, perhaps, like that of a musical score to a performance? The analogies theorists have thus far hit upon have generally invited spelling out the relationship in terms of correlations between components of the two relata. I have already expressed my doubts about the prospects of this approach: nothing need be added on that score. But, in addition there has been difficulty in cashing in the metaphors and analogies for a straightforward, literal statement. These problems don't arise when we begin simply with a consideration of a sentence and the type of occasion fit for its use. This is a further respect in which the correspondence relation is domesticated by a broadly Austinian approach.

The relation, at this typal level, is considerably less controversial than the correspondence relation thinkers customarily have in mind when considering the way in which true propositions correspond to facts. But once in the archives, no further (nonsupervenient) word-world relation at the statemental or propositional level is needed to complete the theory. Thus far, the only other relations we need are, first, that between a sentence and a statement it is used to make, or, more broadly between the sentence and its fully formed token utterances (typically, but not invariably statements), and, second, that between a typal state of affairs and its token. Neither of these latter two relations hold between a semantically evaluable something and another thing that (normally) isn't. Thus, neither is a correspondence relation of the relevant kind. Both are straightforward and easily apprehensible, and, of equal importance, neither generates the sorts of problems distinctive of doubts about the role of the relation in a correspondence theory. However, putting the point this way may seem to disguise the role of deixis in taking us from sentence to statement. That role must be broadened by considering referential relations more generally, and that, it may be contended, is where the problems lie. The point that now requires emphasis is that no such devices rise to the statement-fact level that prompted the doubts embodied in our questions (A)–(D). To elaborate . . .

8.6 The Referential Component

The range of sentences that can become statements shows that more is required than the fixing of indexicals, demonstratives, tenses, and even some elements of context to go from the former to the latter. We may also need the references of singular, plural, mass, and common nouns. Singular terms include not only pronouns (among our indexicals), but also sobriquets and (definite and some indefinite) descriptions. I mentioned in note 5 that the tradition usually treats similar proper names of distinct individuals as akin to ambiguous expressions, not to distinct specifications of indefinite descriptions or indexicals. Thus, the references of proper names are ordinarily taken as determined at the sentential level. But if we decided to leave them unfixed at this stage, there would be no difficulty in including names among the referential devices just listed. All such devices are needed in order to identify the actual state of affairs relevant to the evaluation of the statement. Consider the proposition that the cat is on the mat. Before evaluation is possible there must be a certain cat and, perhaps, a certain mat in question. The reason the extra references are needed is that evaluating a statement requires more than that we be able to assign it some concrete state of affairs or other. It requires the *relevant* one.

The issue of so-called tropes—in the specialized sense of nonrepeatable instances of properties—needn't detain us. If one holds that token states of affairs contain tropes rather than properties, then it is likely that a and b do not share any property when F*a* and F*b*, though they may possess similar particulars. One way to acknowledge this difference is to construe predicates, relational expressions, and the like as referring expressions. Then we need only expand our class of determiners to include these referring expressions. The details don't affect the general procedure.

Once the work of deixis is taken into account we have all that we need for a determination of truth. The resulting statement is true if the type of state of affairs (the one described by the statement's sentence) has a relevant token, if not it is not true. Relevance is determined as follows. If the candidate for a determining state of affairs is such that it contains individuals (or, put otherwise, individuals can be extrapolated from it), the individuals in question will be the ones referred to by the referring expressions of the sentence when it is stated.

The foregoing doesn't aspire to be a complete theory of reference, and my remarks about it are designed to be compatible with any of the major competing theories (e.g., any shades of causal, historical, or descriptivist theories) in the literature. Insofar as the determination of truth is concerned, reference is performing two tasks. It kicks in only when there is at least one token of the type of state of affairs. (If there are none, the theorist has various options, including reference failure and falsehood.) In those circumstances it does the following. First, it selects the relevant token(s). One possibility is that none of them is relevant. In that case, the statement is not true (viz., is false or truth-valueless). Second, where there is a relevant token, reference is used to individuate (or distinguish) it from among any others that might also obtain.

It should be emphasized that adding reference to what is already in the mixture need not yield a complete set of necessary and sufficient conditions for being a state of affairs or for identifying one. It certainly does not amount to an analysis of that notion. Various schemes for identifying states of affairs have appeared in the literature. For example, what has been called "structural" identity requires that states of affairs are identical only if they have the same constituents with the very same structure (Armstrong 1997, 132). On the other hand, on an "empirical" conception, states of affairs are identical iff it is necessary that one exists just in case the other does. (Fine (1982, 58), who holds the view, refers to states of affairs as "circumstances.") My scattered remarks are intended to be compatible with both of these or any other plausible views currently on offer. The sole job of these remarks is to indicate the way in which one from among a circumscribed set of potential candidates for relevance is selected. It is hoped that this explanation will deter certain unwarranted expectations about the theory. Later I briefly take up questions concerning the conditions of identification for states of affairs. Certain questions about them have led to complications, and even to paradox. But other of these details depend on adopting one or another conception of such states, and needn't be decided by a theory of truth as such. However these questions get settled, if states of affairs of any kind are allowed our theory is complete even if the list of conditions given thus far for determining the proper token state of affairs is not. On the assumption of further conditions being met, the referential and deictic devices will suffice to differentiate the relevant state of affairs from other (irrelevant) tokens of the same type.

When raising a question about the truth of a statement, we need, then, only to answer two questions. First, "Is there a token of the type of state of affairs correlated with its sentence?" If the answer is "yes," we need then ask "Is the token the right one, as determined by the references made in the statement plus the context?" Nothing more is needed to assign a definite truth-value.

Thus, reference and deixis are used (to coin a few handy barbarisms) in the first instance to get to a statement and thereby *particularize* a state of affairs, and in the second to *relevantize* that state of affairs. Once the usual referential relationships of subsentential elements have completed their work there is no call for an additional relation of correspondence. That is the extent of the contribution of demonstration (or demonstrative conventions) to truth. If we wish, we may continue to speak of correspondence at this concrete level between a statement and a token state of affairs. But the preceding explanation makes clear that we cannot read much into this. That relation is no longer a working part of the machinery. Moreover, because this relation supervenes on the ingredients and relations already in play, any lingering mystery about it should dissipate.

Although thought-*cum*-world or word-*cum*-world relations of any kind may be found objectionable in certain circles, none of those invoked here are the distinctive brand of statement-to-world relations that some critics have taken to bedevil the correspondence theory. Global objections to referential relations may take their inspiration from a prior antirealist disparagement of any such explanations (or relations). However, the sort of objectors now in our sites—and in fact many of them are metaphysical realists—aren't relying on this general outlook with regard to reference to fuel their doubts. Rather, their objections take off from the difficulty of appropriately describing correspondence, or even from extending well-understood referential devices to whole sentences/propositions. We still require tokens of states of affairs as truthmakers, but not as referents of statements (Forbes 1986, 42). Thus, questions of the relevant kind of correspondence between statements and token states of affairs needn't arise because the devices that make the latter truthmakers all operate elsewhere. On the other hand, if one wants to consider the descriptive connection as the relevant sort of correspondence, then the failures of previous theories can be explained by their having looked in the wrong place. We needn't scrutinize the statement and the world to compare them for fit. As I mentioned earlier, a belief in roughly that procedure has led past thinkers to grope for analogies to portraits, maps, and musical scores in an attempt to understand correspondence. But the engine of correspondence on this account does its work elsewhere. We must look at the relation between sentences and statements on the one hand, between types of states of affairs and their tokens on the other, and (to get at the only other working word-world correspondences) differences between sentences rendering them employable for one sort of occasion rather than another.

If one favors ontologies of states of affairs, acknowledging many complex types can be avoided, as before, by understanding them via truth-functions. One can, though one needn't, refuse to countenance negative, disjunctive, or (truth-functionally) conditional types of states of affairs, just as Russell saw no need for molecular facts as distinct from molecular propositions. Of course, this will take some showing. But if it can be brought off, molecular (compound) propositions will not need molecular facts if the former are made true (false) by the truthmakers (their absence) for their constituent atomic propositions.[8] "Provided we can account for the truth and falsehood of atomic sentences, we can dispense with special truthmakers for, e.g.,

---

8. At one time Russell (1985) tentatively accepted negative facts and required at least one general fact. These issues are still mooted under the topic of truthmaker theory. However, the present scheme avoids those questions of detail, at least regarding truth, by deciding those issues at the level of types of sentences and states of affairs. For example, with respect to negation we need consider only the type being negated by the sentence. If the negated part lacks a token, the negated token statement is true, otherwise false.

negative, conjunctive, disjunctive, and identity sentences" (Mulligan et al. 1984, 280). One advantage of this position is that it would stop before it got started a *reductio* designed to show that there could be only one truthmaker for all truths (see, e.g., Restall 1996.) (I am not suggesting that this is the only way to avoid the *reductio*—see, e.g., S. Read 2000.)

To summarize: Three types of connection do the indispensable work of this account. First, there are relations between sentences (or, as we might call them, abstracted propositions) and types of states of affairs; next, there are those between sentences and statements; and finally there are those between typal states of affairs and their tokens. Going from sentences to statements is mediated by referential and deictic elements. We might illustrate the result as in figure 8.1. However, the story remains incomplete. Suppose more than one token of that type state of affairs obtains. Then we must employ the referential, deictic, and perhaps contextual elements to choose among the candidates for the relevant token. Normally, this will be an easy matter. When a parent scolds a child for not finishing his dinner, it is usually clear that it is tonight's dinner, not last Wednesday's, that determines whether what the parent said is true. This gap in figure 8.1 is the only place for something like demonstration to play a role, and it doesn't require anything like the whole statement (or its sentence) referring. While these devices help explain how a statement gets constructed and how only one among a potentially many tokens of states of affairs can be a candidate, they are not the sorts of relations between complexes that are at the surface of a theory of truth. Rather, they are the common referring expressions studied in the philosophy of language.

```
SENTENCE ———— Description ————▶ TYPAL STATE OF AFFAIRS
   │                                        │
Supplying values                            │
for indices                                 │
   │                                        │
   ▼                                        ▼
STATEMENT ┤------ Demonstration? ------┤ TOKEN STATES OF AFFAIRS
```

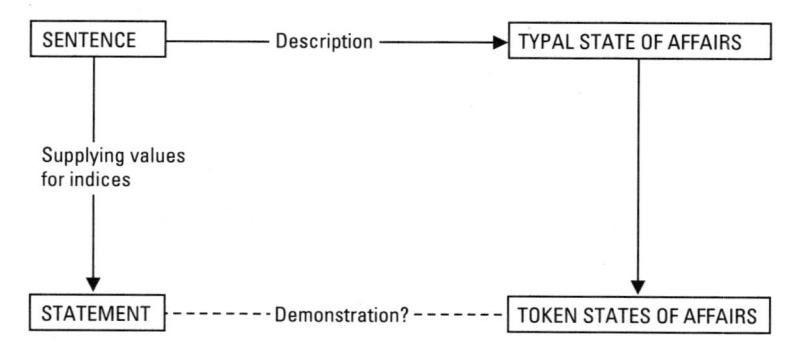

Figure 8.1

The remainder of the theory then falls out smoothly as follows: Given a token of a sentence S (say, an utterance, a statement, or a proposition P), P is true when a certain state of affairs obtains. Which state of affairs? The one whose type is described by the sentence used in making the statement. Where it is possible for more than one token of that type to obtain (viz., when the statement is not made with an eternal sentence), the relevant one for P's evaluation is individuated by deixis and/or referential elements (plus context).

A greatly simplified example will illustrate how this works. Suppose we have a statement made with the sentence "He's a goatherd." Let us say (again for simplicity) that the sentence describes the type of state of affairs *male being a goatherd*. Ignoring issues arising from vagueness and penumbral cases, here is a compendium of the conditions under which the statement in question will not be true.

(i)   There are no tokens of that type (nothing is a goatherd).

(ii) There are goatherds, but none is male.

(iii) 'He', as used in the statement made with our sentence, fails to refer.

(iv) There is one male goatherd, but 'he', as used in the statement, refers to something other than that individual.

(v)   There are multiple tokens of that state of affairs, but 'he', as used in the statement, refers to something other than any of the individuals in those tokens.

Now, (v) is the normally expected case, (iii) the most interesting one. (iii) is the case, again barring considerations of vagueness, for which some are tempted to say that the statement (or "sentence as used") is not even false (= is truth-valueless). But those issues concerning reference-failure do not directly involve Correspondence. However, one decides the question of the conditions under which a putative reference fails to occur, one need not invoke relations (in particular demonstrative conventions) that are brought in only to support a truth theory.

8.7   Revisiting Questions (A)–(D)

We are now prepared to return to the questions posed in section 8.2.

Question (A), the concern about correlating constituents of truthbearers and truthmakers, has been eliminated by opting for congruity over correlation.

Question (B) raised the prospect that a distinct state of affairs had to correspond to a false proposition. It should be clear that no state of affairs other than a token of the type associated with the sentence whose statement is false is needed to account for falsity. The mere absence of a certain relevant particular state of affairs will falsify a proposition just as its presence will confirm it. The befuddlement the query seems to create may rely on the assumption that the basis of correspondence is a relation whose relata occur at the level at which the statement (or proposition) confronts concrete reality. But the prior relation emphasized in the present account shows how it is sufficient for a proposition's falsity (or lack of a truth-value) that the state of affairs selected by its sentence not be (relevantly) tokened. This doesn't rule out other grounds one may have for non-obtaining facts, but they aren't necessary for a correspondence theory of truth as such.

Turning to question (C), we need only observe that the theory doesn't require whole propositions to refer on the model of singular terms. The present view generates no perplexities about what it is that false propositions correspond to. Of course, there are correlations (in a sense other than Pitcher's) between statements and token states of affairs making them true, but those relationships fall out from prior relations to sentences and typal states of affairs, respectively. Any relation at the typal level derives from the simple fact that a given sentence is usable for saying only certain things. Are either of these naming-like relations? That will depend on how fine-grained one's choice of relational taxonomy is. If all such correlations are assimilated to the referential relationship, we will be nudged to concede that sentences and/or statements are kinds of names. And then the long-standing problems about this and about facts being nameables will ensue. However, it appears that the proposal before us has explained these relationships in a way that is both compelling and that needn't tempt us to assimilate them to the relation of a name (that is, a referring expression) to a nominatum (that is, a referent). It is well to bear in mind that any two *things*, be they events, properties, or whatever, can be correlated on some basis or other. Neither term in such a correlation need even be a linguistic expression or its thought counterpart. For example, one might be a guard, the other a prisoner. It would be overreaching to regard all the correlations in this group as a naming relation just because they correlate two things. Why, then, should there be any compulsion to do so just because one of the terms in the comparison is a linguistic expression? *A fortiori*, one will require further justification before supposing the type and token correlatives in this proposal are kinds of name-nominata relations. And this will be needed before we regard the present scheme as involving the various problems and serious questions that the extension of reference to whole utterances is supposed to introduce.

What of question (D)—that is, the fact that, as McGinn puts it, ⟨p⟩ corresponds, say, to both *p* and not-*p*? We seem able to get around this only by opting for the fact that *p* because it is the one that makes the proposition true, thereby revealing "the air of triviality that surrounds the correspondence theory" (McGinn 2000, 91).[9] Frege (1999, 87) makes a similar point in terms of circularity. We can lay it down that "truth exists when there is correspondence in a certain respect.... But in which?" Eventually we would find that we were reduced to specifying the respect in terms of the connection being true, and "the game could begin again."

This difficulty doesn't arise on the present version. The only correlations we have had to take into account are those that (a) a sentence has to the type of state it is used to affirm, that which makes it employable for saying one thing rather than another, (b) subsentential referential and deictic relations, and (c) the type-token relation between that type of state of affairs and its instantiations. (c) should be wholly uncontroversial and not threaten circularity. (b) is generally acknowledged by students of language. Just as important, such relations are quite independent of a theory of truth, even if the theory of truth (and in particular this one) is not independent of them. This asymmetric independence assures us that (b) too doesn't threaten circularity. (a) is perhaps less familiar as an explicit topic in the literature. However, this is accounted for by the fact that it is an irrefutable datum of language use, indeed a starting point, that is simply taken for granted. Nor by itself does it threaten circularity.

The question left about a correspondence relation, then, is whether it too is vulnerable to the surfeit of candidate facts in the conundrum posed by

---

9. In a note attached to this passage, McGinn remarks that he isn't trying to dismiss all forms of correspondence theory by these arguments, and explicitly exempts a form which in general outline resembles the one on offer here. This is noteworthy because his view, thick disquotationalism, although clearly an inflationist form of realism, is certainly a noncorrespondence view. But he offers no other grounds for ruling out the correspondence options he admits that he has not opposed.

McGinn. To suppose that it is, we must overlook, (a), the pedestrian fact that certain forms of speech are appropriate only to certain types of circumstance in lieu of explicit redefinition or stipulation. For that relation assures us that we need be mindful only of tokens of a restricted type. If we denote a typal state of affairs by W, and its tokens by $w_1, w_2, \ldots, w_n$, then let us imagine that statement S is evaluated, say, by w_5. McGinn's point is that S is also related to worldly circumstance not-w_5, as a statement is to its denial. But not-w_5 is not a token of W, and thus lacks any claim to consideration. The many potential correlates of S we can conjure for one or another purpose are beside the point. What matters are only the preexisting relationships in (a), (b), and (c). If we then choose to declare that S corresponds to w_5 in virtue of those relationships, there is no harm, but also little gain, in admitting a type of correspondence, supervenient on our earlier relations, between its statement and token fact (or state of affairs). No relevant puzzlement attaches to (a), (b), and (c), and this addition does nothing to change that.

If one wanted a compact statement of the view developed thus far, the following should suffice:

(V) A statement Σ is true *if and only if* there is a sentence, S, tied descriptively to a type of state of affairs (henceforth SOA) such that
(1) Σ is made with S.
(2) There is a concrete SOA tokening that type to which S is descriptively tied.
(3) The token in (2) is relevant in the context.

Notice that there is no mention of a demonstration (much less demonstrative conventions) in (V). *Relevance*, as we have seen, doesn't smuggle in this relation, but it is determined (if determination is required) by context. Context does this through selecting certain individuals, times, locations, etc. as referents of the singular terms and tenses in the sentences.

We could extend the formula to thought content. One way might be to use the notion of a mental sentence, a sentence in the language of thought. But in the past that notion has not introduced the distinction of levels needed for the machinery of (V). It will be altogether simpler to redeploy our notion of a proposition to cover both thought and linguistic content. But some adjustment is still needed because a proposition too is a fully determined utterance or thought content, akin to a statement, though without the implication that it is or may be stated. So what we lack is the notion of a proposition deprived of all its determinations other than those carried by the thought-equivalents of its proper names. Call that an 'abstracted proposition'. We might then easily rework our formula for a proposition being true as follows:

(∀P) A proposition Φ is true *if and only if* there is an abstracted proposition P, tied descriptively to a type of SOA such that
(1) Φ is a determination of P.
(2) There is a concrete SOA tokening that type to which P is descriptively tied.
(3) The token in (2) is relevant in the context.

And if desired the formula may be qualified to cover what was called in section 2.3 "extended correspondence." There it was suggested that fully fixed propositions of a type such that there were no tokens of that type SOA to which they could be related might still be considered truth bearers by virtue of a relation they bear to propositions which meet the foregoing definition. As such they would be secondary or dependent cases. But their truth-aptness will still be explained ultimately in terms of the correspondence relation in primary cases. This can be achieved by adding a fourth, disjunctive, condition. Affirmations of canonical sentences of mathematics, scientific theory, and ethics, explored again briefly in the next chapter, have been cited as possible candidates. How we decide such cases goes beyond any interest we might have in the basic articles of correspondence.

One further qualification. On (∀) and (∀P), SOAs are necessary conditions for the truth of statements and propositions, respectively. Earlier, I maintained that there is no more reason to suppose we need one kind of truthmaker for all propositions than that we need one kind of referent for all instances of reference. That warning hasn't expired. We can make it consistent with these two formulas in either of two ways. First, we might regard 'state of affairs' merely as a not-too-clumsy cover term (like the terms 'truthmaker' and 'referent') for the broad miscellany of things that make our bearers true. Second, we could retain a more specific understanding of SOAs, but modify the formula to remove the 'only if' clause (the necessary condition for truth). Even with the latter, the formulas would say enough to illuminate the character of truth in a philosophically exciting way. Either option suits me.

8.8 Back to Brief Formulations

Detailed accounts are always preferable, *ceteris paribus*, to sketchy ones. But other than the fact that the theory of this chapter shows that further work is possible, there is really no reason to suppose it is any more defensible than the epigrammatic correspondence summaries examined earlier. Indeed, nothing in these details even so much as indicates that the details couldn't with equal plausibility be developed in a different direction (say, in a system that started from correspondence as correlation). The basic polemical work of defending the correspondence is accomplished in the earlier intuitions on which the epigrammatic formulations were based, and in replying to the various objections raised along the way.

Nevertheless, the foregoing fleshed out account also indicates, if only indirectly, why correspondentists are entitled to stand by the epigrammatic summaries of the view which have guided me through much of this work. Because a relation of correspondence at the level of demonstration is not required, it takes the sting out of the widespread assumption that the summaries lack an essential element. Why such perplexities are thought to arise in the first place is a matter for some speculation. I cannot be altogether certain about what is responsible for that sort of mindset: but because I am accounting for something that has been shown to miscarry (chapter 4), educated guesses may be in order. Here is one.

Let us return again to the Tractarian project. Whether in the end Wittgenstein actually subscribed to the outcome is not at issue. What does matter is that he appears to have assumed, along with a host of others, the following as requirements for completing the project. For one thing, it is assumed that correspondence is brought off by an isomorphism between sentential and factive ingredients (viz., correspondence-as-correlation). We sidestepped that view's difficulties by adopting correspondence-as-congruity as the preferred notion. Nowadays it is generally, though not universally, conceded that we aren't likely to find such isomorphisms, and even opponents of correspondence often don't require it. But while it may seem that by dropping the isomorphism requirement the demands on correspondence have been considerably relaxed, another assumption from the original project, now in the form of unstated desideratum, appears to have survived. For example, at least for some, it is supposed that a correspondence theory must fall out as a consequence of a general theory of sentence meaning, or of a broader semantic enterprise. I can imagine no better reason than this why it is sometimes expected without much argument that correspondentists as such are obliged to resolve problems posed simply for truth-conditional theories of meaning. In this connection, recall that Wittgenstein's version is introduced via the picture theory of meaning. That probably overstates the underlying assumption. Few would acknowledge it in such stark terms. (An exception is Dummett (2003, 21).) The concepts of truth and meaning "must be explained *together*: neither can be taken as given in advance of the other, so that the other can be explained in terms of it.") Of course, it is not hard to find historical reasons for this approach. We needn't delve deeper into them because none holds out a prospect for showing that we cannot offer correspondence as an answer to what makes a proposition true until we have first been given a semantic theory for distinguishing one proposition from another. However the assumption of a combined theory came about, it has fostered expectations that are still in place in various critical circles. Let's trace the implications of that assumption a bit further.

On the assumption's most naive version, if assertive sentences required that their worldly affiliates be settled by virtue of the meanings of those sentences, then only true statements would be meaningful, or, what comes to much the same thing, all statements, including those commonly considered false, would turn out to be true after all. If that weren't enough, the truth of even contingent propositions would be settled by meaning (or content) alone. This industrial-strength truth-conditional semantics isn't at all plausible, and no flesh-and-blood theorist holds it. It is not intended as a serious objection to truth-conditional semantics, but only as a way to illustrate an obvious pitfall theorists are aware of the need to avoid in the design of their theories. Of course, the meanings of sentences (or abstracted propositions) may have a role to play in the identification of those state of affairs relevant to the truth or falsehood of its statements. This is the level at which issues over truth-conditional semantic theories are properly debated. Even if that view is not ultimately accepted, it is not the naive one with which we began. But the conditions determined by such a theory, if any, will be very much like those I have argued attach to sentences—namely, types, not their tokens that determine truth. So too, this sensible semantics is not a candidate for yielding the combined theory of meaning and truth that the assumption under review demanded.

We may, thus, deem this second assumption an overstatement. Still, the view that the semantics of assertoric utterances (including both meaning and truth) form a seamless whole still plays a role, though perhaps only as an unarticulated expectation that we should be able to generate in a systematic and wholly general way the concrete state of affairs that corresponds to any proposition. What is wanted is a method, by which we can tell without *ad hoc* devices, which concrete state of affairs goes with which proposition or statement. This condition, too, is impossible to fulfill, although I strongly suspect it has been one of the inducements for critical puzzlement over how there could be such a relation as correspondence. Why else would some opponents believe that the question "What do false assertions correspond to?" poses a mortal challenge for correspondentists? States of affairs account for the truth of propositions. Why, if this isn't generated by a systematic theory of meaning, should we think there must be a mirror-image relation for false propositions?

It may seem to some unfair to put the blame on earlier exploded expectations for theories of meaning. Well, as I explained, this is merely a speculation. But it does seem to account for certain prominent wayward demands made of correspondence theories. If the model had been *reference* rather than *sense*, such an expectations might never have arisen. For although it is possible to regard instances of proper names, and even some definite descriptions, as having their referents determined by the token expressions themselves, a host of referring expressions—including all indefinite descriptions, indexicals, and demonstratives—can be employed multiply for different referents. They disclose some information about their prospective referents, just as do types of non-eternal sentences for a corresponding state of affairs, but not enough to be able to pinpoint the exact location (in time or space) of the referent. Of course, there is something of a generable relation for compound, truth-functional, assertions. Their relevant states of affairs may be nothing more than those of their components. But this no more demands that we generate relevant (token) states of affairs for noncompound, or nontruth-functional, assertions than that we do so for the referents of indexicals.

If we may provisionally put to one side questions about truthmakers (addressed in the next chapter), with questions (A)–(D) dispatched, and no longer being in the throes of the demand that there must be a systematic device for producing correspondents, it is hard to find further grounds for declaring that brief summaries of correspondence (such as those used and mentioned in earlier chapters) fail to achieve their intended aims. Moreover, the brief statements usefully summarize a host of possibilities for other specifications; for, as we observed, there is a variety of different versions of correspondence, from restricted to extended ones. And although I have claimed that a perfectly defensible variety of correspondence has been presented in this chapter, nothing I have stated thus far rules out divergent, yet unmentioned, developments of the correspondence idea. Other versions might be equally successful in handling questions (A)–(D), and on my estimate both of the compelling intuitions driving correspondence and of the overall strength of the chief objections to it, it would not surprise me if additional forms of the doctrine were equally defensible.

Let us then turn our attention the other side of the attack on correspondence: the case against truthmakers.

9 ... to the World

9.1 The Challenges and Considerations of Constitution

Questions (A)–(D), addressed in chapter 8, concerned the correspondence relation. Another set of critical challenges fixes upon specifications of worldly circumstances. This chapter is devoted to those and to several related matters that appear to have contributed to the bill of indictment against the correspondence project.

One central issue involving truthmakers was handled in section 3.1:

(E) How can the so-called worldly correlates, such as facts, be more than propositions themselves, quasi-linguistic shadows cast by statements?

There I argued that the purported evidence produced to show that facts are nothing more than truths can't withstand closer inspection. The conclusion doesn't follow, and the inference has a false premise to boot. If that was the main reason for dismissing facts, it is even less of a reason for disposing of other kinds of worldly circumstance, such as states of affairs (SOAs), where there is not even an appearance of a convergence with formulations of true statements.

However, other concerns have been raised about the worldly side of this relationship. They forebode serious problems for states of affairs and the like. Here is a short list of questions that encapsulate the concerns I have in mind:

(F) If we lack clear ideas about identifying, re-identifying, and individuating particular SOAs, can we employ them in a theory of truth?

(G) Does Correspondence require worldly situations for all candidates for truth bearer, including counterfactuals, scientific theories, and categorical statements in mathematics or ethics, no matter how controversial?

(H) Doesn't a certain form of *reductio*, the Slingshot, demonstrate that there can be no more than a single state of affairs to which all true propositions must then correspond?

The bulk of this chapter is devoted to replying to these objections and to a few other points that don't strictly fall under the interdiction against states of affairs. However, before examining the objections directly, we should attend to what many consider a more bedrock concern: Even if the earlier objections to facts didn't prove fatal, aren't they, SOAs, or any other truthmaker we can think of, queer, gratuitous additions to anyone's cosmic inventory? Why bother with them?

The last chapter contained what I believe to be an adequate reply: We discriminate sentences (at least when we are using them) by their capacity for latching onto one sort of potential information about the world rather than some other sort. Those abstract circumstances to which our sentences cleave are what I have been calling 'state of affairs' types. This is so solid a datum—indeed, a triviality—that I have taken it to be beyond serious question. It is perfectly neutral with respect to a variety of philosophical treatments, including different proposals for analysis and conflicting views about their ontological status ranging from Platonism to nominalism. And if we have acknowledged the types, there is little basis for withholding the possibility that they have tokens. By this route we arrive at truthmakers.

However, in addition to that inducement, there is another powerful consideration worth bearing in mind, one that may have influenced the prominence Wittgenstein accorded facts in the *Tractatus*. Some non-actual but possible world—call it 'w'—could have all the same individuals and exemplify the same properties as the actual world (= @). For example, imagine these worlds identical save in the following respect: in @ a particular shirt is a shade of green (say, green 238) and a particular car is a shade of red (say, red 96), while in w that shirt is red 96 and the car is green 238. (For simplicity, I ignore counterpart theory and property tropes (Russell's unit properties) whose identity depends in part on that of their possessors. Such wrinkles would complicate the example, but the point could be re-expressed, albeit more baroquely, taking them into account.) How are we to distinguish @ from w? The point of the example is that we can't do this by citing differences of individuals and properties alone: *ex hypothesi* there are none. It seems we must mention some combinations, such as *the shirt having such-and-such a property* in @ but not in *w*. These are precisely the sorts of combinations cited as SOAs and truthmakers.

None of this implies that we need states of affairs as a basic ontological category. In fact, depending on how one chooses to carry out one's inquiry, it doesn't imply that they figure in one's eventual ontology at all: we have not foreclosed on the possibility of further analysis. And, even if we decide there are no such further analyses, this doesn't imply that states of affairs are a more fundamental, or even as fundamental, an ontological category as individuals and/or properties. The most that has been maintained is that appealing to them is indispensable for certain legitimate purposes.

Dodd (2001–2002, 82) replies: ". . . it does not follow from a recognition that objects have properties that there are entities which are objects-having-properties. To put it another way, an acceptance that the things in the world are arranged in certain ways does not entail that there are such entities as arrangements. . . . [W]e have still not come across a good reason for reifying how things are." I am uncertain what to make of this response. Dodd rejects the Wittgensteinian reasoning, but, so far as I can detect, simply tells us that we don't need such a device without explaining *why* we don't need it. It is not that he must be wrong in thinking that the original argument carries a heavy-duty ontological commitment. It may do so, although this too, for reasons in the preceding paragraph, hasn't been demonstrated. And, given that this is the whole of Dodd's immediate printed response to the Tractarian argument, I do not see how we can even begin to speculate about whatever further reasons he might have for his judgment. Thus, we are still left with a decisive reason for the indispensability of appealing to the combinations in question (and with whatever weight one accords that) if we are to distinguish @ from *w*. That is all that is needed in order to show that a picture of the world made up only of particulars and/or exemplifications of their properties (the *how* of the world rather than the *what*) is insufficient for this particular task.

However, we aren't yet out of the woods. For if states of affairs are the truly independent notions we want, we must be able to make their relation to statements and propositions intelligible. And it may be claimed that we have yet to do this. I use Austin once more, but this time to explain how we get ourselves into difficulty. He has claimed that "when a statement is true, there is, of course, a state of affairs which makes it true" (1961, 91). This simply restates a point I made in section 2.3 (item 6): that a worldly circumstance is constitutive of the truth of a proposition. A clear implication of that seems to be that the presence of the truthmaker *necessitates* the truth of the statement. Call that *the truthmaker principle*. (Others have called this *the truthmaker axiom*.) Critics have claimed that there is no suitable form of necessity to elucidate the relationship properly.

The first move (repeating a point from chapter 2) is to notice that the relationship isn't causal. A state of affairs doesn't make a proposition true in the way that an impact dents a car's fender. From this it may be concluded that the necessitation we are in search of cannot be physical necessity. The idea behind this seems to be that causal relations are the only sort that could engender physical necessity. Physical laws cover only causal relations. I agree that the necessity here needn't be physical, but to infer on that basis that physical necessity is ruled out is moving too swiftly. That is not an altogether minor point. For it seems that in at least some instances it is concluded from the fact that the necessity isn't physical that it can only be *logical*. But this too is premature. I will claim at the end of the day that the necessity is *metaphysical*, which (depending on further suppositions) may or may not be the same as physical necessity. The dismissal of physical necessity once we have determined to our satisfaction that the relationship is noncausal may have played some role in overlooking the metaphysical option.

Let me begin by examining why it is at a minimum misleading to characterize the relationship in the truthmaker principle as logical. If we did so characterize it, then, in concert with the reading of necessitation as logical, it is plausible to attempt to precisify the truthmaker principle as follows:

(TM) If ⟨p⟩ is true, there must be at least one thing whose existence entails that ⟨p⟩ is true.

This is how Dodd and members of the Australian school (including honorary members such as David Lewis) construe the revised principle, and it is the sort of revision that first comes to mind. Once done, Dodd writes, quite naturally: ". . . it would be wrong to interpret [(TM)] as saying that entity α entails a truth. The claim, rather, is that ⟨α exists⟩ entails ⟨⟨p⟩ is true⟩" (2001–2002, 71n). It is easy to see that that immediately destroys the intended import of the truthmaker principle. We sought a relation between a proposition and something not essentially propositionlike which made it true: what we have arrived at is an entailment relation between two propositions. It is not uncommon, at least in conversation, to hear those driven to (TM) to proclaim that this is all that finally remains of the truthmaker principle.

Whatever else may be said for entailment, it can't capture the constituting relation. Here is a quick proof of that: "That any omniscient being knows that p"(once more) entails in the very way defenders of (TM) intend "that p is true." But, a tiny sample of very outré contents aside, the former isn't a remotely plausible candidate for what constitutes p's truth. This shows that entailment is unhelpful in spelling out the relation between a truth and its truthmaker. We can try to give it a role by thinking up restrictions; however, in lieu of concrete suggestions, it looks as if any promising candidate one can think of would replace rather than merely supplement the relevant entailment as truthmaker. Nevertheless, once we settle upon logical possibility, the reading of the relation as one subsisting between propositions seems compelling.

It is part of our philosophical heritage to understand logical relations, and therefore noncausal necessitation, as obtaining only between semantically evaluable items. Thus, someone who wants to preserve a general, noncausal necessitation relation between a semantically evaluable item and something that isn't semantically evaluable faces a serious challenge to explain what that could be without violating the precepts of logic. The relations will have to be construed as entailment, consistency, or inconsistency; and how can, say, an entailment relation have something nonpropositional (viz., neither a sentence nor an open sentence) as one of its relata? This puts the essentialist, nowadays the leading proponent of a distinctive metaphysical necessity, at a disadvantage. Either explain the relation between something—in this case the relational property of being true—and its essence via accepted methods of entailment or risk a nonsense claim. Let me approach that issue indirectly by trying to explicate more clearly the sort of necessitation introduced by what I have been calling constitution.

I begin with a (relatively) simple case of constitution that is also, unlike the situation of truthmakers, one of composition. Take a teacup, strike it on a hard surface so that it shatters to pieces. We can see that those pieces (including the microscopic ones) at one time constituted the cup. This is not to say that they did do so by themselves. We must also take into account their former spatial relations, the original intention of the maker of the cup to fashion a teacup—it wouldn't be a teacup, whatever its shape, if it was intended, say, as a home for a mouse—and perhaps other factors omitted here. But the relation all those factors have, when brought together, is to *constitute* the cup. Here is an explication of the sense in which those pieces, etc. necessitate the cup. Call the collection of possible worlds in which the cup (or its counterpart) exists the A worlds, that in which the parts, structural relations, the intention of the maker, etc. (or, their counterparts) exist the B worlds. This combination necessitates the cup *if* every B world is an A world. I avoid "only if" so as not to rule out our having the same cup with a few different parts or modifications.

This may be regarded as metaphysical necessity because the point of it is to say something modal (though not everything that could be said) about the cup's identity. One can regard metaphysical necessity as collapsing into physical necessity if one believes that such relations hold only for worlds with @'s physical laws. In either case, the point of the illustration is that neither term of the necessitation is semantically evaluable. Thus, we have before us a perfectly good sense of noncausal necessitation that can be made clear without propositions. Of course, one could reply that this is all shorthand for ⟨parts a, b, c. etc. are in structural relations y, and devised for purpose w by z⟩ entails ⟨cup x exists⟩; that is, shorthand for relations between those two propositions. But to claim that we must construe the case that way would be a hard slog. I don't see how it improves our understanding of the situation one iota. There may be a tendency among those who devise a modal semantics to construe propositions as sets of possible worlds. In turn, we can then conceive of possible worlds as collections of propositions. This is, no doubt, often a convenience, and it may serve to relieve part of the mystery surrounding the appeal to possible worlds. But consider once again the actual world, which is, of course, a possible world. I maintain, with I believe the great majority of others, that the actual world is more than a collection of propositions. If so, what need is there to regard possible nonactual worlds as collections of propositions? Although this conception is undoubtedly convenient for some purposes, what compels us to make it imperative? Indeed, once a notion of a possible world that may be other than a group of propositions is at hand, it is not even required to have propositions for entailment. For we can now say that for all logically possible worlds containing A and logically possible worlds containing B, B entails A if every B world is an A world.[1]

1. Again, for simplicity, I am ignoring differences between modal systems, accessibility relations, etc.

This leads us somewhat circuitously back to our topic. A truthmaker constitutes the truth of its proposition, thereby necessitating that proposition's truth. This means that the proposition will be true in every world in which that truthmaker obtains. Of course, the case is more complicated than the teacup example for more than one reason. Here are some reasons why we must take the greatest care in our description of it.

First, one of the terms in this relation—the proposition which is made true—*is* semantically evaluable. Nevertheless, the truthmaker is not semantically evaluable, or at least need not be. For present purposes it is helpful (as security against being misled) to ignore the fact that the propositional term is semantically evaluable. As I have indicated, that threatens to lead us to infer that there must be a logical relationship (entailment) in the offing. Thus, we can see how the relation can be one of necessitation—metaphysical necessity—without one proposition entailing another.

Second, one may have doubts about whether propositions must exist in every possible world in which its truthmakers do. It is not easy to picture a situation in which there is a possible world without a certain (counterpart of a) proposition (not necessarily a held one). But if one can find such a world, we can say that the proposition would be true in that world if it existed. We are more interested here in what the appropriate valuation of a proposition would be in various circumstances than we are in the ontology of propositions as such. Perhaps it will help to think of the matter as follows. It is not the proposition itself that the truthmaker is supposed to constitute, but only a property of it—that is, its truth. Where the constituter (in this case the truthmaker) is constituting a property of another thing (in the present case, the proposition) this will depend on the other thing, whose truth is being constituted, being present in the first place. Were it possible for the proposition not to be present independent of that constituting factor, the factor would not be activated as a constituter of its property in those circumstances.

Finally, I am not saying that the analogy holds in every respect. The parts *compose* the cup as well as contributing to constituting it, and it is not easy to see that it is even intelligible to imagine what it would be like for a truthmaker to compose the truth of a proposition. (Of course, metaphorical extensions are always available.) But then the analogy was only supposed to illustrate constitution, not composition.

Thus, we arrive at a truthmaker for which there is perfectly good sense to be made of its necessitating its proposition's truth. Perhaps whenever this relation holds, correlated with it is an entailment between the true proposition and a propositional correlate of the truthmaker. My only claim is that it is not this entailment that accounts for the constituting (for reasons given earlier about the impotency of entailment to bring this off), but the metaphysical relation we have just discussed. On the other hand, if one still wants to insist on a logical modality, one can introduce a modified notion in which an entailment can hold between items other than propositions. That seems to me desperate, but, in any event, it also dilutes the force of the claim that the necessity is logical. Overall, I believe it is best simply to admit that we have here an instance of metaphysical necessity, which (for all that has been said) may or may not be a form of physical necessity. It is necessitation, not entailment, that is driving us to make sense of this relationship, and there is no need to confuse the two notions. We hit upon entailment only as a default, after a failure to understand the relationship in terms of causal laws. But clarity on the issue makes it advisable to expand the narrow menu of options that produces that disjunctive syllogism (i.e., either/or argument).

Let us then proceed to examine issues about SOAs raised by questions (F)–(H).

9.2 Token States of Affairs

I begin with (F), which I shall deal with in parts. A preliminary answer is offered here, and other facets of the issue are addressed in section 9.5.

In treating McGinn's conundrum in section 8.6, I commented on the individuation of SOAs. I claimed that we didn't need a more robust theory of worldly circumstances (or SOAs) than was necessary for the relation of a (type) sentence to its type SOA. Further difficulties may be dealt with as they arise, without necessitating a systematic, complete treatment of these conditions. For the present I hope the following brief observations suffice.

Our standards for truth are, as mentioned, context-dependent. It is true that Iowa is flat for most geographical purposes, not so for those of planar geometry. This has been emphasized by Austin (1962, 142), Lewis (1983), and is at least implicit in Wittgenstein (1969, §§205–206). We can expect our identification and individuation of SOAs to be as rough-and-ready as our standards for truth. The world needn't be inherently vague, but we will be no more scrupulous in our methods for classifying reality than our need for focusing on those aspects that serve daily needs to communicate. Consequently, no very precise carving of reality at the joints, as useful as that may be for other endeavors, is likely to reflect faithfully, or capture the detail of, our humdrum practice of matching world to words. And our present task is just to explicate an intelligible current practice. Moreover, there will be much indeterminacy. We expect it with counterfactuals, but it will infect, if not so extensively, even relatively uncontroversial areas of discourse (McGee 1993). However one decides individual cases, the leading question will be "How far do we extend the model of a type of SOA, first framed for paradigms such as *dinner being served*?" Our inclination to extend it to other classes of utterance will covary rather snugly with our inclination to assign truth-values to utterances in those classes. Thus, the paradigm can serve as a touchstone. That we can carve up the world in a variety of ways doesn't in the least show that in choosing one of them from among other eligible candidates we are carving up something other than the world.

This doesn't resolve every problem about identity for which we are responsible. For example, if specifications of SOAs are extensional, SOAs that are not, at least on the surface, tokens of the relevant type will regularly be relevant truthmakers. Shouldn't that be a problem for the foregoing account? I defer a more detailed answer to section 9.5. For the present I will satisfy myself with stating, with regrettable dogmatism, only that this holds no prospect for conflicting truth evaluations of a single proposition, and that the proposal on offer provides an explanation for such extensional coincidence.

9.3 The Reach of Worldly States

Turning to (G), what is the scope of worldly circumstances? We have encountered this problem before. Do ethical or mathematical sentences describe types of ethical and mathematical states of affairs? What of counterfactuals? Or of the general principles and laws of theories? Contrary to the usual assessment, I believe the difficulties such questions pose do not detract from correspondence in its competition with other views, especially deflationism. Rather they are, at worst, problems which all competitors share, and (on my assessment of the relative seriousness of different ways the problems emerge) may, contrary to usual opinion, highlight correspondence's ability to handle the ramified issues. No doubt, this warrants explanation. I begin by outlining the ways in which deflationists can cope with such questions.

As I noted in section 3.2, typical deflationary theories are syntacticist. That is, they use minimal syntactic criteria—such as permitting negation, and embedding in conditionals and propositional attitudes, plus (perhaps) that the discourse be disciplined—for truth eligibility. This isn't happenstance: it is impelled by the nature of the position. If deflationists had to be more selective about which among utterances meeting these criteria are truth-apt, they would be pushed in a direction that could very well force them to accept substantive truth conditions. How else are they to draw the distinction between truth-apt and non-truth-apt propositions? Consequently, a natural corollary of syntacticism is that canonical ascriptions in the disputed areas are one and all truth-apt. Horwich (1998a, 84) grasps the nettle by commenting that "ethical propositions provide perfectly good and useful instances of the equivalence schema." Wright (1992, 176–178), who may be ranked among deflationists in our sense, if not in his, holds a similar view, as does Hill (2003, 54–56), whose hybrid, deflationist-leaning view resembles Wright's in this crucial respect.

Noncognitivists in ethics hold that ethical discourse is not fact-stating, or, in the end, not a purely objective endeavor. A familiar way to sum up this finding is to say that straightforward ascriptions of ethical predicates (e.g., good, right, evil, duty, ought, obligatory) do not qualify for a truth predicate. Syntacticism precludes this way of putting the noncognitivists' point. It should seize our attention that an account designed for nothing more than modesty about the applicability of a truth predicate has such striking consequences for a traditional dispute remote from its targeted concerns.

With respect to noncognitivism, it seems the deflationist is left with either of two choices: declare neutrality with respect to the issue and hit upon a way to reformulate the traditional differences, or acknowledge that, despite appearances, the equivalences help to resolve the issue in favor of cognitivism. Horwich and Wright choose the first of these. But both responses may be disputed.[2] Perhaps the deflationist can meet these challenges. Nevertheless, that it is an issue which syntacticists, and therefore deflationists, must confront is significant. For the handling of versions of noncognitivism has been raised, almost exclusively, as problematic for correspondence theories, and problematic just because of their view of

---

2. For further discussion, see Jackson 1994; Jackson et al. 1994; M. Smith 1994a,b; Divers and Miller 1994; Horwich 1994, 1998a; Wright 1994a. Also see the appendix.

truth. However, it is noteworthy that deflationism too, for almost opposite reasons, has a comparably delicate problem in dealing with disputed propositions. We appreciate more fully the force of the issue on truth theories when we realize just how this burden is distributed.

Although we will not deal with the other substantive theories, we might just mention that deflationary critiques may regard them just as faulty in this area as is Correspondence. While, say, Coherence and pragmatism may not be required to find ethical, mathematical, etc. facts or SOAs to support ascriptions of truth to those propositions, they do take beliefs as their truth bearers. Given that it is just as easy to talk of Socrates' moral beliefs as it is to talk of the truth of his moral opinions, those views have the same problem, if it is a problem at all, of distinguishing the disputed from the straightforwardly acceptable via their theories of truth as does Corespondence. Furthermore, once classified as beliefs it would be difficult for coherentists and pragmatists to deny truth eligibility to these propositions. Consequently, in both cases the deflationist puts pressure on substantive views to resolve the cognitivism-noncognitivism issue independent of their truth theories.

Let us then shine a light on deflationism. How do the deflationary resolutions proceed? First, Horwich (1998a, 84–85; 1994, 20) suggests that emotivists emphasize the unique character of ethical propositions rather than their lack of truth-value. This won't cover every version of noncognitivism, and other attempts to rewrite that view consistently with truth ascriptions are, at the very least, shrouded in controversy. For example, the pioneers of twentieth century noncognitivism in ethics, the emotivists, thought that the supposed uniqueness of ethical utterances made them akin to cheers and boos. Typically, emotivists supported their claims by showing that such utterances couldn't be in the business of stating truths or falsehoods. Let us say that this form of noncognitivism is reductionist. Its advocates contrived a quite distinct office for the discourse, one that conflicts with Horwich's particular treatment. (We needn't consider the alternative of making commands and/or pure joyous outbursts, such as "hooray," or expressions of disgust such as "boo," truth-apt. First and foremost, the suggestion doesn't pass the giggle test. Second, the utterances in the reductive base don't pass the syntactic tests.)

Next, Wright suggests using Cognitive Command and his supplementary tests (see section 4.3) to moot the further issues between cognitive and noncognitivist views. But this is a further test for utterances that are already truth-apt. Thus, on this alternative, reductionist noncognitivism remains unstatable. Cognitive Command, etc. are supplementary tests designed to get us beyond mere truth-aptness. Moreover, taking this path presupposes that Cognitive Command and/or the supplementary tests are adequate ways to decide the questions of concern for the disputing parties. It would take us too far afield to examine that claim in the detail it warrants. Suffice it to say that Wright puts the tests forward only as hopeful beginnings, and displays quite clearly how their implementations have difficulties to overcome. Some of those difficulties seem to me more life-threatening than they apparently do to Wright (1992, 138–139).

There are two natural reactions to these deflationist proposals for reworking noncognitivism. On the one hand, we may suppose that deflationism is onto something, and its deliberations at this general level, although not initially intended, say, for moral discourse, show that the more extreme forms of noncognitivism (viz., emotivism and implicit command theory) are incoherent. On the other hand, if we are convinced that the radical noncognitivist occupies at least a coherent position, we may suspect syntacticism of glossing over facts that deserve a less dismissive treatment. The deflationist claims as a strength of his view that he is able to account for so much of our transactions with truth on his economical principles. But instead one might take the radical noncognitivist position to argue, via *modus tollens*, that deflationism fails here. I introduce this consideration only as a possibility. I haven't set myself the task of criticizing either deflationary alternative. I only want to situate that view with respect to the noncognitivism issue in general. For the question of present concern is not whether the deflationism has a way into the issue, but to compare its options to those available to the correspondence theory. So let us now turn to the latter.

For starters, note that the correspondence theorist has analogous choices. Correspondence is compatible with the view that these assertoric utterances are truth-apt. It might hold this on the grounds that there are SOAs distinctive of its subject matter or distinctive of a subject matter to which the ethical one is reducible (e.g., naturalism). On this account the noncognitivist is simply mistaken. On the other hand, Correspondence can also mirror the views of Horwich and Wright. For the correspondentist can allow conventional SOAs to support the truth of these utterances. The best attributions of ethical (or mathematical, or counterfactual, or theoretical) discourse aren't altogether unruly. The systems in which they occur seem arbitrary from a broader metaphysical perspective, but within that system there are SOAs, albeit conventional ones, to which those attributions may correspond (or fail to do so). Thus, they are truth-apt, just as much as, say, the statement made by a baseball announcer that a runner is safe at first. And their being truth-evaluative is due to their corresponding or lack of it just as much as that of an imagined utterance of "that peak is snow-capped." The main difference is that the SOA is conventional (in a sense we need not detail here) in the one case, not so in the other. Noncognitivism may be preserved on this outlook because at a meta level it can still be claimed that should basic disagreements occur, there are no further objective means to decide which view is correct. Or the correspondentist can appeal either to Horwich's special features or to Wright's Cognitive Command etc. to bring out the distinctive features of noncognitivism. This too limits the options for the noncognitivist. As with the analogous deflationary move, the version holding that such apparent predications are really disguised expressions of attitude or emotion, or disguised commands, is precluded by this understanding. Still, maintaining that the SOAs are merely conventional, and occur only within a system for which desirable grounding of a certain kind is absent, is another way of bringing out the antirealist direction motivating noncognitivism.

However, the correspondence theorist can distinguish her options from those of the deflationist because she is not forced into either position by truth theory alone. A correspondentist can claim that whether there are worldly circumstances *and* truth-values, say, for ethical sentences may be decided by a separate set of considerations.[3] And it is open to her to come down on either side. It may be a significant clue that users' willingness to extend the terms 'true' and 'false' to such utterances covaries with her willingness to say that their sentences describe kinds of SOAs. That we normally talk about truth in such matters, that we take such propositions as the objects of belief, and that we draw inferences from them can be regarded by

---

3. For an error theorist about morality, such as Mackie (1977), there may be no token worldly circumstances for the relevant class of judgments. But Mackie can accept that the sentences with which such utterances were made are in fact correlated with types of states of affairs (which have no tokens). Indeed, it would be in perfect concert with his correspondentist predilections elsewhere to accept such correlations.

the correspondentist as evidence for ethical SOAs (conventional or otherwise); however, as was discussed in section 3.2, the correspondentist is also free to take these as misdirections subject to correction. Since this may be unguarded talk that relies in an unreflective way on an assumption that worldly circumstances are as appropriate to moral questions as is truth, I don't see how we are to take such evidence until further details of the cases are supplied. Only when we know what happens when users are confronted with that issue can we adequately assess the force of the "common parlance" data to which syntacticists appeal. But, as the earlier options indicate, the correspondence theorist is at no disadvantage whatever the outcome of that further inquiry.

Like the deflationist, the correspondence theorist maintains that these issues aren't basically about truth. But unlike the deflationist, the latter can claim that they are about whether there are ethical or mathematical SOAs (not necessarily irreducible or non-natural ones). Of course, this can't be used as an argument on behalf of correspondence; it presupposes, rather than reinforces, that view. But it is a useful slant for fixing on the differences between the competing views. Both must make hard decisions, but it seems to me that those made from a correspondence perspective are more in line with our expectations that our theory of truth shouldn't force us to take sides on what appears to be at best a remotely related issue. Like the parties to the strictly mathematical, ethical, or counterfactual disputes, a correspondentist can let the matter rest with a closer examination of the internal details of our practices. Of course, if one claims that there are no SOAs correlated with sentences such as, say, "9 × 15 = 135" and "killing is wrong," one will need a different account to distinguish the appropriate from the inappropriate declarations therein. But that doesn't imply that my treatment has skewed, or undermined, a significant philosophical dispute (assuming, once again, that doing so would expose a flaw). Rather, the claim that a mathematical or an ethical sentence has a different relation to its subject matter can, but needn't, be the starting-point for various noncognitivist treatments. It is neither an obstacle nor an encouragement to them. The deflationist, on the other hand, must find a way to reformulate what matters to the noncognitivists in question without using the notion truth, or thinly disguised substitutes such as fact-stating or being objective; and there is at least some basis for a worry that this can't be accomplished without distorting some classical noncognitivist positions.

That doesn't mean that the correspondentist needn't say anything about (G). However, by placing her debating position in clearer perspective vis-à-vis that of her opponents, it shows both that these are not singular burdens of correspondence and that the correspondentist is not in a comparatively disadvantageous position. Of course, the question here isn't whether noncognitivism is correct, or even plausible. We are merely highlighting the alternative ways in which deflationism and correspondence tackle the issues it raises.

We have noted that even interrogative and imperative sentences are associated with distinct types of SOAs, and this is no less true for the assertoric sentences of present interest. 'Lying is wrong' and 'helping others in distress is good' also convey distinct SOAs, as do the sentences 'If $Pr > 0$, then $Pr(A|B) = Pr(B \& A)/Pr(B)$' and 'for any two sets there exists a set to which they both belong'. How, then, can any adherent of this view deny that these sorts of sentences are thereby truth-eligible? Of course, one could maintain that they are covert imperatives, and then give the same reasons we gave for excluding imperatives. (Cf. Field's (2000) nonfactualist rendering of *a priori* utterances as evaluations.) But the roster of candidate explanations is more crowded here. Let's briefly review the main routes taken in the past.

Consider mathematics first. Typically the antirealist side (in mathematics, usually labeled "anti-platonist") concentrates on the status rather than the existence of the relevant SOAs. Antirealists are likely to insist that the semantic values of mathematical propositions, or the crucial terms that classify them as such, are mind-dependent or conventional. It is then of small consequence whether we acknowledge the existence of SOAs so diminished in status. If truth predications are allowed, they may be to a reductive class of sentences. But they may also be truths corresponding to merely conventional SOAs. And, there are other options. An error theorist might maintain that there are typal SOAs, but no tokens. Each of these, as well as the claims that mind-independent mathematical and counterfactual SOAs exist (realism), are available to the correspondence theory as well.

A similar package is available for the correspondentist regarding moral language. Certainly 'lying is wrong' contains a reference to an SOA (lying) as it does in 'lying is stressful'. But what of the whole SOA *lying being wrong*? A noncognitivist correspondence theorist might say that the sentence's grammatical form is misleading: it really amounts to something like 'don't lie' or 'lying, phooey!' Here nothing is predicated of lying. Or, once again, one may be an error theorist: there are typal moral SOAs, but no actual tokens of them (see note 3). Or, once again, such propositions could turn out true even for a noncognitivist because they fit a conventional SOA in the appropriate context. Finally, a correspondentist can be a realist either because she holds that moral sentences are reducible to legitimate nonmoral ones, or that there are token, morally charged SOAs.

Further applications to counterfactuals and theoretical sentences will follow similar, if not identical, lines. But the outcome will be the same: one must make choices with profound philosophical implications. The correspondence theorist has just as many choices, where she doesn't have even more, and none of them seem to be harder, or put her in a less comfortable position, than competing views. When such areas of inquiry are brought up as problems for correspondence, critics have failed carefully to review the alternatives to it as well as the full spectrum of correspondentist options.

9.4 The Slingshot

Finally, on to the objection implied in (H). This is elemental. The charge is, roughly, that there can be at most one fact to which all true propositions must then correspond, further discrimination among facts being futile. A byproduct of our method for identifying facts is that their supposed multiplicity collapses into one all-embracing fact. The objection has been pressed most vigorously by Davidson, who claims to have found its basis in Frege (1960).[4] Davidson (1990, 303) writes: ". . . starting from the assumptions that a true sentence cannot be made to correspond to something different by the substitution of coreferring singular terms, or by the substitution of logically equivalent sentences, it is easy to show that . . . true sentences . . . all correspond to the same thing." The argument, according to Davidson (1999, 106), demonstrates that "there are no interesting and appropriate entities available which, by being somehow related to sentences, can explain why the true ones are true and the others not. There is

---

4. As currently formulated, the objection owes its form to Gödel and/or Church. See Neale 1995; S. Read 1993.

good reason . . . to be skeptical about the importance of the correspondence theory of truth." The objection is commonly known as the Slingshot. For starters, let it stand as stated. Davidson describes it as "the real objection" to correspondence theories (though I provide a somewhat altered, and I believe more balanced, summary of his real objections in section 9.6). How is the proposal before us to avoid it?

Two preliminary points.

First, although we can talk about statements corresponding to token states of affairs, as explained throughout, we needn't do so in order to identify a concrete truthmaker. The view demands only that the concrete state of affairs be a token of a certain type. We can, if we wish, then say that this is the statement's corresponding state of affairs, but it is quite unnecessary to insist on this. Of course, there is an ineradicable word-world relation of a different sort, but that is between two types—sentences and states of affairs. And it seems this connection is too hardy to be undone by Davidson's form of skepticism. In any event, the Slingshot doesn't threaten a collapse here because the state of affairs in question is never concrete (even if it is not a type that carries the possibility of multiple instantiations, as with some general states of affairs such as *all history being cyclical*) and thus doesn't admit unfettered substitution of the kind that blends every state of affairs on the Slingshot. Thus, if by 'correspondence' the usual relation between the statement made and a concrete worldly circumstance is meant, the objection can't take root in the proposal before us. It is also worth keeping in mind that the mysteriousness of a correspondence relation, at a concrete or any other level, is not at issue here. This is noted only to avoid conflating objections. It doesn't disqualify Davidson's complaint, but it does locate his issue more exactly. The Slingshot concentrates on facts rather than the relation of correspondence: it shows that there is at most one fact. Consequently, there could be only one (concrete) truthmaker—a fatal infirmity for any correspondence theory.

Second, Davidson tends to talk in terms of *facts*, but I shall assume that it is of no moment if we think of the predicament instead in terms of Austin's *states of affairs*, or my suggested cover term *worldly circumstances*. This is certainly not unfair to Davidson. If the objection didn't go through on either replacement, it wouldn't be a threat to the current proposal, or to any correspondence view that didn't rely specifically on that one variety of truthmaker. (I return to this topic in section 9.6.)

Against that background, consider again the Slingshot.

A first hitch in the objection is that although we can talk of statements corresponding to token SOAs, unlike facts SOAs aren't designated by propositional clauses. Rather, they are picked out, as are events, by singular terms, frequently gerundives, such as *snow being white* and *coal being black*. But to focus on a more basic issue, let us suppose provisionally that the sentences closest to the specifications of SOAs can go proxy for them. This is required by the objection, but it is not an unreasonable assumption. First, as explained in section 6.6, we often overlook this difference when nothing hangs on it, and, second, there is a structural (interderivability) connection between these singular terms and the associated sentences. Thus, suppose "snow is white" is correlated with the SOA described as "snow being white." We then have

1   Snow is white,

which is logically equivalent to

2   $\iota x(x = \text{Diogenes} \;\&\; \text{Snow is white}) = \iota x(x = \text{Diogenes})$.

But given the truth of "coal is black," by the substitution of singular terms we obtain

3   $\iota x(x = \text{Diogenes} \;\&\; \text{Coal is black}) = \iota x(x = \text{Diogenes})$

which, by logical equivalence, yields

4   Coal is black

correlated with coal being black. Generalizing, any obtaining SOA implies any other. That, in sum, is the Slingshot.

It is unclear what lessons we would be able to draw if we were to replace the concrete facts, to which the argument is meant to apply, by typal SOAs. Imagine it is supposed to teach us that there is at most one such type. If, as I have tried to impress, the relation of a sentence to a typal SOA amounts to no more than that different sentences are fitted to impart distinguishable types of information, it seems that this would argue against the Davidsonian interpretation rather than against the notion of an SOA. Otherwise, how could we ever justifiably prefer to communicate something with one sentence rather than with any other? How is it possible to call into question something so central to all language use? In addition, these really are states of affairs rather than facts. If we scrap our earlier concession about the interchangeability of the noun phrases of SOA descriptions with sentences, there is a difficulty in understanding the role of steps 1 and 4. Singular terms don't take truth-values, so how have we shown that one truth collapses into every truth? Moreover, for the conjunctions inside steps 2 and 3, don't we need either a sentence or an open sentence in the second conjunct to make sense of combining these by a conjunction sign? A singular term—say, 'snow being white'—is neither. Substitutional quantification aside (which should not bother Davidson), what sense are we to make of a (logical) conjunctive operator, which permits names (= constants) as a substituends for its argument places? The question poses a difficulty to seeing how the Slingshot works with these replacements. Indeed, serious questions have been raised about the Slingshot even as it applies to what can be sententially parsed.[5] Nevertheless, for the sake of argument I am prepared to set aside all these misgivings. Let's suppose that the argument works just as intended, and then examine the consequences it has for the current version of correspondence.

For Davidson, *events* are worldly constituents, and are employable, say, as terms in singular causal relations; but methods structurally similar to those in the Slingshot can be adapted to work against there being no more than one event.[6] However, there is no need to resort to a circumstantial *ad hominem* to ward off the objection. Notwithstanding the foregoing concessions, it is sufficient for getting around the argument simply to note that what now makes something a truthmaker of a particular statement is only that it have a certain property—namely, *being a token of the type with which the statement's sentence is correlated*. So if there were only a single SOA, truthmakers would then be the variety of different *properties* possessed by that one universal state.

Even the Slingshot couldn't prevent us from holding that the one actual SOA would make different statements true in virtue of its different properties, the properties corresponding to those which made it a token of one rather than another type SOA. That one state of affairs would be a token of many (very likely, infinitely many!) different types. And its belonging to one rather than another type would be relevant to its being a truthmaker for a particular statement. Accordingly, there would still be something selective

---

5. By, e.g., Cummins and Gottlieb (1972), Barwise and Perry (1983, 24–26), Mackie (1974, 250–256), and S. Read (1993).

6. See Davidson 1980b,d; Vision 1979.

about the world responsible for a statement's truth, although we would now be driven to describe it as a property of the one all-embracing SOA rather than the state itself. The formulation of the view would be more convoluted, but its essential character would survive intact. Conceding the Slingshot and the various features that others have questioned in it doesn't endanger the proposal before us.

9.5 The Identity of States of Affairs

Although supplying a complete account of the principles for identifying SOAs lies outside our charge, we can achieve some clarity by stating just enough to show that a correspondentist scheme of things is compatible with competitive methods for determining identity. Of course, SOAs, facts, and the like may also give rise to skeptical concerns. What are states of affairs or facts, anyway? If an SOA necessitates a truth, and its relevant constitutive role consists in this, does anything else necessitating that it obtains also have a similar role in constituting that truth? Are there conjunctive, disjunctive, conditional, or negative SOAs? Some of these questions have been briefly dealt with insofar as they were directly in lines of inquiry already opened. Others have been ignored, though various writers have addressed them elsewhere. The issue I plan to take up here is rather more specific. On various plausible methods for identifying and distinguishing SOAs, though not on every one, there will be some designations of them that don't display on their face that they are tokens of the relevant state of affairs. How if at all does that bear on our results?

As I understand SOAs, they are (barring a larger intensional context) extensionally specified, although they fail the mereological standard of "same components, same SOA." Our SOAs are structured wholes. The Queen knighting Peter Strawson is not the same as Peter Strawson knighting the Queen. But to raise the present objection we needn't even allot states of affairs unrestricted extensionality within those structural limits. It is sufficient that the identity of an SOA is preserved with certain systematic changes in property and relation designations (accompanied perhaps by changing the order of its constituents) and with free replacement of terms referring to the same individuals. On this account, the Queen knighting Peter Strawson is identical with Peter Strawson being knighted by the Queen. For the sake of argument, I want to go even farther than that, allowing less obvious transformations to preserve an SOA's identity. An example might be the identity of the widowing of Xantippe and the death of Socrates. This surpasses in liberality both the structural and empirical schemes described in section 8.5. The reason for being this accommodating is not that this is the best way to carve up reality, but to give the objection considered below its strongest form by positing the worst case scenario for my proposal. The point is to show that the present view is not endangered even by so promiscuous a scheme for identifying SOAs.

Imagine a sentence S used to make statement Σ, imagine W as the type of state of affairs associated with S, and imagine worldly circumstance w as W's relevant token. Concrete w falling under a certain description makes it a token of W. Now suppose some y, of type Y introduced by a term bearing no obviously relevant descriptive relation to W, but such that $w = y$ (on whatever standard one chooses). Is y also a token of W? I suspect this is a issue over which philosophers will differ: whereas generally it will be accepted that Wellington's victory at Waterloo is a token of the type *victory*, some will not allow that Napoleon's defeat at Waterloo is a token of that type, even if they admit that both select one and the same SOA. Others may say, given the identity, that Napoleon's defeat cannot but be a token of the type victory, although not described in a way that makes manifest its tokening. (And some, who choose the former path, will deny that these could be identical for just that reason. But the reasoning is not promising. Consider a parallel question arising for individual substances. My desk is a token of the type desk. Suppose one maintains that the packing crate in my study is not, as such, a token of that type because "this packing crate" is not specified as a token of the type desk. But it is not plausible to deny their identity as physical objects.[7]) Whichever position one takes about y counting as a token of W, given that $y = w$, y will have to count as much as a truthmaker for Σ as w, and this, it may be claimed, is trouble enough for the proposal under discussion.

We chose w under that description because of a semantic fact that made sentence type S relevant to W rather than to Y. But as long as $w = y$, there will be a specification of y—namely, w—to make Σ true. If there is

---

7. Virtually any claim about identity could quickly engulf us in the quagmire of complications (e.g., relative identity claims). We must avoid getting involved with those here.

no such correlate w for y, Σ is not true. In sum, describing our truthmaker as y has precisely the same bearing on the truth or falsity of Σ as does w. We are entitled to ignore questions of identity in practice because whenever some other correlate, say y, makes Σ true, it will be due to the fact there is some w identical with y and which satisfies our formula. Where $y = w$ (or where they would be identical if either obtained), we will never encounter a case in which the truthmaker described in one way rather than the other will yield a different truth-value for Σ. In explaining our concept or the property of truth—the extent of our inquiry—we need not probe deeper into our practice than to observe that it is because of this connection that we deem y as making the particular statement true. In particular, we need not state a full set of conditions for the identity of a states of affairs as long as this consequence follows for whichever set is chosen.

Of course, if we amend our formulas as suggested earlier to make the conditions sufficient—rather than necessary and sufficient—the problem cannot arise. y could then turn out to be a truthmaker for Σ even if there were no w such that $y = w$. Whichever situation we had, there would no threat of incompatible truth evaluations of a single statement, although we would want to know how this fit the pattern set by (V). One answer might be what I have called extended correspondence.

This by no means exhausts the issues that may be raised about SOAs. For example, I have suggested that their tokens are unrepeatable (concrete) particulars But are they complex or simple? Are the properties and relations which they exemplify tropes or repeatable universals? Different answers to these questions inevitably yield differences over the re-identification of SOAs. (For example, could something other than the actual possessor of a property or relation have possessed that very property or relation? On trope theory, briefly discussed in the last chapter, typically an instance of a property/relation is tied essentially to its subject(s). If Shakespeare wrote *The Tempest*, no one else could have written that very work.) But, fortunately, our limited aims enable us to bypass this cluster of issues. It is easy enough to see how the slight information provided for identity poses no difficulty for the current theory.

No doubt there are still misgivings in some quarters about the existence of SOAs. That they are needed to make sense of this theory isn't likely to put those doubts to rest. For example, Davidson (1996, 266) affirms that "facts or states of affairs have never been shown to play a useful role in semantics." One problem here is to get clearer on what could count as a useful role. Is its role in our current theory sufficient? That aside, suppose our commitments are driven in the first instance by examining our tendency to refer to such things. Much of what Davidson (1980b, 181; cf. Fine 1982, 44) has stated on this head concerning terms for events is equally true of SOAs: both undergo a full panoply of operations distinctive of referential expressions. They tolerate the formation of singular terms as designators ('snow being white'), they can be counted (there have been three recessions in the past twenty years) and quantified (all famines are preventable), they permit definite and indefinite articles (the winter of our discontent, an estrangement) and identity claims (that financial scandal was this administration's undoing), and they take sortal predication (the capture of the murderer was a relief, his remaining silent for the whole lecture was one great achievement). Of course, some of these noun phrases may be expanded into event as well as SOA designators, but that is due to an overlap in these categories. Where a distinction is possible, we can always expand them in ways that make it unmistakable that SOAs are intended. None of this, by itself, proves that SOAs exist; such linguistic tests are fallible guides to ontology. But, then, we have scarcely relied on them in these pages. Rather, we have emphasized the work that they do in the theory of truth. And if that, together with the linguistic appearances, isn't at least a relevant promising start for ontological legitimacy, I find it hard to see what one could be.

9.6 A Final Objection and the Pertinacity of Correspondence

Frege (1999, 87) clearly declares his nihilism: " . . . it is probable that the content of the word 'true' is unique and indefinable." In support of such indefinability, Frege raised, in a telescoped fashion, objections to understanding truth via correspondence. One of those, addressed in section 8.6, took its inspiration from the fact that more than a single state can be correlated with a given sentence. My recent proposal for detecting the appropriate token SOA shows why that needn't be a problem. But a rather different objection is that 'is true' is not a relational expression. Thus, whatever the appearances, there cannot be a relation between a proposition and the world that makes the former true.

If the correspondence theorist had claimed that 'true' has the same sense or meaning as 'corresponds to', Frege's point might require some backtracking on the part of the former. Even so, because meanings can be covert this would be no assurance that *corresponding* isn't carried by the very meaning of 'true'. However, the contention isn't about the meaning of 'true', but about truth's constitution. If it is involved in the meaning of 'true', this is only by way of its involvement in that constitution. And, on that score, there is no more reason to suppose that to say of a proposition that it is true doesn't require something else making it true than there is to suppose that 'is a manager' and 'is a commander', both monadic predicates, don't imply something other than the subject (as such) to be managed or commanded. Of course, a plethora of intransitive forms have transitive counterparts. Thus, we have 'is a manager of' and 'is a commander of', but no natural transitive counterpart for 'is true'. ('Is true of' isn't what we are looking for. But perhaps this is why 'corresponds to' has been introduced.) However, the only point that needs emphasis here is that the nonpresence of a relational expression is no guarantee of the absence of a relation.

It may be helpful to compare the case of 'true' with an older philosophical view that all properties are implicitly related to a class of standard examples. Thus, "this is red," it might have been held, could be expanded to "this is similar to X," where X is a paradigm of redness. This view may be mistaken. However, is the mere fact that 'red' isn't a relational expression enough by itself to defeat this metaphysical thesis? We should be hard pressed to deliver an affirmative answer.

Since Frege brought up the matter, it might be worth mentioning that I have avoided stating my claims as about the meaning of 'true' largely because that approach tends to make us look in the wrong place. (See chapter 2 of Vision 1988.) Those who begin with the question "What does 'true' mean?" and who take this as an adequate way to probe a TRUTH concept aren't likely to discover correspondence just through an examination of that word. More particularly, there is a danger that they will overlook irresistible intuitions such as that summarized by Variability. This needn't prevent us from including correspondence as a component of the meaning of 'true'. However, this will follow from correspondence's constitutive role; it is not a step toward its discovery. So to speak, the evidence supporting correspondence arrives by the workmen's entrance.

Back to the gravamen of Frege's charge. Try to imagine an otherwise Fregean position that leaves no room for a requirement of correspondence. First, Frege grants that truth is a property, even if an unfathomable one. But, second, the predicate determines that its property is nonrelational. How then is truth determined? Either something, albeit an unfathomable something, in the proposition itself must determine this or a proposition's truth (or falsity) must be arbitrary. These are the only alternatives left once (nonreflexive) relationality is eliminated. Frege surely thinks truth is nonarbitrary. Thus, if the monadicity of its predicate is a definitive proof that its constitution is not dyadic, there must be something about the proposition itself that determines its truth or falsity. It is hard to imagine that Frege wouldn't deny outright any thesis in this neighborhood. He may not have thought that the correspondence project could be completed. Truth, for him, might have been so basic as quickly to immerse any promising approach in circularity. But the only option for him is that it is dyadic property, however futilely we must gesture to say so.

Before leaving the topic of how hard it is to abandon correspondence without falling in with even less savory company, briefly consider again Davidson's predicament. He clearly shuns "the folly of trying to define truth." On the taxonomy adopted here, he is a nihilist. The Slingshot aside, his chief objections to correspondence boil down to his rejection of the Socratic search for essences (as distinct from the method of illuminating basic concepts via their interconnections) and his view that any version of correspondence must invoke facts or states of affairs, for which he can find no useful employment. The former reason opens intriguing methodological questions about conceptions of philosophical definition, but we can't pursue them here. For the nonce I'll have to settle for a somewhat unsatisfying "proof is in the pudding" reply. However, although he is not a correspondentist, neither is he a deflationist or an inflationist of a different stripe, and he has no proclivities for the cult of post-modern social constructionism. Reality must have a role to play. Thus, in the course of explaining his middle ground, Davidson writes "what ultimately ties language to the world is that the conditions that typically cause us to hold sentences true *constitute* the truth conditions . . . of our sentences" (1996, 274). Evidently these will not be facts or states of affairs. In other contexts Davidson (1980b, 170) holds that (a) causes are all *events* and (b) "the same event may make 'Jones apologized' and 'Jones said "I apologize"' true."[8] But events are conditions in the world and Davidson (ibid., 180) accepts them as "a fundamental ontological category." So, suppose we drafted a simplified version of correspondence:

A sentence's truth is constituted by its correspondence to an aspect of reality.

It would be difficult for Davidson to deny that this was a version of correspondence on the grounds it fails to mention facts or states of affairs. ("The notion of correspondence would be a help if we were able [to] say, in an *instructive* way, which fact or slice of reality it is that makes a particular sentence true" (Davidson 1999, 106).) If it is not correspondence, what else could it reasonably be? The highlighted formula certainly covers Davidson's remark about the constitution of truth conditions. Is Davidson then a correspondentist? He disclaims being one—we may take him at his word. But the passage just quoted and its striking consequence illustrate just how difficult it is to avoid correspondence while also trying to maintain a nondeflationary realism. The lesson here is basically the one I drew from Quine's similar attempt—at least on the mainline interpretations with which we began—to insist upon a connection to reality while trying to resist taking the final step to correspondence. The main difference is that while Quine may de-emphasize traditional correspondence theories, he doesn't disavow them as explicitly as Davidson.

Conclusion

It may seem that I have devoted an inordinate amount of space to putting down insurrections against the correspondence theory. But in one form or another the theory has been around for a long time, and as we might have expected, it has attracted a good deal of critical reflection. Those who have thought hard and seriously about correspondence have produced a superabundance of questions, qualifications, misgivings, and outright protests. I have chosen to deal with those deemed most salient or important in current discussions. There is always a danger in such reviews of overlooking

---

8. For a similar appeal to events (though a different analysis of an event) see Mulligan et al. 1984. They call their truthmakers "moments", but the class contains a number of quite ordinary events. See also their pp. 295–296 for hints of similar implications in Russell and Ramsey.

the prime concerns of one or another naysayer. But in such matters I am a meliorist: progress doesn't seem well served by awaiting a call from perfection. So I have tried to meet what I have taken to be the most serious challenges.

In the remainder I have attempted to state a promising approach to the topic: one that may indicate why so many have been tied in knots when trying to explicate the elusive correspondence relation. Here, and throughout, I have repeatedly emphasized separating issues that the rich tradition has seemed to me to have confounded. If my proposal is on the right track, part of the problem has been due to theorists believing that they had to solve a variety of other problems just to get clear about truth itself. Once we have hived off these fascinating, but incidental, questions—say about the reasons for the sentence/state of affairs relationship, or about a robust scheme for identifying and individuating concrete states of affairs, or about how we come to *know* that a particular proposition is true, matters that don't properly intrude in delineating a correspondence theory—I think we may see why correspondence deserves its "commonsensical" laurels. This is not to say further details, were they secured, wouldn't be very welcome, but only that their absence does not reflect adversely on our having chosen wisely the best of the options placed before us.

Appendix

The preceding pages have served up a variety of directions in which Correspondence might be developed. An important unresolved question, though by no means the only one, has been how to extend the notion into areas in which there is some inclination to preserve the custom of declaring utterances true or false, but in which philosophers have been wary about acknowledging anything like a fact of the matter. Ethics (indeed, values in general), mathematics, and scientific theory have been flashpoints for recent concerns of this type. The chief point I would have readers take away from that particular portion of the discussion is that the constellation of questions raised about such areas needn't bear on the issues which Correspondence must address. The correspondence theory can be developed in more than one way to yield a competitive account of the place of truth or its absence in each of them. This flexibility doesn't amount to a series of *ad hoc* maneuvers; rather it shows how the issues raised by a choice of a proper truth theory can float largely free of a decision to make such discourses truth-apt. This not to say that these questions must be wholly independent of each other. But for disputed discourses which have been declared truth-apt, the possibilities for incorporating this result into a correspondence theory are plentiful.

Insofar as the subject matters in disputed areas are believed to bear on the correspondence theory, there are two main questions about them. To better understand those, let us introduce the notion of a 'straightforward proposition' for a discourse. A straightforward proposition—assuming we can consider something a proposition before we have decided on its truth-aptness—is one that can be framed by an affirmative indicative sentence, and predicates (putative) properties or expresses subjects distinctive of that discourse. That is a very rough approximation, but it will do for our limited purposes. Thus, we might say that such-and-such an act is morally right, or that this substance contains hydrogen atoms, or that the square of the hypotenuse of a right-angled triangle is equal to the sum of the square of its other two sides. Then our two questions are as follows:

Are the straightforward propositions in those discourses truth-apt?

Do those affirmative straightforward propositions answer to genuine features of the world?

A difficulty for Correspondence posed by pluralists and by its other critics is that one can without inconsistency answer the first question affirmatively *and* answer the second one negatively. This is taken to show that a correspondence theory can't account for the truth of those propositions. Here are the most prominent ways thinkers have found to deal with our two questions about such discourses while not abandoning Correspondence. (As I have stated, the problems only ensue when the first question is answered affirmatively—that is, the discourse does contain straightforward propositions taking truth-value. However, I want to review the full slate of options for a correspondence theorist, including those answering the first question negatively.)

First, one might deny that the first question should be answered affirmatively: contrary to appearances, the problematic discourses don't generate truth-apt propositions, or at least those for which one or another form of antirealism is adopted do not. For whichever discourses one denies truth-aptitude, this will be accompanied by the proviso that there are no facts or states of affairs of the relevant kind enabling one to make a correspondence determination. Thus, a negative answer to the first question is supported by a negative answer to the second one. The theory then need only concern itself with the remaining cases in which there are acknowledged instances of SOAs. This emerges as a prominent option where it goes along with a radical disenchantment of the subject matter, as, say, the one attempted by certain early-twentieth-century emotivists in ethics.

A second option, *error theory*, or, on some versions, *fictionalism*, allows both questions to be answered affirmatively. No SOAs support the truth of such propositions, but whatever there is in the world supports their falsehood. Thus, the utterances in question are truth-apt because false. This is not only consistent with Correspondence, but the failure of truth in this instance has been given a correspondentist explanation. It is also at least conceivable that there be a version of fictionalism or error theory in which the explanation of falsehood is other than correspondentist. But I can't recall an actual instance.

Third is the prospect of reductionism. This would allow a correspondence between the initial propositions and the worldly correlates of their reductive translations. However, broadly acknowledged reductions are rare in philosophy, and it would be risky to pin our hopes on the success of any of them for one of the areas given as examples, much less for all three. Perhaps we can settle for a less-than-rigorous analysis, as has been done in some cases of naturalism in ethics. Whatever the standards adopted, the looming point here is that the fate of any such reduction will be decided on a case-by-case basis, and will not involve us in a decision between truth theories. Thus, although this view is perfectly in line with Correspondence, it is really a side issue for our central topic.

Next, various nonreductive realisms might be mentioned. Suppose it is stated that there are real moral facts, actual scientific laws, or genuine mathematical facts in nature, none of which are reducible to other sorts of actualities. This too is a position that appears often in the literature. Like the preceding view, decisions will be made on a case-by-case basis, but in any event such positions are clearly compatible with Correspondence.

I mention the foregoing views only to emphasize that whatever the pros and cons of the issues they raise, they don't bear one way or another on the plausibility of a correspondence theory. One's views on such issues, whether pro or con, can be crafted to be consistent with correspondence. No doubt, sometimes they haven't been so designed: a view may be described not only as taking sides on one of the above issues, but also as conflicting with the correspondence theory. However, when this happens the latter conflict is always an extraneous addition to the realist/antirealist differences at the heart of the dispute. We must be careful not to believe we are vetting correspondence merely by rejecting facts of a certain kind.

In the remainder of this discussion, I want to concentrate on the comparison of two further prominent correspondence theory options ("fifth" and "sixth" for those counting) for disputed subject matters.

(a) First, we may appeal to what was cited earlier as *extended correspondence*. On that view we make allowance for the truths of propositions in a disputed area, not by discovering purely objective SOAs (reductive classes or otherwise) for them to correspond to, but rather by an extension based on other similarities (that is, other than their corresponding to SOAs) to the core correspondence cases—perhaps features such as satisfying a critical mass of Crispin Wright's other platitudes, such as timelessness and transparency (section 4.5). Their truth may be regarded as secondary or dependent on a core of correspondence truths. (This seems to be Strawson's (1992) most recent view.)

(b) Next, we can discover purely conventional SOAs for such utterances to conform to (or fail to conform to).

I confess a preference for (b) over (a). Let me say more about that option.

Everyday parlance is replete with conventional facts (or conventional SOAs). Unless one is committed to an extreme form of physicalism—believing, say, that the only genuine facts are those of an ideal physics—one will acknowledge facts such as that the ball crossed the goal line, that the mortgage payment is overdue, that a Maserati costs more than a Chevrolet, that Kasparov's position looks unbeatable, that Philadelphia is north of Baltimore, that the truck exceeded the speed limit, and that the year 2002 is past. All of these samples involve conventions, and are unlikely to raise hackles even among rank-and-file naturalists (excluding radical physicalists). Once the camel of conventionality has got its nose under the tent, why not invite in ethical, mathematical, and theoretical SOAs as well?

One reason for not doing so—one I believe we may quickly dismiss—may be the bogy of relativism. While the relational character of rules for trade, customs, games, legal divisions (into cities, etc.) aren't threatening, and are universally admitted, differences in moral codes, mathematical systems (say, of geometry or arithmetic), and conflicting scientific theories are believed by many to pose a serious relativistic problem. I do not wish to deny that at this particular place. (Not because I believe the threat is genuine, but because the issue doesn't bear on our adoption of (b) for the disputed discourses.) However, if relativism in such areas is a threat, that has nothing to do with conventional facts. The very same threat remains even if we remove all conventional SOAs for our currently dominant systems. For example, the removal of conventional ethical facts will not abolish the proliferation of different, occasionally conflicting, ethical codes or systems. And if that was the nub of the difficulty, it remains so without conventional ethical facts. The issues relativism raises will be settled, if at all, by considerations internal to ethics (or whatever area) and not by our vote for or against a correspondence theory of truth.

However, that doesn't put to rest every concern about conventional SOAs. The fact that we acknowledge many of them in our everyday affairs does not mean that the introduction of others might not count as stretching things too far. For example, it would be unwise to plump for astrological, dianetical, or dark magical SOAs to make true the claims of astrology, dianetics, or witchcraft. Only the benighted would consider this an argument for those eccentric views. But the problem there is that we do not want to consider the claims true in the first place. (On the other hand, we have less resistance to regarding them as false, and therefore truth-apt on a correspondentist scheme of things.) And if that is the only difficulty, we can take refuge in error theory or, perhaps, if we regard the claims of the champions of such views as nonsense, noncognitivism. The different problem for our disputed areas is that there is a tendency to regard some of the straightforward utterances or formulas in them as true. And, under that supposition, the question remains about what, if anything, constitutes their truth. Unless we are reductionists, here I think it more plausible to suppose that to the extent we are willing seriously to defend truth—and not merely as a convenience, say, for generalizing over classes of propositions (e.g., Gandhi's beliefs)—we should also be willing to admit ethical facts (or ethical SOAs). And these may very well be conventional in just the same way that it is a fact that I discharge my debt to you by handing you a piece of paper printed by the government.

But I doubt that we have plumbed the bottom of this deep issue. There may be other intuitive restrictions on conventional SOAs. Although it is difficult to describe exactly what may be, one very hesitant stab at an answer might be that when the subject matter reaches a certain level of abstractness, with little or no admixture of the empirical, we are reluctant to acknowledge a state of affairs. This is perhaps a partial underlying explanation why certain antirealists about scientific laws nevertheless allow lower-level laws, or what they call "phenomenal laws", to be treated differently. (Once again, this is no threat to the correspondence theory, but an indirect acknowledgment of it, since it is typical to give something within its precincts as a reason for not regarding the higher reaches of laws, and the explanations in which they figure, as truth-apt.) I doubt that this practice is consistent across the board—other areas of abstraction may not produce the same hesitation. Nevertheless, we might ponder exactly why we intuitively resist more a fact such as that every number has a successor (to make true an axiom of Peano arithmetic) than a fact, say, that White's rook checked Black's king. Is it just that the facts of arithmetic are generally more abstract, less empirically situated than those of chess? Or is it something else? Whatever the answer, I find it hard to doubt that such differences exist, whether or not they amount to more than disposable intuitions. Nevertheless, if there is no firmer basis for recoiling at such conventional facts, and on one's understanding of the material such facts are robust, there seems to me no principled barrier to accounting for truths in some or all of the disputed areas as true on perfectly legitimate correspondence grounds. Of course, one doesn't need to go this far to defend the truth of certain discourses. One might revert to (a), or scrap correspondence altogether. But my purpose here has not been to show that one *must* adopt correspondence if one takes a certain side in these disputes. Rather, it has been to show that correspondence is not ruled out by the stance one takes in such disputes, and that the choice of truth theory is orthogonal to one's decision to declare any such utterances truth-apt.

Thus, although the issues involved in extending the correspondence theory to one or more of the disputed areas are fascinating follow-ups to our inquiry, they don't touch the basic ingredients and don't diminish by so much as a jot the prospects for a correspondence theory of truth.

Works Cited

Alston, William P. 1996. *A Realist Conception of Truth*. Cornell University Press.

Alston, William P. 2002. "Truth: Concept and Property." In *On Truth*, ed. R. Schantz. Walter de Gruyter.

Aristotle. 1941. *The Basic Works of Aristotle*, ed. R. McKeon. Random House.

Armstrong, David. 1993. "A World of States of Affairs." *Philosophical Perspectives* 7: 429–440.

Armstrong, David. 1997. *A World of States of Affairs*. Cambridge University Press.

Austin, J. L. 1961. "Truth." In *Philosophical Papers*, ed. J. Urmson and G. Warnock. Oxford University Press. Original publication: *Proceedings of the Aristotelian Society* suppl. 24 (1950): 111–128.

Austin, J. L. 1962. *How to Do Things with Words*. Harvard University Press.

Ayer, A. J. 1946. *Language, Truth and Logic*. Dover.

Ayer, A. J. 1963. "Truth." In Ayer, *The Concept of a Person and Other Essays*. St. Martin's Press.

Baker, G. P., and P. M. S. Hacker. 1980. *Wittgenstein: Meaning and Understanding*. Blackwell.

Baldwin, Thomas. 1991. "The Identity Theory of Truth." *Mind* 100: 35–52.

Barwise, Jon, and John Perry. 1983. *Situations and Attitudes*. MIT Press.

Berkeley, George. 1710. *A Treatise on the Principles of Human Knowledge*. Dublin.

Berkeley, George. 1734. *Three Dialogues between Hylas and Philonous*. Hackett, 1979.

Bigelow, John. 1988. *The Reality of Numbers: A Physicalist's Philosophy of Mathematics*. Oxford University Press.

Blackburn, Simon. 1984. *Spreading the Word*. Oxford University Press.

Blackburn, Simon, and Keith Simmons, eds. 1999a. *Truth*. Oxford University Press.

Blackburn, Simon, and Keith Simmons. 1999b. "Introduction." In *Truth*, ed. S. Blackburn and K. Simmons. Oxford University Press.

Block, Ned. 1986. "Advertisement for a Semantics for Psychology." *Midwest Studies in Philosophy* 10: 615–678.

Bolton, Derek. 1979. *An Approach to Wittgenstein's Philosophy*. Macmillan.

Bradley, Francis Herbert. 1914. *Essays on Truth and Reality*. Oxford University Press.

Brandom, Robert B. 1994. *Making It Explicit*. Harvard University Press.

Brueckner, Anthony. 1998. "Is 'Superassertible' a Truth Predicate?" *Nous* 32: 76–81.

Carnap, Rudolf. 1947. *Meaning and Necessity*. University of Chicago Press.

Cartwright, Richard. 1987. "A Neglected Theory of Truth." In Cartwright, *Philosophical Essays*. MIT Press.

Cornford, Francis MacDonald. 1957. *Plato's Theory of Knowledge*. Liberal Arts Press.

Cummins, Robert, and Dale Gottlieb. 1972. "On an Argument for Truth-Functionality." *American Philosophical Quarterly* 9: 265–269.

Dancy, Jonathan. 1985. *Introduction to Contemporary Epistemology*. Blackwell.

David, Marian. 1994. *Correspondence and Disquotation*. Oxford University Press.

David, Marian. 2001. "Truth as Identity and as Correspondence." In *The Nature of Truth*, ed. M. Lynch. MIT Press.

Davidson, Donald. 1980a. *Essays on Actions and Events*. Oxford University Press.

Davidson, Donald. 1980b. "The Individuation of Events." In Davidson, *Essays on Actions and Events*. Oxford University Press. Originally published in *Essays in Honor of Carl G. Hempel*, ed. N. Rescher (Reidel, 1969).

Davidson, Donald. 1980c. "Causal Relations." In Davidson, *Essays on Actions and Events*. Oxford University Press. Original publication: *Journal of Philosophy* 64 (1967): 691–703.

Davidson, Donald. 1984. "True to the Facts." In Davidson, *Inquiries into Truth and Interpretation*. Oxford University Press. Original publication: *Journal of Philosophy* 66 (1969): 748–764.

Davidson, Donald. 1990. "The Structure and Content of Truth." *Journal of Philosophy* 87: 279–327.

Davidson, Donald. 1994. "What Is Quine's View of Truth?" *Inquiry* 37: 437–440.

Davidson, Donald. 1996. "The Folly of Trying to Define Truth." *Journal of Philosophy* 93: 263–278.

Davidson, Donald. 1999. "The Centrality of Truth." In *Truth and Its Nature (if Any)*, ed. J. Peregrin. Kluwer.

DeRose, Keith, and Warfield, Ted, eds. 1999. *Skepticism: A Contemporary Reader.* Oxford University Press.

Devitt, Michael. 1991. *Realism and Truth*, second edition. Princeton University Press.

Divers, John, and Alexander Miller. 1994. "Why Expressivists about Value Should Not Love Minimalism about Truth." *Analysis* 54: 12–19.

Dodd, Julian. 1995. "McDowell and Identity Theories of Truth." *Analysis* 55: 160–165.

Dodd, Julian. 2001–2002. "Is Truth Supervenient on Being?" *Proceedings of the Aristotelian Society* 102: 69–86.

Ducasse, C. J. 1940. "Propositions, Opinions, Sentences, and Facts." *Journal of Philosophy* 37: 701–11.

Dummett, Michael. 1978. *Truth and Other Enigmas.* Harvard University Press.

Dummett, Michael. 2003. "Truth and the Past." *Journal of Philosophy* 100: 5–53.

Edwards, Jim. 1996. "Anti-Realist Truth and Concepts of Superassertibility." *Synthese* 109: 103–120.

Engel, Pascal. 2001. "The False Modesty of the Identity Theory of Truth." *International Journal of Philosophical Studies* 9: 441–458.

Field, Hartry. 1974. "Quine and the Correspondence Theory." *Philosophical Review* 83: 200–228.

Field, Hartry. 1977. "Logic, Meaning, and Conceptual Role." *Journal of Philosophy* 74: 379–409.

Field, Hartry. 1986. "The Deflationary Conception of Truth." In *Fact, Science and Morality*, ed. G. MacDonald and C. Wright. Blackwell.

Field, Hartry. 1994. "Deflationist Views of Meaning and Content." *Mind* 103: 249–284. Citations are to the reprint in *Truth*, ed. S. Blackburn and K. Simmons (Oxford University Press, 1999).

Field, Hartry. 2000. "Apriority as an Evaluative Notion." In *New Essays on the A Priori*, ed. P. Boghossian and C. Peacocke. Oxford University Press.

Fine, Kit. 1982. "First-Order Modal Theories III—Facts." *Synthese* 53: 43–122.

Forbes, Graeme. 1986. "Truth, Correspondence and Redundancy." In *Fact, Science and Morality*, ed. G. MacDonald and C. Wright. Blackwell.

Frege, Gottlob. 1960. "On Sense and Reference." In *Translations from the Philosophical Writings of Gottlob Frege*, ed. P. Geach and M. Black. Blackwell. Original publication: *Zeitscrift für Philosophie und philosophische Kritik* 100 (1892): 25–50.

Frege, Gottlob. 1999. "The Thought: A Logical Inquiry." In *Truth*, ed. S. Blackburn and K. Simmons. Oxford University Press. Original publication of this translation: *Mind* 65 (1956): 289–311.

García-Carpintero, Manuel. 1999. "The Explanatory Value of Truth Theories Embodying the Semantic Conception." In *Truth and Its Nature (if Any)*, ed. J. Peregrin. Kluwer.

Goldman, Alvin. 1999. *Knowledge in a Social World*. Oxford University Press.

Grover, Dorothy. 1992. *A Prosentential Theory of Truth*. Princeton University Press.

Grover, Dorothy, Joseph Camp, and Nuel D. Belnap Jr. 1992. "A Prosentential Theory of Truth." In D. Grover, *A Prosentential Theory of Truth*. Princeton University Press.

Gupta, Anil. 1999. "A Critique of Deflationism." In *Truth*, ed. S. Blackburn and K. Simmons. Oxford University Press.

Heidegger, Martin. 1962. *Being and Time*. Blackwell.

Hempel, Carl. 1935. "On the Logical Positivists' Theory of Truth." *Analysis* 2: 49–59.

Hill, Christopher. 2002. *Thought and World*. Cambridge University Press.

Horgan, Terence. 1978. "The Case against Events." *Philosophical Review* 87: 28–47.

Horgan, Terence. 2001. "Contextual Semantics and Metaphysical Realism: Truth as Indirect Correspondence." In *The Nature of Truth*, ed. M. Lynch. MIT Press.

Hornsby, Jennifer. 1997. "Truth: The Identity Theory." *Proceedings of the Aristotelian Society* 97: 1–24.

Horwich, Paul. 1990. *Truth*. Blackwell.

Horwich, Paul. 1994. "The Essence of Expressivism." *Analysis* 35: 19–20.

Horwich, Paul. 1996. "Realism and Truth." *Philosophical Perspectives* 10: 187–197.

Horwich, Paul. 1998a. *Truth*, second edition. Oxford University Press.

Horwich, Paul. 1998b. *Meaning*. Oxford University Press.

Horwich, Paul. 2001. "A Defense of Minimalism." *Synthese* 126: 149–65.

Jackson, Frank. 1994. "Realism, Truth and Truth Aptness." *Philosophical Books* 35: 162–169.

Jackson, Frank. 1998. *From Metaphysics to Ethics: A Defence of Conceptual Analysis*. Oxford University Press.

Jackson, Frank, Graham Oppy, and Michael Smith. 1994. "Minimalism and Truth Aptness."*Mind* 103: 287–302.

James, William. 1907. "Prgamatism's Conception of Truth. " In *Pragmatism and Other Writings*, , ed. G. Gunn (Penguin, 2000).

Joachim, H. H. 1906. *The Nature of Truth*. Oxford University Press.

Johnston, Mark. 1993. "Objectivity Refigured: Pragmatism without Verificationism." In *Reality, Representation, and Projection*, ed. J. Haldane and C. Wright. Oxford University Press.

Kim, Jaegwon. 1993a. *Supervenience and Mind*. Cambridge University Press.

Kim, Jaegwon. 1993b. "Events as Property Exemplifications." In Kim, *Supervenience and Mind*. Cambridge University Press.

Kim, Jaegwon. 1993c. "Supervenience as a Philosophical Concept." In Kim, *Supervenience and Mind*. Cambridge University Press.

Kirkham, Richard L. 1992. *Theories of Truth*. MIT Press.

Kraut, Robert. 1993. "Robust Deflationism." *Philosophical Review* 102: 247–263.

Kripke, Saul. 1980. *Naming and Necessity*. Harvard University Press.

Kripke, Saul. 1982. *Wittgenstein: On Rules and Private Language*. Harvard University Press.

Kvanvig, J. L. 1999. "Truth and Superassertibility." *Philosophical Studies* 93: 1–19.

Leeds, Stephen. 1978. "Theories of Reference and Truth." *Erkenntnis* 13: 111–129.

Lewis, David. 1969. *Convention: A Philosophical Study*. Harvard University Press.

Lewis, David. 1983. "Scorekeeping in a Language Game." In Lewis, *Philosophical Papers*, volume 1. Oxford University Press.

Lewis, David. 2001a. "Forget about the 'Correspondence Theory of Truth.'" *Analysis* 61: 275–280.

Lewis, David. 2001b. "Truthmaking and Difference-Making." *Nous* 35: 602–615.

Locke, John. 1700. *An Essay Concerning Human Understanding*, fourth edition. Oxford University Press, 1975.

Lynch, Michael P., ed. 2001a. *The Nature of Truth*. MIT Press.

Lynch, Michael P. 2001b. "A Functionalist Theory of Truth." In *The Nature of Truth*, ed. M. Lynch. MIT Press.

Mackie, J. L. 1973. *Truth, Probability and Paradox*. Oxford University Press.

Mackie, J. L. 1974. *The Cement of the Universe*. Oxford University Press.

Mackie, J. L. 1977. *Ethics: Inventing Right and Wrong*. Penguin.

McGee, Van. 1993. "A Semantic Conception of Truth?" *Philosophical Topics* 21, no. 2: 83–111.

McGinn, Colin. 2000. *Logical Properties*. Oxford University Press.

McTaggart, J. M. E. 1921. *The Nature of Existence*, volume 1. Cambridge University Press.

Moore, G. E. 1899. "The Nature of Judgment." *Mind*, n.s., vol. 8: 176–193.

Moore, G. E. 1901. "Truth and Falsity." In *The Dictionary of Philosophy and Psychology*, volume 2, ed. J. Baldwin. Macmillan.

Mulligan, Kevin, Peter Simons, and Barry Smith. 1984. "Truth-Makers." *Philosophy and Phenomenological Research* 44: 287–321.

Neale, Stephen. 1995. "The Philosophical Significance of Gödel's Slingshot." *Mind* 104: 761–825.

Nozick, Robert. 2001. *Invariances*. Harvard University Press.

O'Leary-Hawthorne, John. 1994. "Truth-Aptness and Belief." In *Philosophy in Mind*, ed. M. Michael and J. O'Leary-Hawthorne. Kluwer.

O'Leary-Hawthorne, John, and Graham Oppy. 1997. "Minimalism and Truth." *Nous* 31: 170–196.

Oliver, Alex. 1996. "The Metaphysics of Properties." *Mind* 105: 1–80.

Pendlebury, Michael. 1986. "Facts as Truthmakers." *Monist* 69, no. 2: 177–188.

Peregrin, Jaroslav, ed. 1999. *Truth and Its Nature (if Any)*. Kluwer.

Pettit, Paul. 1996. "Realism and Truth: A Comment on Crispin Wright's *Truth and Objectivity*." *Philosophy and Phenomenological Research* 56: 883–890.

Pitcher, George. ed. 1964a. *Truth*. Prentice-Hall.

Pitcher, George. 1964b. "Introduction." In *Truth*, ed. Pitcher. Prentice-Hall.

Plato. 1961. *The Collected Dialogues of Plato*. Pantheon.

Prior, A. N. 1971. *Objects of Thought*. Oxford University Press.

Putnam, Hilary. 1981. *Reason, Truth, and History*. Cambridge University Press.

Quine, W. V. 1953. *From a Logical Point of View*. Harvard University Press.

Quine, W. V. 1960. *Word and Object*. MIT Press.

Quine, W. V. 1969. *Ontological Relativity and Other Essays*. Columbia University Press.

Quine, W. V. 1970. *Philosophy of Logic*. Prentice-Hall.

Quine, W. V. 1987. "Indeterminacy of Translation Again." *Journal of Philosophy* 84: 5–10.

Quine, W. V. 1990. *Pursuit of Truth*. Harvard University Press.

Ramsey, Frank P. 1960. "Facts and Propositions." In *The Foundations of Mathematics*, ed. R. Braithwaite. Littlefield, Adams.

Ramsey, Frank P. 2001. "The Nature of Truth." In *The Nature of Truth*, ed. M. Lynch. MIT Press. Original publication: *Episteme* 6 (1990): 6–16.

Read, Rupert. 2000. "What 'There Can Be No Such Thing as Meaning Anything by Any Word' Could Possibly Mean." In *The New Wittgenstein*, ed. A. Crary and R. Read. Routledge.

Read, Stephen. 1993. "The Slingshot Argument." *Logique et Analyse* 143–144: 195–218.

Read, Stephen. 2000. "Truthmakers and the Disjunction Thesis." *Mind* 109: 67–79.

Restall, Greg. 1996. "Truthmakers, Entailment and Necessity." *Australasian Journal of Philosophy* 74: 331–340.

Richard, Mark. 1997. "Deflating Truth." *Philosophical Issues* 8: 57–78.

Rorty, Richard. 1979. *Philosophy and the Mirror of Nature*. Princeton University Press.

Rorty, Richard. 1986. "Pragmatism, Davidson and Truth." In *Truth and Interpretation*, ed. E. LePore. Blackwell.

Russell, Bertrand. 1985. *The Philosophy of Logical Atomism*. Open Court. Original publication: *Monist* 28 (1918): 495–527; Monist 29 (1919): 32–63, 190–222; 345–380.

Russell, Bertrand, and A. N. Whitehead. 1927. *Principia Mathematica*. Cambridge University Press.

Schiller, F. C.S. 1912. *Humanism*. Macmillan.

Schmitt, Frederick F. 1995. *Truth: A Primer*. Westview.

Searle, John R. 1969. *Speech Acts*. Cambridge University Press.

Searle, John R. 1995. *The Construction of Social Reality*. Free Press.

Sellars, Wilfrid. 1959. *Philosophical Perspectives*. Thomas.

Soames, Scott. 1999. *Understanding Truth*. Oxford University Press.

Smith, Michael. 1994a. "Why Expressivists about Value Should Love Minimalism about Truth." *Analysis* 54: 1–12.

Smith, Michael. 1994b. "Minimalism, Truth-Aptitude and Belief." *Analysis* 54: 21–26.

Steward, Helen. 1997. *The Ontology of Mind: Events, Processes, and States*. Oxford University Press.

Stoutland, Frederick. 1999. "Do We Need Correspondence Truth?" In *Truth and Its Nature (if Any)*, ed. J. Peregrin. Kluwer.

Strawson, P. F. 1949. "Truth." *Analysis* 9, no. 6: 83–97.

Strawson, P. F. 1971. "Truth." In Strawson, *Logico-Linguistic Papers*. Methuen. Original publication: *Proceedings of the Aristotelian Society* suppl. 24 (1950): 129–156.

Strawson, P. F. 1992. *Analysis and Metaphysics*. Oxford University Press.

Tappolet, Christine. 1997, "Mixed Inferences: A Problem for Pluralism about Truth Predicates." *Analysis* 57: 209–210.

Tarski, Alfred. 1949. "The Semantic Conception of Truth and the Foundations of Semantics." In *Readings in Philosophical Analysis*, ed. H. Fiegl and W. Sellars. Appleton-Century-Crofts.

Tarski, Alfred. 1956. "The Concept of Truth in Formalized Languages." In *Logic, Semantics, Metamathematics*, ed. J. Woodger. Oxford University Press.

Urmson, J. O. 1958. *Philosophical Analysis*. Oxford University Press.

Van Cleve, James. 1996. "Minimalist Truth Is Realist Truth." *Philosophy and Phenomenological Research* 56: 289–304.

Vision, Gerald. 1979. "Causal Sufficiency." *Mind* 88, no. 349: 105–110

Vision, Gerald. 1985. "'I Am Here Now.'" *Analysis* 45, no. 4: 198–199.

Vision, Gerald. 1988. *Modern Anti-Realism and Manufactured Truth*. Routledge.

Vision, Gerald. 1996. *Problems of Vision*. Oxford University Press.

Vision, Gerald. 1997a. "Believing Sentences." *Philosophical Studies* 85: 75–93.

Vision, Gerald. 1997b. "Why Correspondence Truth Will Not Go Away." *Notre Dame Journal of Formal Logic* 38, no. 1: 104–131.

Vision, Gerald. 1998. "Perceptual Content." *Philosophy* 73, no. 2: 137–159.

Waismann, Friedrich. 1960. "Verifiability." Reprinted in *Logic and Language*, first series, ed. Antony Flew (Blackwell).

Walker, Ralph C. S. 2001. "The Coherence Theory." In *The Nature of Truth*, ed. M. Lynch. MIT Press.

Warnock, G. J. 1964. "A Problem about Truth." In *Truth*, ed. G. Pitcher. Prentice-Hall.

White, Alan R. 1970. *Truth*. Doubleday.

Wiggins, David. 1980. "What Would Be a Substantial Theory of Truth?" In *Philosophical Subjects: Essays Presented to P. F. Strawson*, ed. Z. van Straaten. Oxford University Press.

Williams, Bernard. 1973. "Imagination and the Self." In Williams, *Problems of the Self.* Cambridge University Press.

Williams, Bernard. 2002. *Truth and Truthfulness.* Princeton University Press.

Williams, Michael. 1986. "Do We (Epistemologists) Need a Theory of Truth?" *Philosophical Topics* 14, no. 1: 223–242.

Williams, Michael. 2001. *Problems of Knowledge.* Oxford University Press.

Williamson, Timothy. 1994. "Critical Notice: *Truth and Objectivity.*" *International Journal of Philosophical Studies* 2: 130–144.

Wilson, Kent. 1990. "Some Reflections on the Prosentential Theory of Truth." In *Truth or Consequences,* ed. M. Dunn and N. Belnap. Kluwer.

Wittgenstein, Ludwig. 1922. *Tractatus Logico-Philosophicus.* Routledge and Kegan Paul.

Wittgenstein, Ludwig. 1958a. *Philosophical Investigations,* third edition. Macmillan.

Wittgenstein, Ludwig. 1958b. *The Blue and Brown Books.* Harper.

Wittgenstein, Ludwig. 1969. *On Certainty.* Blackwell.

Wittgenstein, Ludwig. 1974. *Philosophical Grammar.* Blackwell.

Wittgenstein, Ludwig. 1978. *Remarks on the Foundations of Mathematics,* revised edition. MIT Press.

Woleński, Jan. 1999. "Semantic Conception of Truth as a Philosophical Theory." In *Truth and Its Nature (if Any),* ed. J. Peregrin. Kluwer.

Woozley, A. D. 1966. *Theory of Knowledge.* Barnes and Noble.

Wright, Crispin. 1992. *Truth and Objectivity.* Harvard University Press.

Wright, Crispin. 1994a. "Response to Jackson." *Philosophical Books* 35: 169–174.

Wright, Crispin. 1994b. "Realism: Pure and Simple? A Reply to Timothy Williamson." *International Journal of Philosophical Studies* 2: 327–341.

Wright, Crispin. 1996. "Response to Commentators." *Philosophy and Phenomenological Research* 56: 911–941.

Wright, Crispin. 1998. "Comrades against Quietism: Reply to Simon Blackburn on *Truth and Objectivity.*" *Mind* 107: 183–203.

Wright, Crispin. 1999. "Truth: A Traditional Debate Renewed." In *Truth,* ed. S. Blackburn and K. Simmons. Oxford University Press.

Wright, Crispin. 2001. "Minimalism, Deflationism, Pragmatism, Pluralism." In *The Nature of Truth,* ed. M. Lynch. MIT Press.

Yablo, Stephen. 1993. "Paradox without Self-Reference." *Analysis* 53: 251–252.

Index

Alston, W., 11, 47, 70, 73, 78, 90, 109, 130, 133, 164–165
Antirealism, 13–17, 19–21, 77, 89, 95, 96, 103, 112, 146–147, 158–159, 177, 238
Aristotle, 11, 12, 21, 22, 23, 31, 80, 216, 219
Armstrong, D., 21, 133, 237
Ascriptivism, 135–138, 141–142
Austin, J., 11, 110–111, 133, 160, 161, 220, 221, 226, 253, 258, 267
Ayer, A., 9, 11, 168

Baker, G., 193
Baldwin, T., 5
Barwise, J., 29, 231, 234, 269
Belnap, N., 11, 135–137, 138
Berkeley, G., 13, 61, 68, 79, 80–84, 221
Bigelow, J., 33
Bivalence, 152–156
Blackburn, S., 65, 78, 80, 84
Block, N., 234
Bolton, D., 193
Bradley, F., 5, 7, 41, 221
Brandom, R., 11
Brueckner, A. 104

Camp, J., 11, 135–137, 138
Carnap, R., 64, 65
Cartwright, R., 42, 224
Church, A., 266

Cognition-Independence Intuition, 36–39
Cognitive Command, 95–97, 112, 261–262, 263
Coherence Theory, 5–7, 19, 39–42, 126, 127, 217, 219–220, 261
Coleridge, S., 219
Conceptual Analysis, 48, 50–53, 140–143, 164
Cornford, F., 12
Correspondence
 brief formulations of, 1, 31, 68, 87–92, 107, 121, 123, 246–249
 as congruity, 223–226, 234, 241, 246
 as correlation, 223–225, 235, 241
 extended, 69–70, 99, 245, 281–282
 plain, 92–94
 project, 31, 126, 127
 trivial, 93–94, 106, 108–111
Counterfactuals, 251, 266
Cummins, R., 269

Dancy, J., 11
David, M., 42, 88
Davidson, D., 10, 11, 21, 65, 71, 134, 209, 214, 266–273, 275–276
Deflationism, 8–10, 45, 48
Deixis, 229–231, 233, 236–241
Deontic Justification, 35
Derrida, J., 20
Devitt, M., 64, 88
Disquotationalism, 130, 179, 205, 207

Divers, J., 260
Dodd, J., 11, 65, 253–255
Dummett, M., 193, 247

Edwards, J., 104
Engel, P., 42
Error theory, 263, 280, 281, 283
Equivalences, 8, 33–34, 125, 129, 135, 152, 154, 164–172
Ethical Truth, 44, 73–75, 102, 259–266, 279–284

Facts, 4, 58, 59, 61–77, 173, 179, 214, 222, 251, 267, 281. See also States of Affairs
conventional, 43–44, 69, 226–227, 262–263, 282–284
Field, H., 11, 168, 171, 179–188, 206, 234, 265
Fine, K., 237, 273
Forbes, G., 239
Frege, G., 134, 155, 191, 233, 234, 243, 266, 273–275
Functionalism, 8

Garcia-Carpentero, M., 127
Gödel, K., 199, 266
Goldman, A., 58, 64, 88, 90, 109, 133
Gottlieb, D., 269
Grover, D., 11, 134–136
Gupta, A., 165

Hacker, P., 193
Heidegger, M., 41
Hempel, C., 221
Hill, C., 73, 260
Horgan, T., 65, 69, 88
Hornsby, J., 8, 11
Horwich, P., 11, 17, 47, 50, 92, 117, 121–122, 138–144, 146, 159, 165–169, 172, 175, 177, 179, 188, 205, 211–213, 260–263
Houghton, D., 232

Idealism, 12, 13
Identity Theories, 7, 8

Jackson, F., 149, 159, 220, 260
James, W., 11, 87–91, 105
Joachim, H., 11, 220
Johnston, M., 14, 224
Justification, 149, 159, 220, 260

Kim, J., 65, 116
Kirkham, R., 135, 153–154
Kraut, R., 135
Kripke, S., 43, 193
Kuhn, T., 151
Kvanvig, J., 104

Leeds, S., 156–157
Lewis, D., 21, 22, 55, 93, 171, 254, 258
Liar Paradox, 27–29, 90–91, 127, 170
Locke, J., 234
Lynch, M., 8, 11, 96

Mackie, J., 70, 263, 269
McGee, V., 259
McGinn, C., 11, 88, 90, 109, 130, 176, 223, 243–244, 258
McTaggart, J., 13
Miller, A., 260
Moore, G., 50, 219
Minimalism, 9, 125, 132, 138–150
Moral Truth. See Ethical Truth
Mulligan, K., 239, 240, 276
Multiple Realization, 96

Neale, S., 266
Nozick, R., 88
Nihilism, 9, 10, 45, 46, 92, 188–189, 191–193, 202–203, 273, 275

O'Leary-Hawthorne, J., 49
Oliver, A., 26, 117
Oppy, G., 49, 149, 260

Peirce, C., 11
Pendlebury, M. 62–63
Perry, J., 229, 231, 234, 269
Pettit, P., 104
Pitcher, G., 223–224, 226, 242
Plato, 11, 12, 22, 31, 95, 100, 194, 195–198, 199–200, 219, 223, 228, 245, 256–258
Pluralism, 7, 42–46, 70, 280
Pragmatism, 5–7, 11, 37, 39, 87, 126, 127, 217, 261
Predicates, ungrounded, 154–156
Prior, A., 65
Propositions, 12, 47, 207, 213
Prosententialism 9, 11, 135–137
Putnam, H., 11, 221

Quine, W., 65, 128, 130, 165, 191, 192, 205–217, 276

Ramsey, F., 11, 65, 136, 154, 191, 209, 276
Recognitional Concepts, 162–164
Reductionism, 68
Read, R., 193
Read, S., 240, 266, 269
Restall, G., 240
Richard, M., 72
Rorty, R., 11, 12, 41, 82–84
Russell, B., 11, 50, 68, 69, 71, 193, 199–202, 224, 229, 239, 252, 276

Satisfaction Conditions, 127–128
Schiller, F., 7
Schmitt, F., 85
Searle, J., 11, 54, 67, 70, 88, 90, 130
Sellars, W., 64, 151
Simmons, K., 78, 80, 84
Simons, P., 239–240
Simplicity, 26, 27
Skepticism, 15–21, 46
Slingshot, 62, 65, 252, 253, 266–270
Smith, B., 239–240

Smith, M., 149, 260
Soames, S., 9, 11, 47, 139, 147, 154, 165–170, 172, 175, 179, 182, 186–187
States of affairs, 61, 226–245, 248, 252, 258–259, 262–266, 267, 270–273, 280, 282–284
Steward, H., 67
Stoutland, F., 9, 138
Strawson, P., 19, 65, 70, 135, 155, 160, 161, 231, 282
Strictly Accurate Redundancy Specifications, 132, 133, 137, 142, 175
Superassertibility, 95, 104
Syntacticism, 72–76, 94–95, 260

Tappolet, C., 101
Tarski, A., 21, 22, 23, 31, 60, 127–128, 164–165, 166, 191, 209–211, 215
Truth-Aptitude, 49–50, 260, 262, 280
Truth-Constitution, 5, 12, 15, 53–56, 60, 97–98, 175–179, 212–213, 222, 253–258, 274
Truthmaker Principle, 239, 253–258
Type-Token Distinction, 230–236

Urmson, J., 224

Van Cleve, J., 11, 113, 114
Variability intuition, 33–36, 41, 42, 48, 71, 94, 150, 164, 167, 212–213, 274
Vienna Circle, 50
Vision, G., 5, 67, 77, 83, 121, 230, 269, 274

Waismann, F., 63
Walker, R., 11, 19
Warnock, G., 137
White, A., 131
Whitehead, A., 193, 200
Wiggins, D., 65
Williams, B., 62, 79

Williams, M., 11, 138, 162, 188
Williamson, T., 101
Wilson, K., 135
Wittgenstein, L., 23, 69, 151, 191–205, 217, 224, 246, 252, 258
Woozley, A., 65
Wright, C., 11, 38, 72, 91–120, 122, 123, 141, 145, 149–150, 161, 172, 175, 177, 260–263, 282

Yablo, S., 28